# Lecture Notes in Computer Science

*Commenced Publication in 1973*
Founding and Former Series Editors:
Gerhard Goos, Juris Hartmanis, and Jan van Leeuwen

Pilar Herrero   María S. Pérez
Víctor Robles (Eds.)

# Scientific Applications of Grid Computing

First International Workshop, SAG 2004
Beijing, China, September 20-24, 2004
Revised Selected and Invited Papers

 Springer

Volume Editors

Pilar Herrero
María S. Pérez
Víctor Robles
Universidad Politécnica de Madrid
Facultad de Informática
Campus de Montegancedo S/N
28.660 Boadilla del Monte, Madrid, Spain
E-mail: {pherrero,mperez,vrobles}@fi.upm.es

Library of Congress Control Number: 2005925775

CR Subject Classification (1998): C.2, D.2.12, D.4.3-4, D.4.7, H.3, H.4, H.5.3

ISSN       0302-9743
ISBN-10    3-540-25810-8 Springer Berlin Heidelberg New York
ISBN-13    978-3-540-25810-0 Springer Berlin Heidelberg New York

Springer is a part of Springer Science+Business Media

springeronline.com

© Springer-Verlag Berlin Heidelberg 2005
Printed in Germany

Typesetting: Camera-ready by author, data conversion by Scientific Publishing Services, Chennai, India
Printed on acid-free paper       SPIN: 11423287       06/3142       5 4 3 2 1 0

# Preface

We wish to extend a warm welcome to the reader of this extended postproceedings publication of SAG 2004, the 1st International Workshop on Scientific Applications on Grid Computing. This workshop was held in September 2004, in conjunction with the 2004 IEEE/WIC/ACM International Joint Conference on Web Intelligence (WI 2004) and Intelligent Agent Technology (IAT 2004).

The WI and IAT conferences have provided, for several years, a leading international forum to bring together researchers and practitioners from diverse fields, such as computer science, information technology, business, education, human factors, systems engineering, and robotics, to explore the fundamental roles as well as practical impacts of artificial intelligence (AI) (e.g., knowledge representation, planning, knowledge discovery, and data mining, intelligent agents and social network intelligence) and advanced information technology (IT) (e.g., wireless networks, ubiquitous devices, social networks, the Wisdom Web, and data/knowledge grids), and to examine the design principles and performance characteristics of various approaches in intelligent agent technology.

In the last decade, Grid computing has become one of the most important topics to appear and one of the most widely developed fields. Research into Grid computing is making rapid progress, owing to the increasing necessity of computation resources in the resolution of complex applications. The great challenge is the complete integration of heterogeneous computing systems and data resources with the aim of providing a global computing space. The achievement of this goal will involve revolutionary changes in the field of computation, enabling seamless resource and data sharing across networks. SAG 2004 aimed to provide a forum for novel topics related to Grid computing, providing an opportunity for researchers to discuss and identify key aspects of this important area.

The set of technical papers presented in this volume comprises the SAG 2004 selected papers plus a further 8 invited papers. As for the invited papers, we can say that this extended postproceedings publication gave us the opportunity and the pleasure to introduce the work being carried out by some people who are very well known in the Grid community; and for the SAG 2004 selected papers, we can say that this selection was the result of a difficult and thorough review process. The SAG 2004 workshop received 29 submissions of high quality from which the 10 papers making up the technical program were selected. The number of submissions and the quality and diversity of the resulting program are testimony to the interest in this up-and-coming area.

This publication could not have taken place without considerable enthusiasm, support and encouragement as well as sheer hard work. Many people have earned the thanks of those who attended and organized SAG 2004. In particular, we would like to thank:

- The many supporters of WI and IAT 2004 for their contributions to the conference. Many of these people have been involved with the WI and IAT 2004 conferences for several years.
- The members of the workshop Program Committee who gave their time and energy to ensure that the conference maintained its high technical quality and ran smoothly. The many individuals we owe our thanks to are listed in this volume.
- All the invited authors for their great effort, hard work and support: Konstantinos Karasavvas, Mario Antonioletti, Malcolm Atkinson, Neil Chue Hong, Tom Sugden, Alastair Hume, Mike Jackson, Amrey Krause, Charaka Palansuriya, M. Nedim Alpdemir, Arijit Mukherjee, Anastasios Gounaris, Norman W. Paton, Alvaro A.A. Fernandes, Rizos Sakellariou, Paul Watson, Peter Li, Ilkay Altintas, Adam Birnbaum, Kim Baldridge, Wibke Sudholt, Mark Miller, Celine Amoreira, Yohan Potier, Bertram Ludaescher, Georgousopoulos Cristos, Omer F. Rana, M. Cannataro, M. Comin, C. Ferrari, C. Guerra, A. Guzzo, and P. Veltri, Jose M. Perez, Felix Garcia, Jesus Carretero, Jose D. Garcia, Soledad Escolar, J. Herrera, E. Huedo, R.S. Montero, I.M. Llorente, and Jemal H. Abawajy.
- All those who submitted to the workshop. The standard set was higher than our expectations and reflected well on the research work in the community.

We would also like to acknowledge the organizers of the WI and IAT 2004 conferences, as well as Alfred Hofmann, from Springer, for the support and encouragement they extended to this publication. This volume is the result of a close cooperation and hopefully will allow us to contribute to the growth of this research community.

Pilar Herrero, María S. Pérez, Víctor Robles

# 1st International Workshop On Scientific Applications on Grid Computing (SAG 2004)

## Program Committee

### Steering Committee Co-chairs

Pilar Herrero, Universidad Politécnica de Madrid, Spain
María S. Pérez, Universidad Politécnica de Madrid, Spain

### General Co-chairs

Víctor Robles, Universidad Politécnica de Madrid, Spain
Milena Radenkovic, University of Nottingham, UK

### Program Committee

Abawajy, Jemal, Faculty of Science and Technology, Deakin University, Victoria, Australia
Antic, Dragan, University of Electronic Engineering, Nis, Serbia and Montenegro
Baker, Mark, University of Portsmouth, UK
Benford, Steve, University of Nottingham, UK
Bosque, José Luis, URJC, Madrid, Spain
Buyya, Rajkumar, University of Melbourne, Australia
Carretero, Jesús, UC3M, Madrid, Spain
Corsaro, Angelo, Washington University in St. Louis, USA
Cortes, Toni, UPC, Barcelona, Spain
Del Peso, José, UAM, Madrid, Spain
Dongarra, Jack, University of Tennessee, Knoxville, USA
Dopico, Antonio G., UPM, Madrid, Spain
García, Félix, UC3M, Madrid, Spain
Greenhalgh, Chris, University of Nottingham, UK
Humble, Jan, University of Nottingham, UK
Lord, Phil, University of Manchester, UK
Martín, Ignacio, INTA, Madrid, Spain
Martín, Vicente, UPM, Madrid, Spain
Menasalvas, Ernestina, UPM, Madrid, Spain
Miles, Simon, University of Southampton, UK
Omicini, Andrea, Università di Bologna, Bologna, Italy

Peña, José María, UPM, Madrid, Spain
Rana, Omer, Cardiff University, UK
Rosales, Francisco, UPM, Madrid, Spain
Sánchez, Alberto, UPM, Madrid, Spain
Segovia, Javier, UPM, Madrid, Spain
Stockinger, Heinz, CERN, Geneva, Switzerland
Tari, Zahir, RMIT University, Melbourne, Australia
Zhong, Ning, Maebashi Institute of Technology, Maebashi, Japan

# Table of Contents

## Data-Based Applications

Introduction to OGSA-DAI Services
*Konstantinos Karasavvas, Mario Antonioletti,*
*Malcolm Atkinson, Neil Chue Hong, Tom Sugden,*
*Alastair Hume, Mike Jackson, Amrey Krause,*
*Charaka Palansuriya* .......................................................... 1

Using OGSA-DQP to Support Scientific Applications for the Grid
*M. Nedim Alpdemir, Arijit Mukherjee, Anastasios Gounaris,*
*Norman W. Paton, Alvaro A.A. Fernandes, Rizos Sakellariou,*
*Paul Watson, Peter Li* ....................................................... 13

Mobile Agent-Based Service Provision in Distributed Data Archives
*Christos Georgousopoulos, Omer F. Rana* ........................... 25

A Proxy Service for the xrootd Data Server
*Andrew Hanushevsky, Heinz Stockinger* ............................. 38

A Flexible Two-Level I/O Architecture for Grids
*Alberto Sánchez, María S. Pérez, Víctor Robles, José M. Peña,*
*Pilar Herrero* ................................................................. 50

Data Driven Infrastructure and Policy Selection to Enhance Scientific
Applications in Grid
*Jose M. Perez, Felix Garcia, Jesus Carretero, Jose D. Garcia,*
*Soledad Escolar* .............................................................. 59

## BioApplications

Modelling a Protein Structure Comparison Application on the Grid
Using PROTEUS
*Mario Cannataro, Matteo Comin, Carlo Ferrari, Concettina Guerra,*
*Antonella Guzzo, Pierangelo Veltri* ..................................... 75

Grid Services Complemented by Domain Ontology Supporting
Biomedical Community
*Maja Hadzic, Elizabeth Chang* ........................................... 86

# Applications Architecture, Frameworks and Models

A Generic Architecture for Sensor Data Integration with the Grid
  *Jan Humble, Chris Greenhalgh, Alastair Hamsphire,*
  *Henk L. Muller, Stefan Rennick Egglestone* ...................... 99

Embarrassingly Distributed and Master-Worker Paradigms on the Grid
  *J. Herrera, E. Huedo, R.S. Montero, I.M. Llorente* ................ 108

A Framework for the Design and Reuse of Grid Workflows
  *Ilkay Altintas, Adam Birnbaum, Kim K. Baldridge,*
  *Wibke Sudholt, Mark Miller, Celine Amoreira, Yohann Potier,*
  *Bertram Ludaescher* ........................................... 120

Towards Peer-to-Peer Access Grid
  *Milena Radenkovic, Igor Miladinovic* ........................... 134

A Service Oriented Architecture for Integration of Fault Diagnostics
  *Xiaoxu Ren, Max Ong, Geoffrey Allan, Visakan Kadirkamanathan,*
  *Haydn Thompson, Peter Fleming* ................................ 146

GAM: A Grid Awareness Model for Grid Environments
  *Pilar Herrero, María S. Pérez, Víctor Robles* .................... 158

# Accounting and Market-Based Architecture

Grid Accounting Service Infrastructure for Service-Oriented Grid
Computing Systems
  *Jemal H. Abawajy* ............................................ 168

Mercatus: A Toolkit for the Simulation of Market-Based Resource
Allocation Protocols in Grids
  *Daniel Grosu, Umesh Kant* .................................... 176

# Resource and Information Management in Grid

A Resource Monitoring and Management Middleware Infrastructure for
Semantic Resource Grid
  *Fawad Nazir, Hafiz Farooq Ahmad, Hamid Abbas Burki,*
  *Tallat Hussain Tarar, Arshad Ali, Hiroki Suguri* .................. 188

A Service-Oriented Framework for Traffic Information Grid
  *Guozhen Tan, Chengxu Li, Jiankun Wu* ......................... 197

**Author Index** ............................................... 207

# Introduction to OGSA-DAI Services

Konstantinos Karasavvas[1], Mario Antonioletti[2], Malcolm Atkinson[1],
Neil Chue Hong[2], Tom Sugden[2], Alastair Hume[2], Mike Jackson[2],
Amrey Krause[2], and Charaka Palansuriya[2]

[1] National e-Science Centre, University of Edinburgh, Edinburgh EH8 9AA, UK
{kostas, mpa}@nesc.ac.uk
[2] EPCC, University of Edinburgh, JCMB, The King's Buildings,
Mayfield Road, Edinburgh EH9 3JZ, UK
{mario, neilc, tom, ally, michaelj, amrey, charaka}@epcc.ed.ac.uk

**Abstract.** In today's large collaborative environments, potentially composed of multiple distinct organisations, uniform controlled access to data has become a key requirement if these organisations are to work together as *Virtual Organisations*. We refer to such an integrated set of *data resources*[1] as a *virtual data warehouse*. The *Open Grid Services Architecture - Data Access and Integration* (OGSA-DAI) project was established to produce a common middleware solution, aligned with the Global Grid Forum's (GGF) OGSA vision [OGSA] to allow uniform access to data resources using a service based architecture. In this paper the service infrastructure provided by OGSA-DAI is presented providing a snapshot of its current state, in an evolutionary process, which is attempting to build infrastructure to allow easy integration and access to distributed data using grids or web services. More information about OGSA-DAI is available from the project web site: www.ogsadai.org.

**Keywords:** Data, Databases, Grid, DAIS, OGSA-DAI, Open Grid Services Architecture, Web Services.

## 1   Introduction

Access to and the sharing of data across organisational boundaries is an important requirement for a large number of UK national and international collaborative projects. Instead of requiring each of these projects to individually solve the same data access problem, the OGSA-DAI project was established to produce a common middleware solution that allows uniform access to data resources using a service-based architecture. The initial objectives of the project have concentrated on developing the base data access platform and now, gradually, to

---

[1] A data resource here is taken to mean any entity that can act as a source and/or sink of data together with its associated management framework. Although the framework being developed at the moment works mainly with databases the scope is more general and could encompass file systems and streams.

P. Herrero, M.S. Pérez, and V. Robles (Eds.): SAG 2004, LNCS 3458, pp. 1–12, 2005.

focus on more sophisticated functionality that offers data integration capabilities, such as *distributed query processing* provided by the OGSA-DQP project [OGSA-DQP] using OGSA-DAI services. Up to the advent of OGSA-DAI, provision for uniform data access through service-based interfaces was absent from the then available Grid toolkits, such as the Globus Toolkit 3.0[2] (GT3) and Unicore.

In moving towards these ends the development of OGSA-DAI has been guided by a set of key design principles, mainly:

- *Avoid unnecessary communication between a service and its clients.* In order to minimise the number of message exchanges between a service and its clients, multiple interactions are abstracted into a set of *activities* which are then contained in a single document, referred to as a *perform document*[3] requiring a single message exchange.
- *Avoid unnecessary data movement.* Wherever possible move the computation to the data. Capabilities already available to a data resource, together with additional capabilities implemented at the service layer such as data transformations or third party data delivery, are exposed through the *activities* which can be linked as a series of pipelined tasks through which data flows, all within the same perform document. These activities are then executed within the scope of a single service interaction near or at the data source.
- *Provide an extensible activity framework.* It is unlikely that OGSA-DAI will provide all the base functionality, implemented as activities, that a given project might require. Thus, from the outset, perform documents and the activity *engine* have been designed to be extensible. New functionality can be implemented as activities and incorporated to work within the existing framework.
- *OGSA-DAI does not provide a complete virtualisation of the underlying data resource.* It is still necessary to know what the underlying data resource is and target suitable queries for that type of data resource. The infrastructure does not automatically do this; OGSA-DAI is not attempting to create a new universal query language suitable for all types of data resource.
- *Provide an extensible architecture.* Allow the OGSA-DAI framework to be customised or extended, e.g to add a stronger security model.
- *Build the middleware using existing standards and, where these do not exist, try to produce standards to fill in the gaps.* Up to release 5, the OGSA-DAI middleware has been based on the GGF *Open Grid Services Infrastructure* recommendation [OGSI] and its dependencies. At the time there were no

---

[2] From GT3.2 OGSA-DAI became a contributed component to the Globus Toolkit; an endorsement that such functionality was required. It is also still distributed independently of Globus through the OGSA-DAI project web site, from which there have been over 3300 downloads by approximately a 1000 registered users.

[3] An additional advantage of using a document based interface is that only one operation is required at the interface, *perform*. Functionality can easily be added without requiring a change to the interface, as this can be done inside the document.

standards for service-based interfaces to access data in databases so a GGF Working Group (WG) was established. The *Database Access and Integration* (DAIS) WG, since GGF 5, has been attempting to standardise this in a manner consistent with the OGSA vision. The OGSA-DAI team has been providing a strong lead in this process and aim to produce one of the two interoperable implementations required by GGF for proposed recommendations to become a full GGF recommendation. DAIS and OGSA-DAI are not currently aligned due to the initial rapid movement of the proposed DAIS specifications.

– *Establish a standard, efficient way of moving data between services.* This has become a key concern within OGSA-DAI now that the focus is moving towards data integration where more complex service-to-service interactions are required. No generic solution exists as yet, although the project has developed a *Grid Data Transport* portType[4] to achieve this. The scope of service-to-service data transport is much wider than just within OGSA-DAI and may require further standardisation effort within GGF.

Using the above principles, together with other guiding criteria, five major releases of OGSA-DAI have been produced at fairly regular intervals since early 2003. Each of these releases has increased the functionality, performance, and robustness of the product, as well as keeping abreast of other supporting middleware. The current release, release 5, is based on the GGF 7 version of the DAIS specification [DAIS-GGF7] and the GGF-defined OGSI recommendation. However, within this time frame OGSI has been deprecated and the DAIS specifications have radically changed. Discussion of the implications of this is postponed to section 4. The current release of OGSA-DAI uses the Globus Toolkit 3.2 OGSI implementation (GT3 Core)[5]. A version with a subset of the release 5 functionality that runs over WS-I+ [WS-I+], implemented as the OMII platform[6], is also available. The next few sections of this paper describe the components and operation of OGSA-DAI as found in release 5.

## 2  Architecture

OGSA-DAI has thus far relied on three types of services to provide its functionality: to publish and discover information about services and data resources; to provide persistent Grid proxies for data resources and a service to access and manipulate data resources. The current base OGSA-DAI services are thus:

– **Data Access and Integration Service Group Registry (DAISGR)** – a service allowing other services to publish metadata about any data resources they represent and the capabilities they expose. A client can thus use a

---

[4] A term used within WSDL [WSDL] to collect a set of operations.

[5] Only a modest subset of the facilities of GT3.2 are required for OGSA-DAI and a large number of projects run successfully on this platform.

[6] http://www.omii.ac.uk

DAISGR to identify, by querying its registered metadata, a resource provider that best satisfies its needs.

- **Grid Data Service Factory (GDSF)** – acts as a persistent access point to a data resource and contains additional related metadata that may not be available at a DAISGR. A GDSF creates GDSs to access and manipulate data resources.
- **Grid Data Service (GDS)** – acts as a transient access point to a data resource. It is through a GDS that a client interacts with a data resource.

The GDS and GDSF services were specified in the GGF 7 DAIS draft recommendation. The DAISGR is not specified by DAIS but is based on interfaces specified in OGSI. A typical OGSA-DAI usage pattern is presented in figure 1 below.

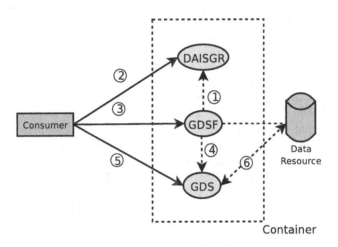

**Fig. 1.** Typical OGSA-DAI interaction

In figure 1 one or more persistent DAISGRs are instantiated at container start-up. Any service implementing one or more of the OGSA-DAI portTypes can register with a DAISGR. There is no requirement for the DAISGR to be co-located in the same container as the services that register with it. Services registering with a DAISGR may register their capabilities, as well as metadata about the data resource's information content.

GDSFs act as a point of presence for one particular data resource on a Grid. The current distribution of OGSA-DAI provides support for a number of different types of data resources amongst which are the relational databases: MySQL, DB2, Oracle, PostgreSQL, SQLServer, Derby (formerly Cloudscape); the XML databases: Xindice (eXist has been shown to work but is not currently supported); as well as some initial support for accessing the content of semi-structured files and file collections. Other types of data resources currently not directly supported by OGSA-DAI have also been employed, such as IBM content manager in the e-Diamond project [eDiamond], and data streams [Data-Streams]. GDSFs are also persistent services configured at container start-up. More than one GDSF can be used to represent the same data resource if necessary but a GDSF can only expose one data resource. Currently GDSFs cannot be dynamically created or configured. On creation, a GDSF may register its service handle with a DAISGR, along with sufficient metadata and capability information to allow service/resource discovery to take place, see (1) in figure 1. Clients can obtain information about available resources (represented by GDSFs) by querying a DAISGR as in (2). They can then ask for detailed information, e.g. the schema of the resource, at a particular GDSF of interest – step (3). A GDSF, in effect, acts as a persistent Grid-enabled wrapper for a data resource but does not provide direct access to that data resource. Access to a data resource requires the creation of a GDS through the GDSF's Factory portType as specified in OGSI – step (4).

GDSs are transient services created at the request of clients who wish to access a data resource. Data resource access is done through the previously mentioned single document-based operation provided by the GDS. A client submits a perform document to the GDS – step (5) – which contains the sequence of activities to be executed on that data resource or the resulting data – step (6). The activities that can be executed by the GDS are defined when a GDSF is configured. The inner workings of a GDS are examined in more detail in the next section.

## 2.1   GDS Low-Level Interactions

The internals of a GDS are schematically shown in figure 2. The *activity engine* is the core component of a GDS. It is responsible for processing requests and generating responses. A request takes the form of a perform document – see section 2.3 for an example, which is an XML document containing one or more activities. An activity dictates the action that the activity engine must

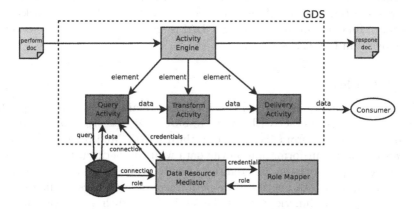

**Fig. 2.** GDS perform document processing and interactions

perform. Activities can be chained together so that the output of one activity becomes the input of another – thus activities read data, process it and write blocks of data to the next activity in the chain. The data blocks are implemented as Java objects which allows efficient streaming between activities and reduces any potential memory overhead. Interfaces are provided for reading and writing between activities – by implementing these interfaces new activities can be added that extend the functionality of OGSA-DAI and work within the same framework.

Figure 2 depicts three activities chained together: the first queries the database, then the results from the query are transformed before being delivered to a third party. In this instance the delivery of data is controlled by the delivery activity. The response document is returned to the client that sent the initial perform document. It contains a result element for each activity contained in the original perform document with its end status. If no delivery activity is explicitly specified in the perform document then the results are included in the response document. Thus in this example three interactions with the service have been reduced to one interaction through the use of the perform document without the client needing to move or organise temporary storage for intermediate results. In addition, the processing of the data has been done close to the data source avoiding any unnecessary data movement.

The *data resource mediator* provides an abstraction layer that governs access to that data resource. It manages the opening and closing of connections. The credentials that a client uses to access the service are mapped to a username and password, via the *role mapper*, which are used to authorise a connection to the data resource. The connection is then returned to the activity to perform the required query or update. This abstraction layer facilitates optimisations such as connection pooling which are performed independently of the engine. New types of data resource can be incorporated to OGSA-DAI by implementing the appropriate mediator.

The GDS engine and activity model are not intended to be, or develop into, a full workflow language. Rather, they are meant to provide an extensible mechanism for supporting common data access, transformation and delivery tasks. The basic unit of functionality within OGSA-DAI is an activity. These are examined in more detail in the next section.

## 2.2    Activities

Activities can roughly be categorised into three main functional groups: (a) *statement activities* interact with a data resource, (b) *delivery activities* deliver data to or collect data from the service to third parties, and (c) *transformation activities* perform transformation on the data while it is still in the service.

Activities expose existing capabilities already provided by a data resource, e.g. allow SQL or XPath queries to be performed on the corresponding type of data resource, or add functionality at the service level, such as transforming the results of a query into another format before passing them to the next activity or returning them to the client, or delivering the results to an ftp server, etc. They

**Table 1.** Supported activities provided with release 5 of OGSA-DAI

| Activity | Description |
|---|---|
| **Relational Activities** | |
| `sqlQueryStatement` | Run an SQL query on a relational resource |
| `sqlUpdateStatement` | Run an SQL update statement on a relational resource |
| `sqlStoredProcedure` | Invoke an SQL stored procedure[8] |
| `relationalResourceManagement` | Create/drop database tables |
| **XML Activities** | |
| `xPathStatement` | Run an XPath statement against an XML database |
| `xUpdateStatement` | Run an XUpdate statement against an XML database |
| `xmlCollectionManagement` | Create/remove collections within an XML database |
| `xmlResourceManagement` | Create/remove resources within an XML database |
| **Delivery Activities** | |
| `deliverFromURL/deliverToURL` | Retrieve/deliver data from/to a URL |
| `deliverFromGDT/deliverToGDT` | Pull/push data from/to a service's GDT portType |
| `deliverFromGFTP/deliverToGFTP` | Retrieve/deliver data to/from a GridFTP server |
| `deliverFromFile/deliverToFile` | Retrieve/deliver data from/to a file in the local file system |
| `deliverToSMTP` | Deliver data in an e-mail using SMTP |
| `inputStream` | Receive data through s GDT portType |
| `outputStream` | Deliver data through a GDT portType |
| `deliverToStream` | Deliver results to a stream |
| **Transformation Activities** | |
| `zipArchive` | ZIP compress the results |
| `gzipCompression` | GNU-ZIP compress the results |
| `dataStore` | Cache parameters and results |
| `xslTransform` | Transform data using an XSLT |
| **BinX Activities** | |
| `fileQuery` | Query a BinX described file |

provide an extensible framework that allows developers to add functionality to a GDS. OGSA-DAI already provides a number of general activities that can be employed to interact with a data resource, see Table 1[7]. If these are found to be insufficient, then more can be added by developers.

Activities are defined and configured at a GDSF and are made available to the GDSs created by that GDSF. Each activity requires a Java implementation together with an XML schema fragment that is used to express the syntax of the XML representation of that activity in a perform document. Release 5 also allows individual activities to be configured when they are used by perform documents–configuration files are placed at the server side and allow the administrator to modify behaviour without having to edit the activity implementation code.

This framework has been found to be sufficient for most purposes. However, more work remains to be done. In the current model the syntax of activities is not complete – there is no typing of the data inputs and outputs that flow in and out of an activity. This makes it hard to automatically connect and thus compose activities together, i.e. the user needs to know what kind of input/output two activities have in order to chain them together. Also, the semantics are not clear – one can add documentation for each activity in the XML schema fragment but that is the only provision for deriving the semantics of that activity other

---

[7] Unsupported activities include file, indexed file, and notification activities.

[8] Currently, this is only supported for DB2 stored procedures.

than through its name. Again this imposes potential difficulties of meaningfully connecting activities together in a generic framework; a human being would be required to do this. In the next section we examine perform documents, which aggregate activities together.

## 2.3    Perform Document

Perform documents collect together an XML representation of a set of activities. It is worth noting that a user would not be expected to craft these documents by hand. Instead, the client toolkit, which offers a programming abstraction of this framework, described in section 3 would be used to generate the required XML. The following listing shows the XML for a perform document that executes an SQL query and delivers the results using ftp to a third party:

```
1    <?xml version="1.0" encoding="UTF-8"?>
2    <gridDataServicePerform
3        xmlns="http://ogsadai.org.uk/namespaces/2003/07/gds/types"
4        xmlns:xsi="http://www.w3.org/2001/XMLSchema-instance"
5        xsi:schemaLocation="http://ogsadai.org.uk/namespaces/2003/07/gds/types
6        ../../../../schema/ogsadai/xsd/activities/activities.xsd">
7
8    <documentation>
9      This example performs a simple select statement to retrieve one row
10     from the test database and then delivers the results to an FTP location.
11   </documentation>
12
13   <sqlQueryStatement name="statement">
14     <expression>
15       select * from littleblackbook where id=10
16     </expression>
17     <resultSetStream name="output"/>
18   </sqlQueryStatement>
19
20   <deliverToURL name="deliverOutput">
21     <fromLocal from="output"/>
22     <toURL>ftp://anon:frog@ftp.example.com/home</toURL>
23   </deliverToURL>
24
25   </gridDataServicePerform>
```

Lines 2-6 contain the root element, **gridDataServicePerform**, and define the appropriate XML name spaces and XML schema the document satisfies – note the location corresponds to the standard server location where the OGSA-DAI XML schema can be found. Lines 8-11 contain documentation – this is purely for human consumption. Lines 13-18 and 20-23 contain the two chained activities; the first one queries a relational data resource and streams the results to the second activity, which delivers them to the specified URL. A data pipe is established from one activity to the other by naming the output stream of the query activity in line 17, **resultSetStream**, and connects this to the second activity by specifying the same name in the sink **fromLocal** element that serves as the input to the delivery activity on line 21. Thus, the connection is established. Note that the username and password are explicitly embedded in the document – you would not do this unless you were employing message or transport level security and entertained a certain level of trust with your service provider. Although in principle this sounds relatively simple you would not want to craft such documents by hand, which is tedious and error prone. Instead, you would use the client toolkit, which is described next.

## 3   Client Toolkit

The client toolkit provides a Java client side library that allows perform documents to be easily constructed and used by applications wishing to communicate with OGSA-DAI services. In addition, the toolkit manages the communications with the OGSA-DAI services so the user need not concern themselves with this. Part of the motivation for having this library is to provide an API that shields developers from changes in OGSA-DAI. Developers need only learn this single API to be able to write client software to access OGSA-DAI.

As an example consider the perform document that was outlined in the previous section. In this instance the whole process of using the OGSA-DAI services is considered. First of all, one must know the service handle for a GDSF or obtain one from a DAISGR – the client toolkit provides abstractions to do this too. Here we assume that we already know of a suitable GDSF handle which is used to create a factory object which in turn is used to create a GDS:

```
String handle = "http://example.com:8080/ogsadai/GridDataServiceFactory";
GridDataServiceFactory factory = ServiceFetcher.getFactory(handle);
GridDataService        service = factory.createGridDataService();
```

The **service** object can be used later to destroy the GDS, in order to release any resources no longer being used, using **service.destroy()**. Now the activities for the request are created and chained together so that the output of the SQL statement activity is streamed into the input of the delivery activity:

```
SQLQuery     query   = new SQLQuery("select * from littleblackbook where id=10");
DeliverToURL deliver = new DeliverToURL("ftp://anon:pass@ftp.example.com/home");
deliver.setInput( query.getOutput() );
```

Finally these activities are aggregated into a composite request and sent to the GDS where it is executed. The **response** object contains the status of each activity in the request sent back to the user by the service.

```
ActivityRequest request = new ActivityRequest();
request.add( query );
request.add( delivery );
Response response = service.perform( request );
```

The contents of the response object may be accessed in various ways, e.g. we can get a JDBC **ResultSet** from a relational query activity, or a XML:DB **ResourceSet** from an XPath query activity. To simply view the results we can get them as string by using the **getAsString()** method of the **response** object.

From this example one can see how easy it is to construct a perform document and how the library manages all the communication and infrastructure mechanisms. This improves usability and shortens the learning curve to develop an OGSA-DAI client. The client toolkit is also extensible: new client-side activities, corresponding to new server-side activities, can be added. In essence a new client toolkit activity must serialise into the appropriate XML fragment that trigger the corresponding server side activity – an abstract class must be extended to do this. More information about the client toolkit is available in the OGSA-DAI release documentation.

## 4   Future Directions

The deprecation of OGSI and changes to the DAIS specifications [WS-DAI, WS-DAIR, WS-DAIX], no longer a single document, will require changes to the underlying OGSA-DAI model. Moreover, OGSA now explicitly aim to align with the *Web Services Resource Framework* (WSRF) set of standards [WS-RP, WS-RL, WS-SG, WS-BF] being developed within OASIS. Globus is moving towards WSRF as well. In the UK, there is a push towards using an extended set of standards to those addressed in the *Web Services Interoperability (WS-I) Basic Profile* [WS-I], termed WS-I+ [WS-I+], as an interim position until the standards space settles down.

Technical preview versions of WSRF and WS-I+ of OGSA-DAI already exist and are available. However, long term support for each of the OGSI, WS-I+ and WSRF versions of OGSA-DAI is not tenable. Development of the OGSI version will stop after release 6, although there will still be support available for projects using the OGSI version of OGSA-DAI. The OGSA-DAI distribution is being refactored to allow support for a combined WS-I+ and WSRF OGSA-DAI distribution. The client toolkit will have to be generalised to take these changes into account. Now that DAIS appears to be stabilising some early prototyping of the DAIS specifications will be undertaken – a relational prototype already exists. As with all other Grid based projects a lot of changes are about to take place. However, we feel that these are for the better and we aim to try and carry our existing users with us and gain some new ones in the process.

Future releases will continue to extend the functionality of OGSA-DAI, particularly in the directions of transaction handling, heterogeneity management, higher-level integration facilities, and performance improvement. This will involve changes to the underlying architecture to increase concurrency and exploit pipelined operations.

## 5   Conclusions

This paper has given a high-level overview and snapshot summary of the current state and some future directions of OGSA-DAI. Readers are warned that much detail and important information has been omitted, and the new releases and previews represent significant changes. Those considering using OGSA-DAI are therefore encouraged to obtain up-to-date and full information from the website, www.ogsadai.org, and to contact the team, if they still have questions. Those planning to use OGSA-DAI or already using it are warmly invited to join the OGSA-DAI users' group in order to help steer the future development priorities. We also run regular training events.

A key question often asked is: *'What is the point of using OGSA-DAI when you already have a perfectly viable solution in JDBC?'*. OGSA-DAI manages JDBC access in the context of security mechanisms, exploits the emerging strengths of Web Services and provides:

- Language independence, you do not necessarily have to use Java at the client end[9].
- Platform independence, you do not have to worry about the underlying operating system that is being used or connection technology, drivers, etc.
- Multiple data models, XML resources can be handled within the same framework as relational and other types of data resources, such as indexed file collections.
- Extensibility through the addition of functionality at the service end such as transformations and third-party delivery, etc. avoiding unnecessary data movement.
- The OGSI based provision for metadata is powerful and generic, and will be carried forward to new infrastructure platforms.
- Usefulness of the registry for performing dynamic service or resource discovery based on service and resource metadata.
- Dynamic service binding process allowing binding to data resources.
- Composability, as services can be coupled to operate in combination to offer more powerful capabilities such as distributed query processing. Composable activity invocation within a perform document can be used to avoid round trip latency and to handle convenient handling of intermediate results.

So, it is clear that using an OGSA-DAI solution does offer potential advantages over a pure JDBC solution. If the extra facilities are not used, there is a performance penalty for some relational operations. Work is underway to reduce the penalty. OGSA-DAI is pioneering the new architectural possibilities for data access and integration, and is supporting a large and growing number of projects and will advance in capability and functionality as an extensible open framework, to which contributions are very welcome.

*Acknowledgements.* This work is supported by the UK e-Science Grid Core Programme, whose support we are pleased to acknowledge. We also gratefully acknowledge the input of our past and present partners and contributors to the OGSA-DAI project including: EPCC at the University of Edinburgh, IBM UK, IBM US, NeSC, University of Manchester, University of Newcastle and Oracle UK. All trademarks acknowledged.

# References

[DAIS-GGF7]     Chue Hong, N.P., Krause, A., Malaika, S., McCance, G., Laws, S., Magowan, J., Paton, N.W., Riccardi, G.: Grid Database Service Specification. Presented at GGF 7, 16th February 2003.

---

[9] As yet, unsupported client toolkits have been developed for Perl, SML, and C.

[Data-Streams]  Plale, B.: Using Global Snapshots to Access Data Streams on the Grid, In proceedings 2nd European Across Grids Conference (Ax-Grids04), Springer Verlag Lecture Notes in Computer Science, Vol. 3165, January 2004.

[eDiamond]  Oevers, M., Collins, B., Knox, A., Williams J.: The Use of OGSA-DAI with IBM DB2 Content Manager for Multiplatforms in the eDia-MoND Project. Appeared at *The Future of Grid Data Environments Workshop* at the Global Grid Forum 10 meeting, March 2004.

[OGSA]  Foster, I. (editor), Berry, D., Djaoui, A., Grimshaw, A., Horn, B., Kishimoto, H. (editor), Maciel, F., Savva, A., Siebenlist, F., Subramania, R., Treadwell, J., Von Reich, J.: The Open Grid Services Architecture, Version 1.0. 12th July 2004. Global Grid Forum.

[OGSA-DQP]  Alpdemir, M.N., Mukherjee, A., Gounaris, A., Paton, N.W., Watson, P., Fernandes, A.A.A.: OGSA-DQP: A Grid Service for Distributed Querying on the Grid, Proc. 9th International Conference on Extending Database Technology (EDBT), 858-861, 2004.

[OGSI]  Tuecke, S., Czajkowski, KI., Foster, I., Frey, J., Graham, S., Kesselman, C., Snelling, D., Vanderpilt, P.: Open Grid Services Infrastructure, Version 1.0, March 13, 2003.

[WS-RP]  Graham, S. (editor), Treadwell, J. (editor): Web Services Resource Properties 1.2 (WS-ResourceProperties) Working Draft 04, 10 June 2004.

[WS-RL]  Srinivasan, L. (editor), Banks, T. (editor): Web Service Resource Lifetime 1.2 (WS-ResourceLifetime). Working Draft 04, 11 November 2004.

[WS-SG]  Maguire, T. (editor), Snelling, D. (editor). Web Services Service Group 1.2 (WS-ServiceGroup). Working Draft 03, 10 November 2004.

[WS-BF]  Tuecke, S. (editor), Liu, L. (editor), Meder, S.: Web Services Base Faults 1.2 (WS-BaseFaults). Working Draft 02, June 24, 2004.

[WS-DAI]  Antonioletti, M., Atkinson, M., Krause, A., Laws, S., Malaika, S., Paton, N.W., Pearson, D., Riccardi, G: Web Services Data Access and Integration (WS-DAI). May 21st 2004.

[WS-DAIR]  Antonioletti, M., Collins, B., Krause, A., Laws, S., Magowan,, J., Malaika, S., Paton,N. W.: Web Services Data Access and Integration - The Relational Realisation (WS-DAIR). May 21st 2004.

[WS-DAIX]  Antonioletti, M., Hastings, S., Krause, A., Langella, S., Malaika, S., Laws, S., Paton, N. W.: Web Services Data Access and Integration: The XML Realisation (WS-DAIX). May 21st 2004.

[WSDL]  Christensen, E., Curbera, F., Meredith, G.,Weerawarana, S.: Web Services Description Language (WSDL) 1.1. W3C Note 15 March 2001,

[WS-I]  Ballinger, K., Ehnebuske, D., Gudgin, M., Nottingham M., Yendluri, P. (eds.): Basic Profile Version 1.0. Final Material. See: http://www.ws-i.org/Profiles/BasicProfile-1.0.html.

[WS-I+]  Atkinson, M., DeRoure, D., Dunlop, A., Fox, G.,Henderson, P., Hey, T., Paton, N., Newhouse, S., Parastatidis, S., Trefethen, A.,Watson, P., Webber, J.: Web Service Grids: An Evolutionary Approach. See: www.omii.ac.uk/web_service_grids.htm for more details.

# Using OGSA-DQP to Support Scientific Applications for the Grid

M. Nedim Alpdemir[1], Arijit Mukherjee[2], Anastasios Gounaris[1],
Norman W. Paton[1], Alvaro A.A. Fernandes[1], Rizos Sakellariou[1],
Paul Watson[2], and Peter Li[2]

[1] Department of Computer Science,
University of Manchester,
Oxford Road, Manchester M13 9PL, UK
[2] School of Computing Science,
University of Newcastle upon Tyne,
Newcastle upon Tyne NE1 7RU, UK

**Abstract.** The data management problems in grid computing are often
challenging in many aspects such as data volumes, heterogeneity, structural complexity and semantic content. Thus, e-Scientists and scientific
application developers stand to benefit from tools and environments that
either hide, or help to manage, the inherent complexity involved in accessing and making concerted use of the diverse resources. This paper
describes OGSA-DQP, a high level data integration tool for service-based
grids, and illustrates how it can be used to support grid users, via an
example scientific study in bioinformatics. The paper also discusses various options for employing OGSA-DQP to handle data integration tasks
as service orchestrations involving both data and analysis services.

## 1  Introduction

Both commercial and scientific applications increasingly require access to distributed resources. Grid technologies have been introduced to facilitate efficient
sharing of resources in a heterogeneous distributed environment. However, from
its inception, grid computing has provided mechanisms for data access that lie at
a much lower level than those provided by commercial database technology [7].
This is despite the fact that the data management problems in grid computing
are not likely to be less complex, rather the contrary, insofar as in all relevant
aspects (viz., data volumes, structural complexity and semantic content) data in
the grid is likely to be at least as complex as that found in current commercial
environments. Furthermore, in those applications for which grid solutions seem
particularly appropriate (e.g., scientific ones), data is often more fragmented
and more in need of computationally-demanding analyses than in classical Web
applications (e.g., e-commerce ones). Thus, high-level data access and integration services are needed if applications that have large amounts of data with
complex structure and complex semantics are to benefit from the grid. This
paper briefly describes OGSA-DQP [1], a high level data integration tool for

P. Herrero, M.S. Pérez, and V. Robles (Eds.): SAG 2004, LNCS 3458, pp. 13–24, 2005.

service-based grids, and aims to illustrate how it can be used to support grid users in accessing distributed resources in a bioinformatics context. The paper also discusses how OGSA-DQP can be exploited to provide a relatively low-cost implementation of complex scientific applications for the grid.

The rest of the paper is structured as follows: Section 2 briefly introduces the service-oriented approaches to resource utilisation on the grid; Section 3 describes the architecture and usage of OGSA-DQP as a high-level data access and integration tool for service-based grids; Section 4 illustrates how OGSA-DQP can be exploited to support e-scientists in conducting their studies, through an example bioinformatics application; Section 5 briefly discusses various options for employing OGSA-DQP in more complex grid applications and finally Section 6 presents a number of conclusions.

## 2    Service-Oriented Architectures for Resource Utilisation

Service-based approaches [4] (such as Web Services and the Open Grid Services Architecture) have gained considerable attention recently for supporting distributed application development in e-business and e-science. The service-based approach seems to many a good solution to the problem of modelling a virtual organisation as a distributed system, and is perceived to offer a convenient paradigm for resource sharing through resource virtualisation. Web Services, in particular in conjunction with the resource access and management facilities of grid computing, show considerable promise as an infrastructure over which distributed applications in e-business and e-science can be developed. As such, it is argued that uniformly treating the diversity of resources and applications as services significantly simplifies their use and management [5].

One particular impact of service-oriented approaches on application development, is the introduction of new techniques that permit various models for aggregating distributed software modules as loosely-coupled compositions of coarse-grained services to construct more complex applications [6]. Workflow languages such as Business Process Execution Language (BPEL) appear to be central to service aggregation approaches. However, It is worth noting that although it is likely that workflow languages will have a prominent role, service-based Distributed Query Processing (DQP) also offers service orchestration capabilities, accomplishing system-supported optimisation of declarative requests with implicit parallelism, a combination that should yield significant programmer productivity and performance benefits for large-scale, data intensive applications. OGSA-DQP is one approach to provide such capabilities.

## 3    OGSA-DQP: A Grid Service Framework for Data Integration and Analysis

### 3.1    Overview

OGSA-DQP [1] is essentially a high-throughput distributed data-flow engine that relies on a service-oriented abstraction of grid resources and assumes that data sources are accessible through service-based interfaces. OGSA-DQP relies on infrastructure support from other grid Middleware at two distinct levels: it uses the reference implementation of Open Grid Services Architecture (OGSA) [3] viz., Globus Toolkit 3 (GT3) [8], which implements a service-based architecture over virtualised resources referred to as Grid Services (GSs), thus enabling dynamic allocation of resources necessary for efficient evaluation of a distributed query; it also builds upon OGSA-DAI [2] which implements Grid Data Services (GDSs) that insulate users from certain aspects of data source heterogeneity, ensuring that metadata and data held in a particular data source are accessed via a standard, well-defined and uniform interface. By building on those layers, OGSA-DQP delivers a framework that

- supports declarative queries over many *Grid Database Services* (GDSs) by creating a union of the database schemas of the participating data sources.
- supports calls to external web services through insertion of the web service operation invocations into a query, thereby combining data access with data analysis;
- adapts techniques from parallel databases to provide implicit parallelism for complex data-intensive requests; and
- automates complex, onerous, expert configuration and resource utilisation decisions on behalf of users via its query optimisation module.

OGSA-DQP provides two services to fulfil its functions: The *Grid Distributed Query Service (GDQS)* and the *Grid Query Evaluation Service (GQES)*. The GDQS provides the primary interaction interfaces for the user, collects the necessary metadata, and acts as a coordinator between the underlying query compiler/optimiser engine and the GQES instances. The GQES, on the other hand, is used to evaluate (i.e. execute) a query sub-plan assigned to it by the GDQS. The number of GQES instances and their location on the grid is specified by the GDQS, based on the decisions made by a query optimiser and represented as an execution schedule for query partitions (i.e. sub-plans). GQES instances are created and scheduled dynamically, to evaluate the partitions of a query constructed by the optimiser of the GDQS.

Figure 1 illustrates the high-level architecture of OGSA-DQP, where the client application queries multiple data resources via a global schema that presents a union of the schemas of the participating data sources. Notice that OGSA-DQP utilizes the computational resources and data resources available to it, via services provided by a core grid middleware (i.e. OGSA and OGSA-DAI). As such, by virtue of this core middleware support the query execution engine is constructed dynamically (i.e. at run time) by instantiating GQESs for each section (or partition) of the distributed query plan, as stipulated by the query optimizer encapsulated within the GDQS.

## 3.2   Using OGSA-DQP for Querying Distributed Data Sources

This section describes, briefly, how OGSA-DQP can be used in practice as a high-level tool for retrieving and combining data from multiple data sources, as well as feeding retrieved data into analysis services if desired.

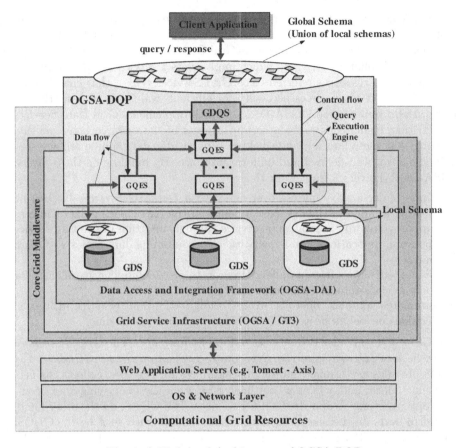

**Fig. 1.** A High-level Architecture of OGSA-DQP

**Starting a Query Session.** Preparing OGSA-DQP for query submission involves identifying the data sources and the analysis services to be used in a
query session. This process may start with a search and discovery phase at the
end of which the user finds the set of resources s/he is interested in. OGSA-
DQP does not currently offer direct support for this initial discovery process,
largely because this is conceived to be an application level functionality. Instead,
it is assumed that the user has already identified the required resources. Thus,
the user submits an XML document containing the list of the data sources and
analysis services as illustrated by the following XML fragment:

```
<GDQDataSourceList>
    <importedDataSource>
        <GDSFactoryHandle>
            http://host:port/ogsa/services/ogsadai/ProteinDBGDSFactory
        </GDSFactoryHandle>
    </importedDataSource>
    <importedDataSource>
        <GDSFactoryHandle>
            http://host:port/ogsa/services/ogsadai/GenesDBGDSFactory
```

```
      </GDSFactoryHandle>
    </importedDataSource>
    <importedDataSource>
      <GDSFactoryHandle>
          http://host:port/ogsa/services/ogsadai/MicroarrayDBGDSFactory
      </GDSFactoryHandle>
    </importedDataSource>
    <importedService
      name="EntropyAnalyser"
      wsdlURL="http://host:port/services/EntropyAnalyserService?wsdl"/>
</GDQDataSourceList>
```

Note that the data sources are indicated by the Grid Data Service Factory
(GDSF) handles of the services that wrap those data sources. The analysis services are indicated by URLs that point to the WSDL documents describing those
services.

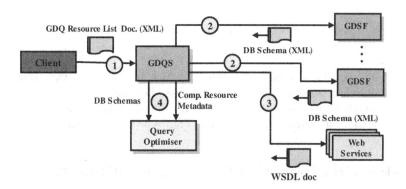

**Fig. 2.** Metadata Retrieval During OGSA-DQP Set-up Phase

As illustrated in Figure 2, on receipt of the XML document containing the
resource list (interaction 1), the GDQS obtains metadata about each resource
in the list (interactions 2 and 3) to aid the query optimiser in generating an
efficient execution plan. This metadata includes database schemas (both the
logical structure of the data and some physical characteristics such as index
information, cardinality, row sizes, etc.) that are obtained from the data sources,
and WSDL documents that are obtained from the web services.

**Submitting Query Requests.** After the GDQS is set-up with a resource set
and a query session is initiated, the user can submit multiple query requests
until the GDQS instance is destroyed, which effectively terminates the session.

As illustrated in Figure 3 (a), for each query request a GDQS instance com-
piles, optimises, partitions and schedules the query to generate a distributed
query plan optimised for specific requirements of the submitted query. Each
partition in the distributed query plan is assigned to one or more execution
nodes. The GDQS, then, commands the creation of GQESs as stipulated by the
partitioning and scheduling decided on by the compiler (Figure 3 (b), interaction
1), and co-ordinates the GQESs into executing the plan. Each execution node

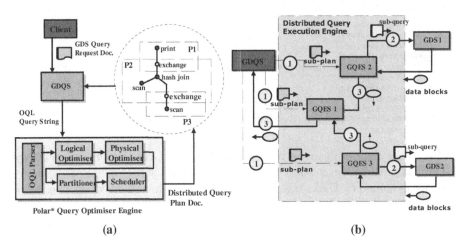

**Fig. 3.** Query Optimisation and Execution Process

corresponds to a GQES instance, each of which initiates its evaluation upon receiving its plan partition. The whole process effectively constructs a tree-like data flow system with the GDQS instance at the root, GDS instances at the leaf and a collection of GQESs in the middle (Figure 3 (b), interactions 2-3).

## 4   How Grid Users Can Benefit from OGSA-DQP

This section illustrates OGSA-DQP in use as part of the solution to a bioinformatics problem. First a brief explanation of the problem is provided in Section 4.1, followed by a description of how OGSA-DQP is put into use to aid in providing a solution, in Section 4.2.

### 4.1   An Example Bioinformatics Application: The Graves' Disease Scenario

The myGrid project (www.mygrid.org.uk) has developed an application that uses a number of middleware services to build in-silico tools for a study that seeks to identify genes and SNPs associated with a genetic autoimmune condition known as *Graves disease (GD)*. The condition is an disease of the thyroid in which the immune system of an individual attacks the cells of the thyroid gland resulting in hyperthyroidism (thyroid overactivity).

Researchers studying human genetic disease such as this, ultimately wish to establish which genes are affected in the diseased state, the changes in those genes between individuals and the underlying molecular mechanisms that lead to the autoimmune response. The hypothesis is that single nucleotide polymorphisms (SNPs) are instrumental in the disease mechanism. Thus, there are three objectives:

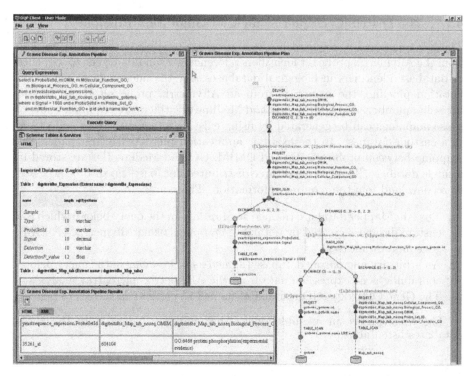

**Fig. 4.** OGSA-DQP GUI Client Screen Shot showing the Query Plan and the Results

1. Investigate what genes and loci are involved in GD.
2. Examine which single nucleotide polymorphisms (SNPs) located in genes are involved in GD.
3. Develop genotyping experiments to test the above hypotheses.

One of the several in-silico experiments designed for the whole study is an annotation pipeline that aims to help the user establish which genes in the candidate gene pool may be involved in the diseased state [9]. In other words, the main purpose is to retrieve information associated with candidate genes that were differentially expressed in GD. The user can assimilate the information provided and make a decision as to which gene or genes they wish to examine in more detail, and ultimately take back to laboratory studies. To achieve that, however, it is necessary to return links to annotation data from a range of genomic databases and the literature, for each gene in the dataset. A *distributed query* over grid enabled databases can achieve the required data integration at a relatively low cost compared to other approaches that require a separate, isolated interaction with each of the databases and do the integration as a custom postprocessing step (e.g. application-specific scripting solutions, or workflow-based solutions that either include application-specific logic in each of the data-access services or a separate service in the workflow to perform the integration).

## 4.2   The Distributed Queries for the Annotation Pipeline

The key functionality required in the annotation pipeline is the ability to map from the Affymetrix probe set identifiers referencing a candidate gene to sequence or database identifiers in biological databases. For the nucleotide sequence annotation pipeline, the mappings from an Affymetrix probe set ID to EMBL accession number, and OMIM, GO and Medline identifiers are required. Some of those mappings can be generated by using existing annotation tools and stored in a custom database. In the example application presented in this paper, the mapping between probe set IDs and OMIM, GO and Medline IDs are stored in a single database. Thus, in total three distributed databases need to be accessed to retrieve and join the required information. Those are:

1. The AffyMapper database (named as *Map_tabs* in the query below) which is a custom database created by obtaining mappings using Affymetrix's NetAffx gene annotation tool.
2. An arbitrary microarray database (named as *expressions* in the query below) containing gene expression data from the Affymetrix microarray analyses.
3. The Gene Ontology (GO) database (named as *goterms* in the query below).

The following is an example query that integrates data from the three databases listed above:

```
QUERY1:
select
    e.ProbeSetId, m.OMIM, m.Molecular_Function_GO,
    m.Biological_Process_GO, m.Cellular_Component_GO
from
    e in expressions, m in Map_tabs, g in goterms
where
    e.Signal>1000 and e.ProbeSetId = m.Probe_Set_ID and
    m.Molecular_Function_GO = g.id and g.name like <input  name>
```

The query selects those Affymetrix probe set IDs which have an expression signal over 1000 and which have also been annotated with a given GO ID. In other words, the query answers questions such as *"which genes are expressed in my samples and have a molecular function activity x?"*.

Figure 4 illustrates the OGSA-DQP GUI client that was used to execute the example query. The GUI client supports an administrator mode where a system administrator can create and save configurations with a resource set and pre-defined queries, and a user mode where a more novice user can load a configuration, execute pre-defined queries or add more queries if necessary. The screen shot illustrates the user mode and includes three small windows on the left representing – from top to bottom in order– the query text, the tabular representation of the union of the database schemas of the participating data sources, and the query results in tabular form. The figure also shows a graphical representation of the query execution plan on the right hand side of the window. The plan is dynamically generated for each executed query and is annotated to indicate the partitioning and scheduling of the distributed plan (denoted by dashed rectangular boundaries), algorithms employed to evaluate each sub-plan (denoted by circular nodes with textual annotations such as HASH_JOIN, TABLE_SCAN,

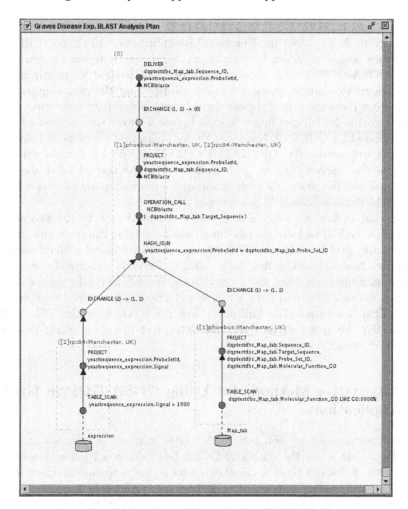

**Fig. 5.** The Query Plan with the BLAST Call

etc.) and the location of the servers that were used to execute a particular sub-plan (denoted by textual labels above the dashed rectangular boundaries).

OGSA-DQP can also be used to implement another step in the GD study which involves applying the Basic Local Alignment Search Tool (BLAST) analysis service. The BLAST call here can be used for identifying PDB records that might provide information on the structure of the protein that is encoded by the nucleotide sequence of the candidate gene. An example query is given below:

```
QUERY2:
select
     e.ProbeSetId, m.Sequence_ID, NCBIblast(s.sequence)
from
     e in expressions, m in Map_tabs, s in sequences
where
     e.Signal > 1000 and e.ProbeSetId = m.Probe_Set_ID and
     m.Molecular_Function_GO like <input GO:Id>
```

This query includes a call to a Web Service that wraps the BLAST analysis program hosted by the European Bioinformatics Institute (EBI) (see http://www .ebi.ac.uk/blastall/index.html) and it demonstrates a powerful feature of OGSA-DQP; that of combining invocations to analysis programs with data retrieval in a single query statement. Notice that the gene sequences retrieved from the *sequences* database (which may potentially constitute a set), are fed into the NCBIblast function call. Figure 5 shows the distributed query plan generated for QUERY2. Note that the sub-plan that contains an invocation to BLAST web service (i.e. OPERATION_CALL operator) is parallelised across two nodes (i.e. servers) on the grid (indicated by the textual label above the rectangular box in the middle with two machine names separated by a comma), since BLAST is a relatively high-cost operation.

Note that during execution of the queries, the databases are accessed via grid services (i.e. GDSs) and the intermediate data processing computations are also carried out by grid services (i.e. GQESs) all of which are linked with dynamically forged data-flow and control-flow paths, which effectively constructs a service orchestration framework. Note also that with the second query, the service orchestration is extended beyond data services and internal query evaluator services (i.e. GQESs) to external (i.e. third party) analysis services, making OGSA-DQP a declarative (i.e. query-driven) alternative to procedural (e.g. workflow-based) service-orchestration systems.

## 5   Alternative Methods for Using OGSA-DQP in Grid Applications

Although Section 4 described how OGSA-DQP can be used via a stand-alone GUI client, this is not the only way OGSA-DQP delivers its functionality. As OGSA-DQP is itself a Grid Service, exposing a programming interface in conformance to interaction patterns specified by the OGSA-DAI project, it can be integrated into higher-level applications in at least two other ways:

1. An application can discover the GDQS from public service registries, and interact with it via its service interface to submit the list of resources required for the distributed queries, and subsequently to pass the query requests themselves. The results received as a response to the query requests can then be transmitted to other processing modules in the application or presented to the user via application-specific user interfaces.
2. The GDQS can be invoked in an intermediate step in a more complex workflow involving calls to other services. This is a particularly interesting case as it leads to simplified workflows due to the replacement of many interlinked activities (i.e. a sub-workflow) with a call to OGSA-DQP as a single task, and could potentially result in performance gains, since OGSA-DQP optimizes and parallelises its query plans.

# 6   Conclusions and Future Work

This paper has described a distributed query processing service, namely OGSA-DQP, for service-based grids, and demonstrated how it can support the development of scientific grid applications via an example application from the bioinformatics domain. In summary, developers and users of scientific applications for the grid can stand to benefit from OGSA-DQP from several angles:

1. The users of the grid can benefit from OGSA-DQP as a generic data integration and analysis tool. A typical use-case involves deploying OGSA-DQP to a virtual organisation application server and configuring it with a set of frequently used data and analysis resources; a procedure most likely to be carried out by a system administrator. The configured OGSA-DQP can then be used to pose queries against the resource set. Section 4.2 described how the user mode of the OGSA-DQP GUI client allows one to query a set of resources.
2. The developers of scientific applications for the grid can delegate data integration tasks to OGSA-DQP, to implement a distinct functional part of a sophisticated application. It is worth noting that since a GDQS is fully compliant with data delivery and transformation patterns specified by OGSA-DAI, the application can command the GDQS to channel the results to another Grid Data Service, to send the results to a remote file system via FTP, to compress and save the results to the local file system, or to deliver the results asynchronously in blocks via streaming. See the OGSA-DQP user guide at www.ogsadai.org.uk/dqp for details.
3. As programming practice evolves from traditional coding models to service composition or service coreography, the developers of scientific application workflows can employ the GDQS to undertake the orchestration of a sub-set of services required for the overall solution. Our future work plans include integrating OGSA-DQP into various workflow execution environments, and carrying out more quantitative research on comparing performance characteristics of the two.

**Acknowledgements.** The work reported in this paper has been supported by the UK e-Science Programme.

# References

1. M. Alpdemir, A. Mukherjee, N. W. Paton, P. Watson, A. A. Fernandes, A. Gounaris, and J. Smith. Service-based distributed querying on the grid. In M. E. Orlowska, S. W. M. P. Papazoglou, and J. Yang, editors, *the Proceedings of the First International Conference on Service Oriented Computing*, pages 467–482. Springer–Verlag, 15–18 December 2003.
2. A. Anjomshoaa et al. The design and implementation of grid database services in OGSA-DAI. In S. J. Cox, editor, *Proceedings of UK e-Science All Hands Meeting Nottingham*. EPSRC, 2–4 September 2003.

3. I. Foster, C. Kesselman, J. Nick, and S. Tuecke. The Physiology of the Grid: An Open Grid Services Architecture for Distributed Systems Integration. Technical report, OGSI-WG, Global Grid Forum, 2002. Draft 2.9, June 22, 2002.

4. K. Gottschalk, S. Graham, H. Kreger, and J. Snell. Introduction to Web Services Architecture. *IBM Sys. Journal*, 41(2):170–177, 2002.

5. S. Graupner, V. Kotov, A. Andrzejak, and H. Trinks. Service-centric globally distributed computing. *IEEE Internet Computing*, 7(4):36 – 43, July/August 2003.

6. R. Khalaf and F. Leymann. On web services aggregation. In B. Benatallah and M. C. Shan, editors, *Proceedings of VLDB Technologies for e-Services Workshop*, LNCS 2819, pages 1 – 13. Springer–Verlag, 2003.

7. R. W. Moore, C. Baru, R. Marciano, A. Rajasekar, and M. Wan. Data-Intensive Computing. In I. Foster and C. Kesselman, editors, *The Grid: Blueprint for a New Computing Infrastrcuture*, chapter 5, pages 105–129. Morgan Kaufmann, 1999.

8. T. Sandholm and J. Gawor. Globus Toolkit 3 Core  A Grid Service Container Framework. Technical report, 2003. www-unix.globus.org/toolkit/3.0/ogsa/docs/.

9. R. Stevens et al. Performing in silico experiments on the grid: a users perspective. In S. J. Cox, editor, *Proceedings of UK e-Science All Hands Meeting Nottingham*, pages 43 – 50. EPSRC, 2–4 September 2003.

# Mobile Agent-Based Service Provision in Distributed Data Archives

Christos Georgousopoulos and Omer F. Rana

University of Wales, Cardiff (UK)
{geolos, o.f.rana}@cs.cf.ac.uk

**Abstract.** An agent-based architecture of an active Digital Library (DL) is first described, to illustrate how electronic service provision can be supported through the use of agents. The use of mobile agents is presented as a key enabler for allowing services to be combined from a variety of providers, each of which provide a subset of the total required service. Load balancing approaches are then used to illustrate how particular performance criteria can be achieved in service provision. Extrapolation of the approach to the general Service-Oriented computing model is also discussed. A DL composed of multi-spectral imagery of the Earth, as part of the Synthetic Aperture Radar Atlas (SARA) is then used to illustrate the concepts described. The load balancing technique proposed is based on a combination of the state and model-based approaches. Experimental results demonstrating the distribution of agent load among the servers that constitute the DL, and the optimization of performance provided by the adaptability of the model employed is presented. Such an approach is particularly suited to Grid environments, which can involve a composition of services from a variety of distributed data resources.

## 1 Introduction

Digital Libraries (DL) provide a useful way to group a collection of services and digital objects that may be used in a particular context. DL research has often focused on providing static content that may be subsequently accessed in a variety of ways. Recent focus on active DLs, whereby content from a collection of different repositories may be aggregated, provides useful parallels with work in Service-Oriented computing. Such repositories can be implemented using specialized hardware, and often support domain-specific interfaces. Accessing the content available within such a DL through the use of intelligent agents provides an important step in re-purposing such DL content. An agent, in our work, is seen as software capable of conforming to FIPA standards[1], and having a very specific functionality (role) within a larger system. Interaction between such agents is then based on demands made on them by other agents. In this way, a collection of agents can be

---

[1] FIPA: http://www.fipa.org/.

P. Herrero, M.S. Pérez, and V. Robles (Eds.): SAG 2004, LNCS 3458, pp. 25–37, 2005.
© Springer-Verlag Berlin Heidelberg 2005

used to provide a service-based layer to access the contents of a DL in a variety of different ways. The service-based architecture is demonstrated in the context of the Synthetic Aperture Radar Atlas (SARA), described in section 2. Load balancing issues to support performance-sensitive service delivery are described in section 3. Section 4 presents the proposed approach of load balancing for an active DL, followed by performance results in section 5. Conclusions follow in section 6.

## 2   The SARA Agent-Based Architecture

SARA is an active DL of multi-spectral remote sensing images of the Earth from the SIR-C Shuttle mission. Web-based online access is provided to a library of data objects at Caltech and the San Diego Supercomputer Center in the US, and the University of Lecce in Italy. The objective of the SARA project is to develop an infrastructure for a high-speed, high-volume, multi-protocol distributed database, together with a means to attach distributed computing resources for data conversion, visualization and knowledge discovery [13]. A prototype Multi-Agent System (MAS), which comprises both intelligent and mobile agents, has been developed to manage and analyze data in the SARA DL [8]. The SARA architecture is composed of a collection of *information* and W*eb* servers, each of them supporting a group of agents. Information servers support Local Interface Agents (LIA), whereas Web-servers support User Interface Agents (UIA). The information-servers manage the computational resources and data repositories to support the SARA active DL – where the data repositories generally contain pre-processed images or geospatial data about a given region. Figure 1 represents the SARA architecture and the multi-agent interaction. Our approach is based on localizing the most complex functionality in non-mobile LIAs, which remain at one location, providing resources and facilities to lightweight mobile agents that require less processor time to be serialized, and are therefore quicker to transmit. LIAs are stationary agents that provide a set of pre-defined services. The primary motivation for using mobile agents are: (a) the avoidance of large data transfers – of the order of Terabytes, consisting of sometimes proprietary data, (b) the ability to transfer user developed image analysis algorithms, and (c) the ability to utilize specialized parallel libraries.

SARA may be accessed by users via a Web-based GUI or via other FIPA-compliant agents (as part of an application) via an intermediate gateway; the gateways provide the interoperability layer of the architecture, described in detail in [5]. The Web-based interface allows a user to query a collection of SAR images, and provides the ability to further fuse the results with data available locally to the user. Such a request is received from UAA – trace the numbers in figure 1 – that creates a mobile agent i.e. URA on behalf of the user and forwards the request. After dispatch, the mobile agent is responsible of migrating to the information-servers and interacting with the local stationary agents to fulfill the user's request. The stationary agent LAA is responsible for supplying the URA with information about accessing the data repository at the local server, whereas the LRA's objective is to execute a query on the data source on behalf of the URA.

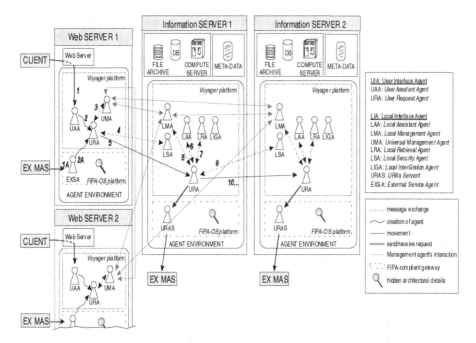

**Fig. 1.** The SARA agent-based architecture

Every stationary agent implementation consists of a number of different Java classes – allowing modularity and extensibility of the agent. In this instance, the amendment or introduction of a new service provided by an existing agent may be easily achieved without affecting the rest of the agent's code and a new Java class may be attached to an agent. For example, the maintenance of an information-server's data repository by a future DBMS may require updates only to a part of LAA code. Details of the architecture, describing system integration and data management issues can be found in [12,17].

## 3  Load Balancing

Generally, load balancing aims to improve the average utilization and performance of tasks on available servers, whilst observing particular constraints on task execution order. Assuming agents have a set of tasks to execute, it is necessary to identify how these tasks may be distributed across available servers. Hence, workload distribution must consider both the number of agents on a server and the number of tasks being executed by each agent. Load balancing can be either static or dynamic [9] according to the multi-agent system in which it is being considered. In static load balancing tasks cannot be migrated elsewhere once they have been launched on a specified server. In dynamic load balancing a task may migrate to another server, utilizing the agent's mobility. Keren and Barak [2] show that dynamic load balancing outperforms the static case, with a 30-40% improvement over the static placement scheme.

There are two basic approaches to distribute tasks among servers: the state-based and the model-based approach. In the state-based approach, information about the system state is used to determine where to start a task. The quality of this decision depends on the amount of the state data available. Gathering the data is expensive, but leads to a more accurate decision. In the model-based approach, load balancing depends on a model which predicts the system state and which may be inaccurate. Model-based approaches are more difficult to implement as they involve the derivation of an initial model, and the need to adapt the model over time.

In state-based load balancing, a common approach for managing system state and load is the *market* mechanism to value resources and achieve an efficient match of supply and demand for resources. Examples include Spawn [3] (based on a negotiated auction protocol), Dynast [10] and OCEAN [11] based on non-negotiable pricing mechanisms. System state may be accumulated in different ways, via specialized monitoring agents, such as Mats [14] and Traveler [6]. In the FLASH [16] system a *system* agent maintains information about the whole system state and passes it to *node* agents on each server in the network. Node agents monitor locally residing mobile agents. *User* agents (which are mobile) are responsible for the load balancing of the parallel application, and migrate through a cluster searching for free resources. Their migration decisions are based on internal states as well as internal and external events.

Almost all the systems that explore the model-based approach use distribution of CPU load and expected process/task lifetime to decide if and when to migrate. Malone's Enterprise [15] uses a market mechanism, and Challenger [1] uses a learning-based approach. Eager et al. [7] utilize concurrent execution to improve resource usage. Most of these approaches however cannot easily adapt to changing system workloads.

## 4  The SARA Load Balancing Mechanism

The SARA load balancing mechanism combines model-based and state-based approaches. The agents' tasks are classified into simple and complex. Simple tasks involve data gathering procedures. Whereas complex tasks filter the data retrieved from a simple task e.g. based on an image processing algorithm. Complex tasks require more processing power and time, and are assumed to less in number than simple tasks.

State-based load balancing in SARA is similar to the FLASH [16] approach, as specialized management agents (MAs) maintain a global view of the system, and are positioned in every server. They are used to gather, disseminate and update the system state information. This is because an active DL may be composed of a collection of different information and computation resources (though some might be replicated) and where the resources needed by each task are unknown before its initiation, efficient load balance may only be achieved with a global view of the system. In our system, decisions on load balancing are supported though the MAs and not the mobile agents (in contrast with FLASH). The advantages of the MAs having control over such decisions leads to: (a) minimization of information transmitted over the network, (b) minimization of the mobile agents' size, and (c) better overall system optimization, as discussed in [4].

## 4.1  Model-Based Load Balancing

The model-based approach in SARA is mainly based on the servers' CPU utilization, and emphasis is given to the prediction of an agents' task lifetime. The model adapts over time due to the information gathered from the state-based approach. Reliable capture of system state is important, and therefore the information exchanged between the MAs is a very important factor for prediction. Firstly because the efficiency of the model depends on it (i.e. quality of information), and secondly because the greater the amount of information the higher the risk for an increase in network load. The main information exchanged in state-based approaches, is the number of agents on each server and the number of available servers along with their utilisation indexes. A second factor in either state-based or model-based approaches is the utilization of the servers used in a network, in relation to their processing power. Irrespective of the algorithm used for the distribution of tasks among the available servers, a common policy is that a task should be assigned to the least loaded server i.e. the one with less utilization – assuming that servers are of equal processing power. Consequently, the more accurate the estimation of a server's utilization, the better the load balancing decision.

## 4.2  Estimation of a Server's Utilization

The utilization of a server at any point of time is directly correlated with its load i.e. the tasks being executed at that time. Malone [15] defines the utilization of a system by the expected amount of processing requested per time unit, divided by the total amount of processing power in the system, and give by: $U = (\alpha \cdot \mu)/L$; where, $\alpha$ is the average number of job arrivals per time unit, $\mu$ is the average job length, and $L$ is the total processing power in the system. In the SARA algorithm-model this formula is used to evaluate the utilization of each server separately. Therefore for a given server, $\alpha$ corresponds to the number of agents on that server (assuming that there is a one task per agent), $\mu$ to the average task time of the $\alpha$ agents, and $L$ to the total processing power of the hosting server. A server's utilization in relation to its processing power $L$, can be estimated. Such a comparison on utilization values helps identify a server that will be unloaded first i.e. will accomplish all of its tasks sooner than any of the rest of the servers. Accuracy of estimating a server's utilization is based on a perfect estimation of the agent task lifetimes. The more accurate the average task time $\mu$ of agents $\alpha$, the more reliable the corresponding server's utilization.

The actual utilization of a server can be measured by using specialized routines/utilities (like *xload* or *ps,* available on the Unix operating system) that provide the percentage CPU usage. FLASH makes use of such a scheme to acquire the servers' utilization. The difference between those kinds of routines and Malone's approach is that while the former provides the current utilisation (CPU usage) of a server the latter also denotes a value of when a server will be unloaded, and may be used as a predictive tool. As a server's CPU usage changes frequently, decisions on load balance should not only rely on the current utilization of each server, but rather on which server will be unloaded first in the future. The advantage of using Malone's formula is that apart from estimating utilization, it is also possible to predict it before the assignment of a new task to that server, given that the lifetime of the corresponding task is known.

### 4.3  The Model

Load balancing decisions are based on a model which accepts as input an agent's requirements and the system state information, and gives as output the appropriate server(s) where the particular agent should migrate to in order to fulfill its task. The model is a function of the: (1) agents' tasks, (2) servers' utilization (workload), (3) availability of resources at the server, and (4) network efficiency. The model may be better expressed with reference to the agents' task as a tree structure, depicted in figure 2. For each of these cases indicated by numbers 1-7, the itinerary of a mobile agent is constructed based on the factors stated above.

As described earlier, an agent task might be simple or complex. A simple agent task which undertakes the acquisition of data composed of a collection of SAR images may be either completely new, exactly the same or similar (part of it) to a task performed by another agent in the past. The coordinates of the images that have to be collected contribute in comparing simple agent tasks. A complex agent task may be considered as an extension of a simple one since it concerns the filtering of the results acquired by a processing algorithm that exists on a compute server, referred to as fixed filter, or by a custom one provided by the user.

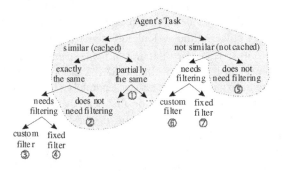

**Fig. 2.** Representation of all possible cases of an agent's task as a tree structure

The itinerary of an agent is constructed by its local MA each time before the initiation of its task. The itinerary of an agent with a simple task comprises a list of server addresses, with the appropriate resources in descending order, based on the servers' workload which can serve the agent's task. The first server on the list is characterised as the ideal one where the agent can accomplish its task fastest, and the rest provide alternative option of migration.

Since the acquisition of information precedes its filtering, the construction of an agent's itinerary with a complex task requires input from the MA twice. Initially, an itinerary composed of suitable servers is created for the acquisition of the appropriate data (a simple agent task for instance), subsequently a second itinerary for the processing of the data (after they have been collected) consists of a list of compute servers. The existence of two separate itineraries is compulsory. Firstly because it is impossible to decide on which compute servers a filtering task can be performed, as the amount and kind of data to be processed is unknown. Secondly, on a dynamic environment where server/resource conditions change frequently, decisions on load balancing must be taken directly before the initiation of a task. Hence, the construction of an agent's itinerary with a simple task is mainly based on the current utilization of the available servers, whereas the itinerary of an agent with a filtering task (since its lifetime can be estimated) is mainly based on the predicted utilization of the available servers i.e. the utilization of the servers that would result after the execution of the particular task on each of them. Cases 1 to 5 in figure 2 occur when an agent's task is similar to a task performed by another agent in the past, whereas cases 5 to 7 occur when a task has not been performed previously.

### 4.4  Adaptability of Model

The Enterprise and Challenger model-based approaches to load balancing use Malone's formula of system utilization. Their model is based on the distribution of CPU load and expected lifetime of tasks. However, it is sometimes impossible to estimate task lifetimes beforehand (e.g. the time a user is running a remote application) or such estimates may be erroneous. To deal with such errors in estimation, the Enterprise system uses an *estimation error tolerance* parameter. If a task takes significantly longer than it was estimated to take (i.e. more than the estimation error tolerance), the server running the task aborts it, and notifies the user who initiated the task that that task has been *cutoff*. This cutoff feature prevents the possibility of a few users or tasks monopolizing an entire system. Challenger on the other hand introduces learning behavior in the bidding agents to deal with errors in estimating task completion times. In Challenger, those agents who misestimate the lifetime of their tasks are penalized. Therefore, during a bid evaluation process, each agent's bid (i.e. lifetime of its task) is adjusted by multiplying it by the agent's current inflation factor. For instance, if an agent has recently been making perfectly accurate bids, its inflation factor will be 1.0 and its bid will not be altered. Otherwise, if an agent has been recently turning in task completion times that are twice as long as what it estimated, then its bid will be multiplied by an inflation factor of approximately 2.0.

The SARA model is based on simple agent tasks for which the lifetime is predicted to be equal to the average task completion time in previous runs. For complex tasks, lifetime can be estimated based on calculations on the collected data to be filtered. The major parameter on distributing tasks among the servers is the workload on the available servers. If the lifetime of complex tasks was unknown, then the model would not function properly, since complex tasks influence the utilization of a server significantly more than simple tasks. In order for the model adopted in SARA to be applicable to other systems in which the lifetime of complex tasks is impossible to estimate or predict, or where lifetime of tasks are erroneous, the model should provide a means of self-adapting to such error estimations. The policy of Challenger system on penalizing the agents for misestimating the lifetime of their tasks based on prior recorded estimations cannot be followed by the SARA model, because in SARA each user request (task) is represented by a different agent. Whereas the approach of the Enterprise system on setting a threshold value, which when exceeded leads to task termination is impractical for tasks with unknown lifetimes. The adaptability in the SARA model is intended for systems in which the lifetime of complex tasks cannot be estimated. The algorithm is activated by the MAs and its objective is to monitor the utilization of every server and amends it when it is miscalculated, due to the introduction of agent tasks with unknown lifetime in the servers.

### 4.4.1 The Adaptation Algorithm

The utilization of a given server has a direct relation to the average task completion time of the agents on that server (as utilization is the server's agent load divided by its processing power). Furthermore, assuming no other operations are being performed on a server, the utilization of a server only changes when its agent load changes i.e. when an agent enters or leaves the server. Since the lifetime of complex tasks is unknown, the selection of servers on which agents can fulfill their tasks is based on the current utilization of suitable servers and not on their predicted utilization (after the complex task has been run on them). This implies that the utilization of a server on the arrival of a complex task is not actually affected, since the lifetime of the corresponding complex task is not added as extra time to the server's agent load, resulting in an incorrect evaluation of a server's utilization.

The algorithm runs on each server separately. On the arrival of the first agent on a server, the algorithm sets a timer which after a predefined time calls a procedure *check_AvTaskComplTime*. Initially the timer is set equal to the average task completion time of agents on the corresponding server. The *check_AvTaskComplTime* procedure monitors the transit of agents on a server. If no agent has left the server up to the time where *check_AvTaskComplTime* has been initialized, it means that the number of agents on that server has been either increased or remained unchanged. This implies that the agents present on the server (or even the first agent that arrived on the server) have not accomplished their task by the expected time i.e. the time corresponding to the average task completion time of an agent. The average task completion time of agents on a given server (and therefore its utilization) are updated only after the departure of an agent from that server. Therefore, until an agent accomplishes its task the utilization is unchanged. Provided that the agents require more time to complete their task, the algorithm's objective is to update the utilization of that server based on the increase in the average task completion time of those agents that have completed, and publish this information to the rest of the MAs. This updated must be repeated after regular intervals. Once an agent leaves the server, the lifetime of its task is used to update the average task completion time of agents on that server, and calculate the utilization of the server. The timer of the algorithm which activates the *check_AvTaskCompl Time* procedure is triggered in different time intervals due to the change in the average task completion time of agents. It is stopped when there are no agents left on the server.

## 5   Experimental Results

Experimental results on balancing the load of mobile agent tasks among the information-servers is presented in this section. The top graph of figure 3 displays the utilization of each of the five information-servers used in the SARA prototype during the launch of 200 agents. Agents consisted of simple tasks and the graph demonstrates the even distribution of agent load among the servers.

The load balancing experiments were performed on a 100Mbit/s Fast Ethernet network with six Sun Ultra 5 Workstations of a 270 MHz UltraSPARC-IIi 64-bit processor running on Solaris 8, utilising the Voyager 4.5 agent platform from Recursion Software. Of the available machines, five were used as information-servers and one as a Web-server. Every information-server had a data repository maintained by the Oracle DBMS, composed of replicated test-data. Each server had identical computational capabilities.

Note that the utilization of a server in the SARA load balancing model does not represent its actual CPU usage, but its agent load (or the expected time when the server will become unloaded). Since the utilization of a server is updated after the arrival of an agent from that server, small changes are expected to appear due to the intervals of sampling values recorded.

The introduction of agents with complex tasks in the agent load resulted in higher deviations of a server's utilization. Complex tasks apart from the data gathering procedure included the fusion of agent's results against different filtering algorithm on-site. The second graph of figure 3 illustrates the utilization of the information-servers on which 15% of the agents launched had complex tasks.

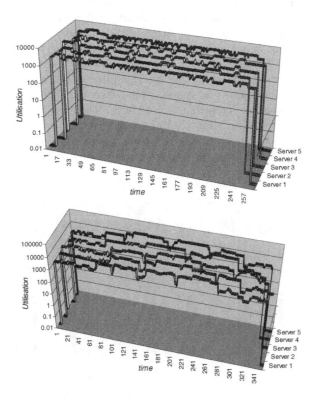

**Fig. 3.** Utilisation of Information-servers on the execution of simple and mixed agent tasks

The variations in utilization of each server are higher in comparison with the previous graph, due to the arrival/departure of agents with complex tasks that require more time to be processed. Though it can be observed that the utilization of each server fluctuates at the same level as the other servers, where after a high drop in utilization of a server caused by the completion of one or more complex task(s), there is a rise to set the server's utilization equivalent to the utilization of the other servers.

Since a server of which has a lower utilization can handle more tasks that with a higher utilization, and the objective of load balancing is to evenly utilize the resources of each server, more tasks are assigned to the least loaded servers. Therefore, the rise on a server's utilization results from the constant assignment of agents with either simple or complex tasks to that server, increasing in that way its utilization until the agent load in every server is balanced.

### 5.1 Adaptability of Model

In order to explore the efficiency of the adaptability algorithm, three different load balancing schemes have been developed; labeled as LB scheme No.1, No.2 and No.3 in figures 4, 5, and 6. LB scheme No.1. LB scheme No.1 represents the default load balancing scheme adopted in the SARA system. LB scheme No.2 is an alternative version of scheme No.1 in which the lifetime of complex agent tasks is unknown, and therefore not used the in calculations, and LB scheme No.3 is an alternative version of scheme No.2 in which the adaptable algorithm is utilized for amending the server's utilisation due to the introduction of agent tasks with unknown lifetime in the servers.

The purpose of the experiments is to examine at what percentage LB scheme No.3 reaches the performance of LB scheme No.1; in other words, test the functionality of the adaptability algorithm by systems within which the lifetime of complex tasks cannot be estimated or predicted successfully. The performance of each load balancing scheme on distributing 200 agent tasks among five information-servers, according to the total time required by those agents to accomplish their tasks is presented in figure 4. The experimental tests performed on each load balancing

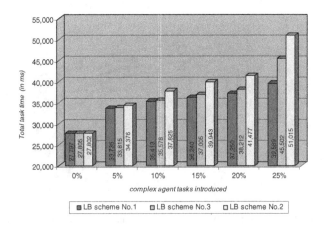

**Fig. 4.** Total task time required by agents to complete their tasks

scheme within the SARA system have been based on a variable introduction of complex tasks to test the efficiency of the algorithm.

The lower the value of each bar in the graph of figure 4, the lower the time required by the agents to complete their tasks in total, thereby resulting in better load balancing. The value of each bar corresponds to the mean value sampled from the conduction of four experiments on each of the three load balancing schemes for six different variable introductions of complex tasks in agent load, resulting in the launch of 14,000 mobile agents in total. As it would have been expected, LB scheme No.1 which is based on known or correctly predicted lifetime of agent tasks, disseminates properly the agent load among the servers by evenly utilizing each server, and therefore resulting on the fastest completion of agent tasks in comparison with the other two LB schemes; where obviously when there are no complex tasks involved all of the three LB schemes behave the same.

The difference in performance between LB scheme No.1 and LB scheme No.2 and No.3 is expressed in figure 5. The chart compares LB scheme No.1 with LB schemes

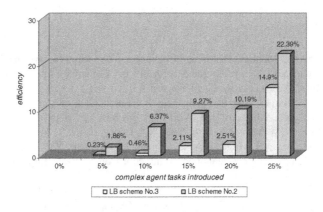

**Fig. 5.** Efficiency between LB scheme No.2 and No.3

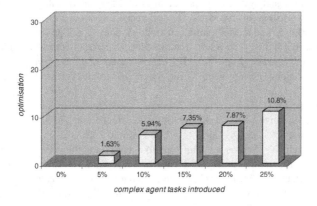

**Fig. 6.** Optimization of LB scheme No.2, based on the utilisation of the adaptability algorithm

No.2 and No.3, where the difference in performance between LB scheme No.2 and No.3 is due to the utilization of the adaptability algorithm is depicted in figure 6.

Figure 6 reveals the optimisation in performance arising from the use of the adaptability algorithm. From figures 4, 5 and 6 it can be inferred that the higher the introduction of complex tasks of unknown lifetime in a system (from 5% to 25%), the better the load balancing by the use of the adaptability algorithm – with an improvement of between 1.63% to 10.8%.

# 6   Conclusion

The design of a load balancing model depends on the properties and functional needs of the agent-based system. The proposed model may be employed by other systems utilizing active archives, in which the lifetime of complex tasks cannot be estimated or tend to be erroneous. System developers can take advantage of the adaptability of the model to cater for variable system workloads.

# References

[1]   A. Chavez, A. Moukas, P. Maes, "Challenger: A multi-agent system for distributed resource allocation.", in proceedings of the 1$^{st}$ Int. Conference on Autonomous Agents, ACM Press, Marina del Ray, CA, USA, 1997.

[2]   A. Keren, A. Barak, "Adaptive placement of parallel java agents in a scalable computing cluster", in proceedings of the Workshop on Java for High Performance Network Computing, ACM Press, Palo Alto, CA, USA, 1998.

[3]   C.A. Waldspurger, T. Hogg, B.A. Huberman, J.O. Kephart, W.S. Stornetta, "Spawn: a distributed computational economy", transactions on Software Engineering, 18(2):103 117, 1992.

[4]   C. Georgousopoulos, O.F. Rana, "Combining state and model-based approaches for mobile agent load balancing", in proceedings of Symp. on Applied Computing (SAC03), ACM press, ISBN 1-58113-624-2, held in Melbourne, Florida, USA, 2003, pp. 878-885.

[5]   C. Georgousopoulos, O.F. Rana, A. Karageorgos,  "Supporting FIPA interoperability for legacy multi-agent systems", in proceedings of 4$^{th}$ Agent Oriented Software Engineering (AOSE) workshop of AAMAS'03 conference, Springer-Verlag LNCS 2004, ISBN 3-540-20826-7, held in Melbourne, Australia, Sydney, 2003, pp. 167-184.

[6]   C.Z. Xu, B. Wims, "Traveler: a mobile agent infrastructure for wide area parallel computing", in proceedings of the IEEE Joint Sump. of 1$^{st}$ Int. Symp. on Agent Systems and Applications (ASA'99) and 3$^{rd}$ Int. Symp. on Mobile Agents (MA'99), Palm Springs, 1999.

[7]   D.L., Eager, E.D. Lazowska, J. Zahorjan, "Adaptive load sharing in homogeneous distributed systems", IEEE Trans. on Software Engineering,vol SE-12,1986,pp.662-675.

[8]   http://www.cs.cf.ac.uk/Digital-Library/, last viewed 2003

[9]   J. Gomoluch, M. Schroeder, "Information agents on the move: A survey on load-balancing with mobile agents", in Software Focus, vol. 2, no. 2, Wiley, 2001.

[10]  M. Backschat, A. Pfaffinger, C. Zenger, "Economic-based dynamic load distribution in large workstation networks", in proceedings of the 2$^{nd}$ Int. Euro-Par Conference, volume 2, Lyon, France, 1996, pp. 631-634.

[11] OCEAN - Open Computation Exchange & Auctioning (or Arbitration) Network, http://www.cise.ufl.edu/~mpf/ocea n/index.htm, last visited 2004.

[12] O.F. Rana, Y. Yang, C. Georgousopoulos, D.W. Walker, R.D. Williams, "Agent based data analysis for the SARA Digital Library", in proceedings of the Int. workshop on advanced data storage/management for high performance computing, ISSN 1362-0223, held at CLRC-Daresbury laboratory, Warrington, U.K., 2000, pp. 211-210.

[13] R.D. Williams, B. Sears, "A High-Performance Active Digital Library", Parallel Computing, special issue on Metacomputing, 1998.

[14] R. Ghanea-Hercock, J.C. Collis, D.T. Ndumu, "Co-operating mobile agents for distributed parallel processing", in proceedings of the 3rd Int. Conference on Autonomous Agents, ACM press, Mineapolis, USA, 1999.

[15] T.W. Malone, R.E. Fikes, K.R. Grant, M.T. Howard, "Enterprise: A market-like Task Scheduler for Distributed Computing Environments", in: The Ecology of Computation. Ed. Huberman, B. A. Elsevier, Holland, 1988.

[16] W. Obeloeer, C. Grewe, "Load management with mobile agents", in proceedings of the 24th EUROMICRO Conference, IEEE, 1998, pp. 1005-1012.

[17] Y. Yang, O.F. Rana, D.W. Walker, C. Georgousopoulos, G. Aloisio, R.D. Williams, "Agent based data management in Digital Libraries Remote-Sensing Archive", published in Parallel Computing Journal, Elsevier Science, vol. 28, issue 5, 2002, pp. 773-792.

# A Proxy Service for the xrootd Data Server

Andrew Hanushevsky and Heinz Stockinger

Stanford Linear Accelerator Center (SLAC), Stanford University,
2575 Sand Hill Road, Menlo Park, CA-94025, USA
{abh, Heinz}@slac.stanford.edu

**Abstract.** In data intensive sciences like High Energy Physics, large amounts of data are typically distributed and/or replicated to several sites. Although there exist various ways to store and access this data within a Grid environment, site security policies often prohibit end user access to remote sites. These limitations are typically overcome using a proxy service that requires limited network connections to and from remote sites. We present a novel proxy server for the xrootd data server that provides access to data stored in an object-oriented data store (typically in ROOT format). Our proxy service operates in a structured peer-to-peer environment and allows for fault tolerant and reliable access to remote data.

## 1 Introduction

In a Data Grid environment security is one of the main issues. On the one hand, data needs to be securely stored in specific data stores to guarantee local site security as well as data integrity. On the other hand, network access imposes additional security concerns that might not be directly addressed by the storage system. Grid middleware, file servers as well as database specific client-server or peer-to-peer applications need to deal with network security. One of the most commonly applied solutions is to set up firewalls and restrict the number of in- and/or outbound network connections.

Often, client applications in a Data Grid are executed in an Internet Free Zone (IFZ) or run on machines that do not allow for outgoing network connections. However, due to the nature of a Data Grid, data is distributed and/or replicated to several data stores outside the LAN where the client application needs to execute. In addition, a client application may need to access non-local data and therefore requires access to remote sites without compromising the local security infrastructure. One way to overcome this issue is to apply a proxy server that relays client requests to a remote machine outside the local firewall.

A proxy server adds an additional point for retrieving and temporarily caching data, and thus potentially means a slight overhead, appearing as increased latency, in data transfer. However, this overhead is often accepted in cases where security concerns are more important than very high speed data access.

One of the most commonly used data stores for data intensive sciences in the High Energy Physics community is the ROOT framework [9]. It allows for data storage, retrieval, physics specific data analysis, etc. Remote data access is usually done via a ROOT data server called rootd (ROOT daemon). Recently, this data server has been

P. Herrero, M.S. Pérez, and V. Robles (Eds.): SAG 2004, LNCS 3458, pp. 38–49, 2005.

enhanced by xrootd [6], an extended, high performance data server. Xrootd was partly developed to access ROOT files, but it can be considered as a general data server that provides POSIX like file access to any kind of data. Although xrootd is a very reliable and secure server, the problem of outbound network connectivity still needs to be tackled.

In this paper, we describe another extension to the xrootd data server system where proxy servers take care of local client requests and then serve the data from a remote site if required. In this way, application clients only need to have network connectivity to the local proxy server(s) and access to remote data is guaranteed.

## 2 The Problem Domain

Several data intensive sciences like High Energy Physics require access to remote data. However, site administrators do not always allow client applications to directly access remote files because of network security issues. This is particularly true for Data Grids where client applications are executed on a worker node that is in an Internet free zone.

Several Grid data management solutions in major Grid projects do not directly address this problem, and mainly deal with entire file transfers [15,1] rather than POSIX like read/write file access. Given that a majority of physics data is stored in object stores such as ROOT [9], there is a clear need for a high level file access in order to analyze data. Due to the distribution of both, users and data (potentially all over the world), remote access is of major importance. In addition, partial and random file access is needed in order to reduce network traffic and increase end user access performance.

Physics experiments such as BaBar [12] at SLAC or Large Hadron Collider experiments at CERN generate large quantities of data that are stored both on disks and on tertiary storage devices that include low-latency tape and hierarchical storage systems [5]. Although our proposed system takes care of interaction with such systems, we limit our discussion to disks only.

If no direct access to remote data is allowed, proxies are one way to allow for reading remote data. This implies that a proxy server acts on behalf of a user, contacts a remote data server, reads the requested data and sends the result back to the client. Proxies are very common in the Internet and typically used by web servers. In a Data Grid environment where data security is of major importance, proxies can be used for all possible services that would need data or information from a remote site.

## 3 General Overview of xrootd

### 3.1 The Basics of the Data Server

The basic purpose of the xrootd data server is to provide access to files stored on secondary (disk) or tertiary storage devices (tape or hierarchical storage devices). The files do not have to be organized in special formats since the data server provides file I/O similar to a POSIX file system interface. In particular, files that reside in a certain file system are served by the xrootd data server. Using the xrootd, end users that want to access files in a certain domain need to connect to the server which then provides read or write access to a client. Client-sever communication is done via the xrootd protocol [6].

A typical example for such a client-server communication is depicted in Figure 1. The xrootd server runs on a certain machine and serves all files that are located in a specific directory: in our example it is /data. Assume a remote user on the same local area network but without direct access to the disk of the xrootd server. This user now wants to open the file /data/file1 (using a POSIX like *open* command), get the file size (using *stat*) and then read 1,000 bytes of that file starting from offset 3,000 (using the *read* call). In order to achieve all this, a client connects to the server using the xrootd protocol via respective client libraries. All previously mentioned calls are then sent to the server which in turn reads the file from disk and sends the requested bytes back to the client.

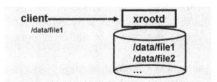

**Fig. 1.** Basic client-server interaction with an xrootd server

The xrootd request/response protocol contains more file system related calls such as chmod, getfile, putfile and write. For more details we refer the reader to [6].

## 3.2 Design Principles

xrootd is a high-performance data server where several hundred user requests can be served in parallel, depending on the hardware configuration. However, a single data server is often not resilient to many kinds of server, network or hardware failures. Therefore, the xrootd system is designed to allow for several data servers where client requests get automatically redirected to a different data server for load balancing and fault tolerance reasons. In other words, multiple data servers located on multiple machines can serve client requests potentially for the same file. Based on the load of a single data server and the location of a requested file, a client request gets redirected to one of the servers that is potentially able to serve the request with minimal latency.

Given that the xrootd system is not a single client-server system but requires servers to be coordinated, we can distinguish the following main interactions in the system.

- On the one hand, the system needs to find out where data is located and which server is least loaded to provide the requested data. We refer to this as **control flow**. Part of the control flow can be compared to replica lookups with redirection as we reported in [12].
- Once a suitable data server is selected, the actual data needs to be transferred between the data server and the client. We call this the **data flow**.

The distinction between control and data flow is rather common and is found in many peer-to-peer file sharing systems (BitTorrent, GnuTella), distributed file systems (Google, Lustre, PFS) and data transfer protocols such as FTP. One of the main design principles of the xrootd is a separation of **data flow** and **control flow** when serving data to a client.

In order to allow for separation of concerns, data flow is achieved by data servers (i.e. the **xrootd** discussed in Section 3.1) whereas the control flow is done by servers that are dedicated to that purpose. Since the main purpose of such servers is to locate data and balance the load they are called **open load balancers** (**olb**) in this context. Simply put, data severs and load balancers work together to serve client requests. An end user only needs to know about data servers and their locations in order to retrieve data. Therefore, whenever we talk about the xrootd system in this paper, we refer to the entire system that consists of data servers and load balancers.

### 3.3 Basic Architecture

The overall architecture of the xrootd system consists of several components that are implemented in either the data server or the load balancer. The orchestration and interaction of these main servers are implemented as a **structured peer-to-peer system**, where data servers and load balancers can have different roles to achieve the overall goal to serve data. Before we go into the details of the server interaction, we describe the different roles that servers can have, as depicted in Figure 2.

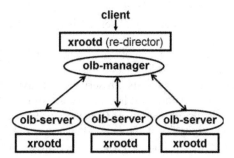

**Fig. 2.** Interaction in the xrootd structured peer-to-peer system. It shows the clear distinction between control and data flow as well as the different roles

A data server (xrootd) can act either as a pure data server or as a redirector:

- A **pure data server** knows the xrootd protocol and can only serve data located on a certain file system. Its task is to handle a client request for data and directly transfer data to the client. On the bottom of Figure 2, we have three pure data servers named xrootd, each potentially located on a different machine in the same local area network.
- A **redirector** knows the xrootd protocol and accepts client calls for file access but rather than serving data directly, it interacts with load balancers in order to find a suitable data server that can serve the client request.

The interaction of load balancers, also referred to as the **control network**, consists of identifying where data is located and which of the pure data servers (xrootds) will serve data to the client. In order to structure the interaction in the control network, a load balancer (olb), can have one of the following roles: manager or server.

- An olb-manager (also referred to as **manager**), has the task to accept data location requests from an xrootd redirector. Next, the manager needs to interact with olb-servers to check the current load and the availability of files.
- An olb-server (also referred to as **server**), subscribes to an olb-manager and thus is committed to provide data location information to the manager. Once a data server is located, the redirector redirects the client to that server.

Note the difference between olb-server and data server. Whereas the olb-server only provides the location information (control flow), the xrootd data server really serves the actual data (data flow). In addition, the interaction between olb-managers and olb-servers is done using the olb protocol rather than the xrootd protocol.

We call this architecture structured peer-to-peer because at any instance has a specific role. This provides critical administrative predictability to the system. On the other hand, it is peer-to-peer since servers act as clients under certain conditions.

### 3.4  Request Flow

We now extend our example from Section 3.1 in order to explain the request flow (control and data flow) for a typical read request.

1. The end user client contacts an xrootd server that, typically unknown to the client, acts as a redirector.
2. The redirector asks its associated olb-manager, which may or may not be co-located, for the location of the file.
3. The olb-manager interacts with all its olb-servers that have subscribed to the control network. Each olb-server reports if it has an instance of the requested file.
4. The olb-manager collects all responses. If a suitable data server has been reported, the olb-manager returns the hostname of the data server to the redirector.
5. The redirector sends the hostname back to the client, indicating that the client request is redirected to a new xrootd.
6. The client contacts the xrootd server indicated by the redirection response of the redirector. If the current xrootd is configured to be a pure data server, the requested bytes for the read request are sent back to the client. Otherwise, the process is repeated until the client is redirected to a pure data server.

The design and implementation of the system allow that olbs and xrootds can be used with other systems like Objectivity [18] and thus allow for a wide range of interoperability. The current servers can be re-used as long as they speak either the xrootd or the olb protocol.

### 3.5  Data Security

Up to now, we mainly discussed network security issues related to firewalls and network connections. Within a site, secure access to data is fundamental, in particular for the interaction with the xrootd. The xrootd allows for a secure access to data via authentication of clients as well as authorization policies on the server side. The authorization is handled via ACL like access permissions that are stored in a separate configuration file. By means of a generic security interface, several security protocol implementations can be used, i.e. dynamically loaded at startup time of the xrootd server.

The basic request authentication is done when the client contacts the server to open a file. The xrootd protocol internally requires a login as well as an authentication procedure for this purpose. The flexible security interface allows for several authentication steps, based on the used security protocol. Currently, the system has implementations of Kerberos security, but is also extensible to the more commonly used Grid Security Infrastructure (GSI).

# 4  The Proxy Service

The architecture presented in Section 3 allows for a flexible system of data and load balancing servers distributed to several locations within a local area network or spread around in a Grid environment. The system also allows for access to replicated data in several locations. However, in all cases, a redirection request to a new data server requires that a client (used by an end user application) has external network connectivity to a remote data server. In addition, the load balancer control network requires potential outbound network connectivity if load balancers of remote sites (olb-servers) have subscribed to the local load balancer (olb-manager), i.e. olb-manager and olb-server reside in different sites. In the following section we introduce a proxy service that extends the presented architecture.

## 4.1  Architectural Overview

The main aim of the proxy service is to act on behalf of a client (in this case also on behalf of the end user). The proxy service retrieves the requested data from a remote data server and sends it back to the client. The basic concept is rather straight forward. However, the challenge is to integrate the proxy service with the existing peer-to-peer system of data servers and load balancers outlined above.

Basically, the xrootd data server is extended to contact a remote xrootd data server. Since the original data server acts as a client to the remote data server, it needs to use the xrootd protocol like any other client. Therefore, in our peer-to-peer system we allow for an additional interaction between a pair of xrootd servers to exchange data.

We recall that the xrootd acting as a pure data server only knows about its local files, and it does not know about any other hosts. Only a redirector knows about an olb-manager and can contact it in order to obtain the location of a file served by a pure data server[1]. Given this, we extend the functionality of a redirector such that an xrootd can serve as a **proxy**. In detail, a proxy-capable xrootd (also referred to as proxy server) first needs to ask its corresponding olb-manager for the location of a file. This lookup is equivalent to the lookup for a potential redirection. However, rather than returning a redirection response to the client, the proxy-capable xrootd directly connects to the remote data server and relays the received client request to the

---

[1] We restrict our discussion to this simple arrangement. In fact, the xrootd may redirect a client to a virtual data server, sometimes called aggregator, that will in-turn redirect a client to a pure data server. This scenario is outside the scope of this paper.

remote server, acting on behalf of the client. Once the proxy server has received the requested data from the remote server, it can send it back to the client. This simplified information flow is depicted in Figure 3. Note that although the proxy has now the feature of a redirector in the sense that it can ask the control network for the location of a remote file, the proxy is also similar to a pure data server since it also serves data to the user rather than redirecting the client request.

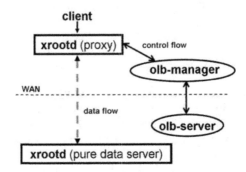

**Fig. 3.** Simplified interaction between client, proxy and remote data server

The minimal peer-to-peer topology presented in Figure 3 allows for shielding the client completely from the Internet in case the remote data server is located in a remote site only reachable via a wide area network connection. Therefore, a client has potential access to data distributed all over the globe but only needs to access a local proxy server that then retrieves the requested data.

Since both the olb-manager as well as the proxy server requires outbound network connectivity to the Internet, only two network ports have to be opened to the "outside" world: the port where the olb-manager talks in order to retrieve data location information, as well as the port where the proxy server sends its data requests to a remote data server. The client itself, typically located in the Internet Free Zone (IFZ), only needs to have access to the proxy server and does not require any further outbound network connections.

The described architecture so far only requires a modification/extension for xrootd data servers whereas load balancers are unchanged. In other words, no modification to the code of the olb was required. This is fine for a simple scenario with a single proxy server. However, if there is a conventional redirector in the local area network, a potential client request might still get redirected to the remote data server since the control network system does not distinguish between servers within the local domain and remote domain when selecting file locations. This apparent problem is readily solvable by a simple configuration options. We can impose the configurable rule that local data servers and remote data servers may not subscribe to the same olb-manager.

### 4.2 Configuration/Deployment Options

Both, xrootds and olbs are configurable and allow for several different deployment scenarios. For simplicity, we previously mentioned only the minimal number of servers in the structured peer-to-peer system to explain the basic interaction. However, in a real deployment environment where thousands of users and potentially millions of files are distributed to several sites in a Grid environment, a single proxy and/or a single data server per site is not sufficient. One can also have several redirectors or several proxies per site. Furthermore, while we always coupled xrootds with olbs (manager or server) on the same machine; one can use any number of xrootds and olbs on any number of machines. Further, as mentioned previously, olbs can act as aggregators for other olbs. Thus, one olb might actually report file information for several xrootd data servers.

The xrootd data server can either serve data directly from a disk location or contact a mass storage system such as HPSS [5] to stage the file. Once the file is staged, the xrootd can serve it to the client. Since a data server acts as a proxy, we still provide this configurable option that files can also be staged. In addition, a proxy first tries to find a file on a potential local disk and only if it fails, it requests the file from remote data server. In this way, potential transfer latencies are reduced if the file can be served locally. This also allows administrators to configure pure data servers to act as proxies as a matter of last resort.

### 4.3 Implementation

The entire xrootd system has been implemented in C++ and ported to several platforms (Sun Solaris 8, 9, Linux RedHat 7.x (currently the most commonly used Linux platform in HEP), Linux RedHat Enterprise edition 3.0) using native Solaris, GNU, and Intel compilers.

The standard xrootd system as presented in Section 3 has been fully implemented and is used in production in the BaBar experiment. Although the data servers are implemented using the xrootd protocol, the actual servers allow for other protocols by dynamically loading a protocol implementation compatible with a client's first interaction with the server.

For the proxy server, the most important xrootd methods have been implemented, i.e. login, open, read, stat, auth etc. in a synchronous, blocking environment. The xrootd dynamically loads a proxy object, which implements the xrootd client code, when the olb-manager returns the hostname and port information of a remote data server.

## 5  Experimental Results

The testbed we used for our experimental results corresponds to a typical Data Grid setup where an end-user client application gets executed on a worker node of a computing element [15]. For simplicity, we only assume one worker node that is behind a firewall and requires access to local data on the same local area network as well as remote data accessible via a proxy server. We used four different sites as indicated below. The client was deployed at SLAC with servers at each of the four sites. The numbers in brackets correspond to the Round Trip Time (RTT) of TCP packets from SLAC to the given site:

- *SLAC: Menlo Park, California (RTT local)*      *CERN: Geneva, Switzerland(RTT 165ms)*
- *Caltech: Pasadena, California (RTT 13ms)*      *Pisa: Pisa, Italy (RTT:170ms)*

Note that both links between SLAC and CERN as well as SLAC and Pisa represent high-latency, wide area network links. We used the following hardware for the performance tests of the xrootd system where each machine had a 100Mbps Fast Ethernet card:

- *Client (SLAC): Sun Fire V.240, 1 GHz, 2 GB RAM*
- *Proxy (SLAC): Sun Fire V.240, 1 GHz, 2 GB RAM*
- *Server (SLAC): Dual Pentium III, 1.4 GHz, 2 GB RAM, 512 KB cache*
- *Server (Caltech): Intel Xeon, 4 CPUs, 2.8 GHz, 1GB RAM, 512KB cache,*
- *Server (CERN): Dual Intel Pentium III, 800 MHz, 256 KB cache, 512 MB RAM*
- *Server (Pisa): Intel Xeon, 1.7 GHz, 1 GB RAM, 512 KB cache*

All Intel-based machines ran either RedHat Linux 7.2 or 7.3 with gcc 2.95.2, 2.95.3 or gcc 3.2 whereas the Sun based machines used Sun Solaris 9 and the native Sun compiler. All server machines above ran both the xrootd data server as well as a corresponding olb-server. The olb-servers were all subscribed to the olb-manager on the Proxy machine (Sun Fire). In addition, the proxy machine also hosted the xrootd proxy which was the main contact (proxy) for the client application residing on a second Sun Fire machine on the same LAN. This corresponds to the scenario depicted in Figure 3.

In order to measure the performance of the newly introduced proxy server for read requests, we first isolate a few latency parameters. Note that the system has a certain start-up time because all peers need to talk to each other. Once an olb-server subscribes to an olb-manager, a certain interaction takes places where the manager collects information about the server. We call this the *start-up latency*. Once this is done, the manager knows about all its servers and which name spaces they are serving, i.e. which file path on disk is addressed. Next, each time a client requests a file for the first time (i.e. an open request is sent to the xrootd proxy), the olb-manager checks for the file location at the site of the olb-server. We call this the *look-up latency*: this time is a configurable parameter and is set to 5 seconds by default at the server startup. The olb-manager caches all the file locations it has looked up and keeps them for a default of 8 hours in its local cache.

We are mainly interested in the performance of the proxy server and the potential overhead it implies as compared to a potential direct data transfer between the client and a remote server. We therefore compare the time of a read request on an open file. In the first experiment, the client requested to read all bytes of a 9.5 MB file issuing a read starting from offset 0. The results are depicted in Figure 4. "proxy" corresponds to reading data via a proxy and "direct access" corresponds to reading the file directly from the remote data server where the file is located. In both cases, the client was located at SLAC.

From the results in Figure 4 we see that for high- latency links like California (SLAC) to Europe (CERN, Pisa), the proxy server did not impose any additional overhead whereas for fast links between SLAC and Caltech, a small overhead can be seen. Note the logarithmic scale on the time axis. This overhead is also true for a local read.

We compared the read time to the transfer time of the same file via scp as well as bbcp [17] in order to see how much we can potentially improve the access time over the wide area network. Transferring the same 9.5 MB with scp (single stream, no window size tuning) between SLAC and CERN resulted in a transfer rate of about 370KB/s. The transfer rate of xrootd is ~277 KB/s.

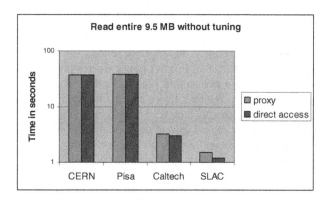

**Fig. 4.** Read 9.5MB file via the proxy server from a remote site compared to read the file directly from the remote data server

Next, we studied the effects of tuning the network transfer with bbcp and experimented with different window sizes and various parallel streams. We reached the optimum using 20 parallel streams and a window size of 1 MB. We gained an effective transfer rate of 1128 KB/s, which also includes the security handshake. The raw transfer rate, which corresponded to only reading the file, was 5232 KB/s. Consequently, we see that on the WAN link we needed to optimize the transfer rate by window size tuning and the usage of parallel streams.

In our current implementation of xrootd we only allow for window size tuning and thus all subsequent tests were run with a TCP window size of 1 MB. We therefore redid the pervious test and gained a transfer rate of ~355KB/s for the SLAC-CERN link, i.e. almost equivalent to scp. There is clearly more improvement possible once we apply parallel stream transfer as used in bbcp.

In the next test depicted in Figure 5 we tested partial file reads. We used the same 9.5MB file but only read 100 KB starting from offset 50,000. We observe that the raw transfer rate is higher with tuned window sizes.

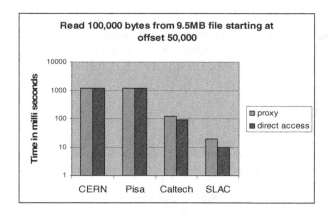

**Fig. 5.** Read parts of a file with tuned TCP window set to 1 MB

# 6  Related Work

There has been considerable work done on proxy servers for web-based content with [7][8] spanning a decade of research. Proxies now exist for practically all protocols in many contexts; from protocol conversion [14] to dealing with firewall issues [16]. Considerable work in caching methodologies in distributed file systems, peripherally related to proxy services, represents a closely related area [2][3][10][11]. Perhaps the closest work in terms of what xrootd tries to do, though in many different ways, is the Google File System [4]. However, we know of no on-going work that uses a proxy service, let alone a structured network of control and data proxies, to address a typical quandary that develops in peer-to-peer file services: what happens when a file that was expected to be found in the local domain can only be found in a remote domain? While clients in unstructured, non-fire-walled, P2P systems can easily solve this problem by simply getting the file, structured systems are rarely so lucky. We feel that our approach, while not theoretically new, is technically novel and represents a significantly effective solution to a relatively recent problem in data management.

# 7  Conclusions and Future Work

We have presented a proxy server for the xrootd system that can be used to address network security issues related to in- and outbound network connections. This is an important solution to data intensive science applications like High Energy Physics.

Our current server only imposes a small, expected overhead for read access over wide area networks in a Data Grid. In order to reduce the overhead further, we might also add parallel streams for the actual data transfer. There is also the future potential to call external file transfer protocols like bbcp or GridFTP in case nearly the entire file needs to be read by the client. Other plans are to implement more proxy functionalities such as write access or to allow for asynchronous communication with the server.

## Acknowledgements

We thank Flavia Donno and Kurt Stockinger for useful comments on the paper. This work was supported by Stanford Linear Accelerator Center and Stanford University under contract DE-AC03-76-SF00515 with the US Department of Energy.

## References

1. B. Allcock et al. Secure, Efficient Data Transport and Replica Management for High-Performance Data-Intensive Computing. *IEEE Mass Storage Conf.*, San Diego, Apr. 2001.
2. M. Blaze, Caching in Large Scale Distributed File Systems, PhD thesis, Princeton University, Nov. 1992.
3. J. Howard, et. al., Scale and performance in a distributed file system. *ACM Transactions in Computer Systems*, 6(1):231-244, 1988.

4. S. Ghemawat, H. Gobioff, S. Leung, File and storage systems: The Google File System, *19th ACM Symposium on Operating Systems Principles*, Bolton Landing, Oct. 2003.
5. A. Hanushevsky, M. Nowak. Pursuit of a Scalable High Performance Multi-Petabyte Database. *IEEE Symposium on Mass Storage Systems*, San Diego, Mar. 1999.
6. A. Hanushevsky. eXtended ROOT Daemon (xrootd), http://www.slac.stanford.edu/xrootd
7. A. Luotonen and K. Altis, World-wide web proxies, Computer Networks and ISDN systems, *Int. Conference on the World-Wide Web*, Elsevier Science BV, 1994.
8. V. S. Pai, L. Wang, et. al., The dark side of the Web: an open proxy's view, *ACM SIGCOMM Computer Communication Review*, 34(1): 57-62, Jan. 2004.
9. ROOT Framework, http://root.cern.ch
10. M. Satyanarayanan, The evolution of Coda, *ACM Trans. on Computer Systems*, 20(2):85–124, May 2002.
11. F. Schmuck, R. Haskin, GPFS A Shared-Disk File System for Large Computing Clusters. *Int.Conf. on File and Storage Technologies (FAST)*, USENIX, Monterey, Jan. 2002.
12. H. Stockinger, A. Hanushevsky. HTTP Redirection for Replica Catalogue Lookups in Data Grids. *ACM Symposium on Applied Computing*, Madrid, Mar. 2002.
13. H. Stockinger, A. Samar, S. Muzaffar, F. Donno. Grid Data Mirroring Package (GDMP). *Scientific Programming Journal - Special Issue: Grid Computing*, 10(2):121-134, 2002.
14. http://de.samba.org/samba/samba.html
15. http://www.edg.org
16. http://www.ftpproxy.org/
17. http://www-iepm.slac.stanford.edu/monitoring/bulk/bbcp.html
18. http://www.objectivity.com

# A Flexible Two-Level I/O Architecture for Grids

Alberto Sánchez, María S. Pérez, Víctor Robles, José M. Peña, and Pilar Herrero

Computer Science School,
Universidad Politécnica Madrid,
Madrid, Spain
{ascampos, mperez, jmpena, vrobles, pherrero}@fi.upm.es

**Abstract.** One of the major advantages of Grid Computing (GC) technology is the use of geographically distributed resources. Nevertheless, just like any kind of systems, GC environments have a great problem: I/O system is the bottleneck of the whole system. In order to obtain a better performance, it is necessary and advisable to improve the data access. This problem could be solved by introducing a parallel data access to grid resources.

Since GC consists of many resources and some of them are clusters, it would be possible to exploit the parallelism among the different nodes of each cluster. We propose to use two levels of parallelism in a Grid environment to improve the data access and therefore the whole system performance. The low level will be represented by the nodes of each cluster, and the high level will include all the clusters. This paper shows a new architecture for grids, which is based on the parallel file system MAPFS, designed for high performance clusters.

**Keywords:** Grid Computing (GC), Grid Services (GS), parallel I/O systems, Grid Architecture.

## 1   Introduction

A Grid system is defined by Foster in [Fos02] as coordinates resources that are not controlled by a centralized entity, by using standard, open, general-purpose protocols and interfaces to deliver nontrivial qualities of services. If we extend this definition, a Grid environment could be understood as the result of the computing and storage resources offered by all elements which make up the grid. We must try to get the best performance in any kind of access to any grid element or the whole environment.

The system performance can decrease, mainly due to the underlying I/O system. While the process capacity has been duplicated each 18 months, according to the Moore law, the data access has not been correlated with this increment. Thus, it is critical to improve the I/O system to enhance the whole system performance.

A proposed solution to improve the I/O system is accessing data in a parallel way. Different approaches have been defined within the field of parallel file systems, such as PVFS [CLIRT00] or MAPFS [PCG+03].

MAPFS (*Multi Agent Parallel File System*) has been developed at the Universidad Politécnica de Madrid in 2003 [DISPH03]. Since MAPFS uses an agents paradigm - which has been designed for Distributed Artificial Intelligence (DAI) systems- to access

P. Herrero, M.S. Pérez, and V. Robles (Eds.): SAG 2004, LNCS 3458, pp. 50–58, 2005.

data in a parallel way, MAPFS could be considered as an innovative approach to I/O access in I/O systems.

The main contribution of MAPFS is the conceptual use of agents to provide applications with new properties, with the aim of increasing their adaptation to dynamic and complex environments. MAPFS is based on a multi-agent architecture that offers features such as data acquisition, caching, prefetching and use of hints.

MAPFS can be adapted to complex environments. As a proof of that we have adapted MAPFS to a Grid environment, having therefore what we have called MAPFS-Grid [PCG+04].

This paper pretends to define the architecture which allows applications to get two levels of parallelism in MAPFS-Grid: intercluster and intracluster. This requires a flexible architecture, which exploits both levels, with the aim of improving the whole system.

The remainder of this paper is organised as follows: Section 2 defines the main concepts of the Grid technology related to our work, as well as the GC trends. Section 3 describes our proposal, which is based on the trend shown below. Finally, Section 4 explains the main conclusions and outline the ongoing and future work.

## 2    Current Grid Technology

Nowadays, the Grid community is changing its directions towards a services model, as is described in [FKNT02]. The new architecture OGSA (*Open Grid Services Architecture*), defined by the organization that standardizes the Grid technology (GGF (*Global Grid Forum*))[GGF], introduces an abstract view of the new trend of Grid environments. OGSA provides support by the creation, maintenance and lifecycle of services offered by the different VOs (*Virtual Organizations*). A Virtual Organization can be defined as a set of persons, users, individuals or institutions that share the same access policies [FKT01].

A new trend tries to fuse Web Services and services defined by OGSA services to get what is known as *Grid Services (GS)* in a single development line. The GGF and the organization in charge of Web Services, W3C (*World Wide Web Consortium*), are making great efforts to make possible this union. It is expected that GS will be included in next version 1.2 of WSDL (*Web Services Description Language*).

The Grid Services Architecture defined by OGSA is implemented in the version 3 of Globus Toolkit (GT3) (see Figure 1). It has the following levels:

- High level services. There are no GT3 Services that are based in the GT3 architecture.
- GT3 Data Services. They provide both data and replica management.
- GT3 Base Services. They supply the jobs management and a reliable file transfer. In addition, they contain Monitoring and Discovery Services [MDS], called Index Services (IS), which provide a way to produce and query service data, mainly used in discovery operations.
- GT3 Security Services. They give basic access control to the grid by means of Grid Security Infrastructure (GSI) [FKTT98]. If fine-grained access policies are required, the Community Authorization Service (CAS)[PWF+02] can be used.

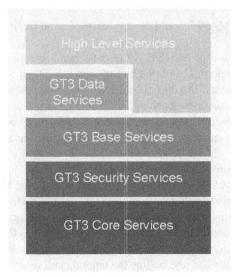

**Fig. 1.** GT3 Architecture

- GT3 Core Services. They provide the basic features to distinguish Grid and Web Services, like factories, notifications and lifetime management. We analyse in depth these differences below.

The use of GS makes easier the access to the resources associated to a specific Virtual Organization. Thus, GS pretend to be the front door of the VO resources, hiding how these resources are internally managed.

Unlike Web Services, GS are stateful, allowing grids to store internal information corresponding to very complex operations. Grid environments are built to run very complex applications with a large lifetime and that usually execute complex operations. In case of failure, it is very important to have internal results for recovering the operation without restarting it. This is the main reason why GS are stateful services.

Moreover, GS can be characterized by the following features:

- They support event subscription and notification.
- GS are asocciated to a lifetime.
- Several instances of a service can be created.

As we can see in Figure 2, GS are similar to factories, since it is possible to create different instances of the same service. Each instance has its own state and clients can connect to the instance in which they are interested to share information and run jobs.

As we could see above, GS are the front doors to the use of resources. It could happen that several GS having the same interface were different. This can be due to:

- They use different resources.
- They have different implementations.
- They have different internal structures.

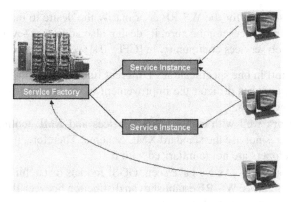

**Fig. 2.** Grid Service factory

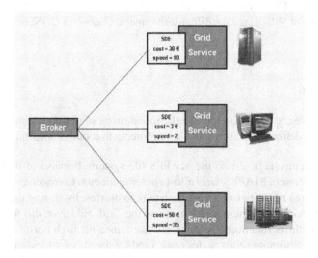

**Fig. 3.** Service Data Elements

Since many GS have the same functionality but different performance, the existence of IS is essential for making possible the search of the most suitable GS amongst registered GS based on the application requirements.

This selection is not trivial. In fact, the existence of Service Data, collecting structured information about GS, makes this selection much easier. For this purpose, each GS instance has its own sort of associated information, called Service Data Set, which can contain zero or more SDE (*Service Data Elements*) of different types. Figure 3 shows how a broker selects the most suitable GS that meets the applications requirements, using the Service Data associated to such service.

Since development started on OGSI, the Web Services world has evolved significantly. Specifically, a number of new specifications and use patterns have emerged that simplify and clarify the ideas expressed in OGSI, called WS-Resource Framework (WS-RF).

While the motivation for the WS-RF is primarily the desire to integrate recent developments in Web services architecture, its design also addresses several criticisms of OGSI from the Web services community. In [CFF⁺04] we can see these criticisms:

1. "Too much stuff in one specification". Different functions are not clearly separated in OGSI. This makes difficult the improvement of the existing functions and the inclusion of new ones.
2. "Does not work well with existing Web services and XML tooling". OGSI uses XML but it does not use the standard XML Schema. Therefore, there are problems because developers are not familiarised with it.
3. "Too object oriented". As we have seen, OGSI models a stateful service, but Web Services are stateless. WS-RF establishes an distinction between the service and the stateful entities called WS-Resources.
4. "Introduction of forthcoming WSDL 2.0 capability as unsupported extensions to WSDL 1.1". OGSI uses constructs from WSDL 2.0, but delays in the publication of this version of WSDL makes difficult the interact between OGSI and Web services tools.

## 3   Proposal

In this section we are going to establish the foundations of our architecture. First of all, we are going to define the features and requirements that our architecture has to meet:

– Our architecture is based on the MAPFS file system, because of its features. The implementation of MAPFS-Grid allows heterogeneous servers connected by means of a wide-area network to be used as data repositories, by storing data in a parallel way through all the clusters which make up the Grid. However, this feature must not interfere with its functionality as an infrastructure for high performance clusters, composed of homogeneous nodes connected by means of a local-area network. In short, it should be possible to access to MAPFS in the same way that was accessed before. Thus, our approach is being implemented as a new layer in the MAPFS architecture, keeping the MAPFS interface. This new layer has been called MAPFS-Grid, as we mentioned above. Both layers, MAPFS and MAPFS-Grid, are accessed by applications, according to their requirements.
– It seems logic that the MAPFS-Grid implementation follows the new philosophical trends of the Grid community shown in section 2, being close to the *Grid Services* technology. Therefore, our approach proposes publishing all the functionality of the file system by means of a GS that we will denote MAPFS_GS (*MAPFS Grid Service*). Thus, an external application to the cluster can access to the functionality of MAPFS system through this service. Thanks to IS, clients or the broker can search the most suitable GS, according to their features (described by their SDEs) for I/O operations. Read and writes operations in MAPFS system are made on a set of data servers of the cluster, called Storage Groups [SPSP⁺04]. Before using MAPFS in a Grid environment we must extend the definition of storage groups, including both clusters and data servers.

– MAPFS-Grid, as MAPFS, manages the parallelism logic on the client, using data servers as data repositories solely. In this case, clusters are seen like data repositories, hiding the parallelism at low level. Conceptually, the only difference is that MAPFS-Grid considers the clusters as data repositories, and one of the nodes of every cluster must support the *MAPFS Grid Service*.

We can take advantage of the two levels of parallelism of MAPFS-Grid, by using MAPFS_GS in a node of every cluster, and MAPFS to access data in parallel (see Figure 4).

### 3.1    Fitting the Two Different Technologies

As it can be observed in [GLO], Grid Services technology uses a programming language that contributes to the platform independence and is widely used within the Web Services technology (Java language). However, MAPFS file system is implemented in a programming language that allows to reach a low level of abstraction of the hardware, very advisable from the point of view of the file system designer (C language).

This implies that it is necessary a new layer in the MAPFS-Grid architecture, which is denominated MAPFS_Adapter. This layer makes possible the adaptation between MAPFS-Grid and MAPFS, providing the interconnection between different programming languages (see Figure 5). Furthermore, this layer will hide complex details of the MAPFS implementation to the grid users by means of the use of internal tables that connect file descriptor returned by MAPFS-Grid with the more complex data structure, necessary for storing a file in MAPFS.

This implies that it is necessary a new layer in the MAPFS-Grid architecture, which is denominated MAPFS_Adapter (see Figure 5). This layer makes possible the adaptation

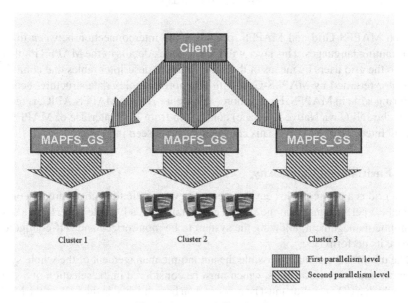

**Fig. 4.** Two parallelism levels

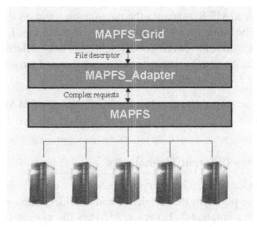

**Fig. 5.** Adaptation between MAPFS-Grid and MAPFS

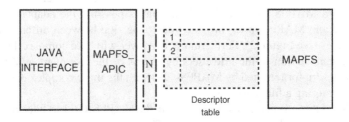

**Fig. 6.** MAPFS_Adapter

between MAPFS-Grid and MAPFS, providing the interconnection between different programming languages. This layer will hide complex details of the MAPFS implementation to the grid users by means of the use of internal descriptor tables that connect file descriptor returned by MAPFS-Grid with the more complex data structure, necessary for storing a file in MAPFS. Furthermore, a new class, called MAPFS_APIC, is required to hide the JNI (Java Native Interface) conversion from Java Interface of MAPFS-Grid to the C Interface of MAPFS. This conversion can be seen in Figure 6.

### 3.2    Environment Complexity

Since a grid is a very complex environment, it is very difficult to configure it in order to get the best performance that the system can obtain. It is advisable to perform a system autonomic management, allowing the system to be monitorized and self-configured to improve its performance.

The use of GS can make possible the autonomic management of the whole system. The most important parameters, which must be considered in the selection of a storage group which a I/O operation must be made in, can be published in the SDE of the MAPFS Grid Service associated with each cluster. In this way, we can know externally different values that affect to the performance of the whole cluster. For instance, the total number of nodes of a cluster is a value externally unknown. With this method, the number of nodes of the cluster could be published in the SDE. Other different values that define a cluster, like the network bandwidth among the internal nodes or its workload, could be also known by an Grid application external to the cluster. In this way, the broker could take a better decision about which are the most suitable resources to make a I/O request.

## 4  Conclusions and Future Work

In this paper we have deeply analyzed the way of obtaining a better performance in data access in a Grid system. We propose to make two levels of parallelism exploiting the existing clusters in a Grid environment. The high level provides parallelism among the grid's clusters, and the low level provides parallelism among all the nodes of each cluster. Furthermore, we have shown an architecture that adapts a parallel file system MAPFS designed to its use in clusters to a Grid environment.

As ongoing and future work, we are currently working with the aim of making a prediction about the future behavior of the system, according to the analysis of the current system state. The analysis of the SDEs values of each GS, especially those internal values of a cluster, can help to know the system behavior and make predictions based on logs and mathematical models.

An overview of the modifications made when moving from OGSI to the WS-Resource Framework can be found in [CFF$^+$04]. We present details about the mappings from OGSI concepts and constructs to equivalent WS-RF ones. In this sense, as future work we think to extend this model to WS-Resource Framework following the guidelines explained in such paper.

## Acknowledgments

This research has been partially supported by Universidad Politécnica de Madrid under Project titled "MAPFS-Grid, a new Multiagent and Autonomic I/O Infrastructure for Grid Environments".

## References

[CFF$^+$04]  K. Czajkowski, D. Ferguson, I. Foster, J. Frey, S. Graham, T. Maguire, D. David Snelling, and S. Tuecke. From Open Grid Services Infrastructure to WS-Resource Framework: Refactoring & Evolution, 2004.

[CLIRT00]  P.H. Carns, W.B. Ligon III, R.B. Ross, and R Thakur. PVFS: A parallel file system for linux clusters. In *Proceedings of the 4th Annual Linux Showcase and Conference*, pages 317–327, October 2000.

[DlSPH03]  María De los Santos Pérez Hernández. Arquitectura multiagente para E/S de alto rendimiento en clusters. Master's thesis, Universidad Politécnica de Madrid, 2003.

[FKNT02]  I. Foster, C. Kesselman, J. Nick, and S. Tuecke. The Physiology of the Grid: An Open Grid Services Architecture for Distributed Systems Integration, 2002.

[FKT01]  I. Foster, C. Kesselman, and S. Tuecke. The Anatomy of the Grid: Enabling Scalable Virtual Organizations. *International Journal of SuperComputer Applications*, 15(3), 2001.

[FKTT98]  Ian T. Foster, Carl Kesselman, Gene Tsudik, and Steven Tuecke. A security architecture for computational grids. In *ACM Conference on Computer and Communications Security*, pages 83–92, 1998.

[Fos02]   Ian Foster. What is the Grid? A Three Point Checklist. *Grid Today*, 1(6), July 2002.

[GGF]     Global Grid Forum. *http://www.ggf.org/*.

[GLO]     The Globus Alliance. *http://www.globus.org*.

[MDS]     The Monitoring and Discovery Services. *http://www.globus.org/mds/*.

[PCG⁺03]  María S. Pérez, Jesús Carretero, Félix García, José M. Peña, and Víctor Robles. A flexible multiagent parallel file system for clusters. In *International Workshop on Parallel I/O Management Techniques (PIOMT'2003) (Lecture Notes in Computer Science)*, June 2003.

[PCG⁺04]  María S. Pérez, Jesús Carretero, Félix García, José M. Peña, and Víctor Robles. MAPFS-Grid: A flexible architecture for data-intensive grid applications. *Grid Computing (Lecture Notes in Computer Science)*, 2004.

[PWF⁺02]  L. Pearlman, V. Welch, I. Foster, C. Kesselman, and S. Tuecke. A Community Authorization Service for Group Collaboration, 2002.

[SPSP⁺04] María S. Pérez, Alberto Sánchez, José M. Peña, Victor Robles, Jesús Carretero, and Félix García. Storage groups: A new approach for providing dynamic reconfiguration in data base clusters. In *Proceedings of the IASTED International Conference on Parallel and Distributed Computing and Networks (PDCN 2004)*, Austria, 2004.

# Data Driven Infrastructure and Policy Selection to Enhance Scientific Applications in Grid

Jose M. Perez, Felix Garcia, Jesus Carretero, Jose D. Garcia,
and Soledad Escolar

Computer Architecture Group, Department of Computer Science,
University Carlos III de Madrid, Spain
jmperez@arcos.inf.uc3m.es

**Abstract.** Most works on Grids have taken an approach where the system is a mixture of clusters and other resources put together with the help of some services. But this solution is a simplistic one that tries to grow from the cluster perspective. We think that the Grid model should be different and near to the p2p model, especially in the I/O field where the network and the heterogeneity of the infrastructure play an important role. In this paper we present a model to organize the DataGrid Infrastructure using concepts as data phases and a p2p approach, in order to select the adequate working policies. These concepts allow the definition of a clearer model for our DataGrid Architecture than a mixture of resources. We present a model relying on the former concepts, their implementation in an I/O middleware for Grids, called GridExpand, and the evaluation of some of the concepts presented.

## 1 Introduction

Nowadays, a trend for high-performance computing is to use all available computational resources in several centers under a common set of services to provide high computational performance. The resulting entity from that trend has been called a *Grid*.

A Grid [1] is a huge bundle of resources geographically distant that try to coordinate their efforts to provide computational services. Currently a huge computational power can be obtained using clusters and grids, however I/O has become a major bottleneck, as it already was in high-performance computing [2]. In Grids, this problem is more important due to the distances among resources (latency problem) and the low speed of some networks. An approach to alleviate this problem is the *DataGrid*, a set of storage resources and data acquisition instruments that try to feed the applications running in the Grid with the necessary data. To alleviate the bandwidth problem most DataGrid projects [3][4] rely on special networks that interconnect several computational centers. And to alleviate the latency problem most DataGrids have adopted the usage of replicas, but this solution raise other questions: When should be replicated? How much replication should be done? Where the replicas should be placed? Much work has been done in the Grid replica field, but usually all the work performed de-

P. Herrero, M.S. Pérez, and V. Robles (Eds.): SAG 2004, LNCS 3458, pp. 59–74, 2005.

scribes a read-only replica system, which invalidates this model for cooperative applications that need to update the replicas.

Replicas were also an approach in clusters and distributed systems [5][6]. Clusters and old MPPs have evolved to use much more sophisticated systems, as caches [7][8][9], which can be seen as fine-grain replicas, partial replication, etc.

Another problem related to grid data replication is that the datasets used in grids may be huge, in the order of Gigabytes or Terabytes; which may make replication very costly, or even impossible, causing delays in the execution of an application due to the lack of data. Deferred data access, in order to get the data in background, has been proposed [10] to alleviate part of the problem.

Most emphasis has been done in the issues related to initial data access, specially the so called *famous datasets*, but we think that the access to remote famous datasets is not the only role of the DataGrid. Once the application has the initial data, the DataGrid must be used to storage temporal results, checkpointing, results datasets, etc. It usually means using several heterogeneous resources from one or several sites in a coordinated and efficiently way, which depends on the datasets, the infrastructure, the application), the DataGrid's load, etc.

Heterogeneity creates a major problem, because established policies are mostly though for homogeneous environments, and, at the moment, this problem has not been addressed by the DataGrid community. Some related works can be found in the high-performance storage community [11][12], but most of them work with homogeneous systems and remote storage play a second role.

In this paper a data driven architecture for the Grid is presented. Section 2 shows the data cycle of an application, from initial acquisition to final results. Third section emphasizes the work that must be done with data after their acquisition, analyzing the factors that have impact on the access to data in heterogeneous storage resources. Section four presents an implementation of our theoretical infrastructure model. Section five shows some evaluation results. And finally, section six presents the conclusions and future works.

## 2   Data Application Phases

Three phases can be distinguished related to data in the execution of an application: reading of initial data ($I_P$), writing of intermediate results and checkpoints ($W_P$), and writing of the result data ($R_P$) (Fig. 1).

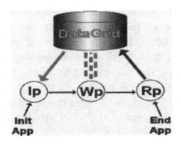

**Fig. 1.** Data Phases during application running

In a local environment, or in small clusters, the management of these phases and the policies used to manage data can be the same. However, as we shift to a huge distributed environment with high level of heterogeneity, the policies of each phase may vary widely.

Another important parameter in the execution of grid applications is the location of the application's processes, and the *distance* to the data. In order to analyze a Data-Grid infrastructure we must take into account if the application is running in one or several sites, and if the data are local, in a close place, or in some remote place. Several techniques have been proposed to enhance data access: replicas, site caches, local caches, parallel I/O, etc. The performance of the storage system may be influenced by the techniques selected. Their usage must be based on the characteristics of the infrastructure, the data location and the application being running. Below we study the dataset phases with some detail.

## 2.1 Initial Dataset Phase

The initial dataset phase deals with the acquisition of initial data, which we can categorize in two classes: famous data and common data. Famous data are generated from some important sources, as experiments or huge simulations. Those data are accessed from a great number of clients and they usually occupy a great amount of read-only storage space. Common data are not so popular datasets that can proceed from other applications, usually related applications.

Usually, access to initial data is made through replicas, but it seems clear that we can not replicate everything everywhere. For this reason most DataGrid architectures only replicates famous datasets. However, we also have to take into account the access to other initialization data. In order to increase the access performance to those data other techniques must be used.

Another problem with replicas is their actualization when a dataset is updated. Replica updating arises two kinds of problems: a consistency problem if we want to run an application using the nearest replica and it is not updated and a concurrency problem if an application runs concurrent tasks simultaneously in several sites and each site access to different replicas, some of them updated and other with old versions.

A traditional solution to solve the data replication waste of space and the consistency of data has been the usage of caches and consistency protocols. Another trivial solution is to avoid the consistency problem and to access directly to the data through the network. This is the solution used in most parallel file systems, but this solution may be costly in time terms. Table 1 shows strategies for an application to access the initial data, taking into account whether data are available in the site where the application is executed, and whether the application has tasks in one or several sites.

As shown in Table 1, access to initial data residing in the same site does not create problems. If the computation is running through several sites some problems may arise whether the data are not updated in all the places, so, replica and cache consistency must be checked.

Major problems arrive when data are not available in the execution site. If that case data must be obtained from remote sites. Based on the mechanisms used for accessing data, different issues must be taken into account:

- If replica mechanisms are used, a close replica must be localized or a new replica must be created in the site. If the application runs in several sites, the problem is bigger. Several works has been done in order to find the better placement of replicas [13][14] trying to alleviate the cost of replica creation.
- The cache solution has similar problems but at a smaller scale, as only some blocks are cached. But this creates a new problem: what *blocks* must be cached to have a good hit ratio? In order to solve this problem, some kind of informed requests or prediction methods for next requests are needed.

Direct access methods may be a good solution in some cases. But it can be a costly one if all the applications that run in a site access the same remote datasets. In this scenario, a replica or cache system may alleviate the data load. Direct access storage can be enhanced using techniques as Parallel I/O and informed/intelligent prefetching techniques.

**Table 1.** Strategy rules for accessing initial data

| | Data available on the site | | | Data unavailable on the site | | |
|---|---|---|---|---|---|---|
| | Replica | Cache | Direct | Replica | Cache | Direct |
| Computation performed in one site | Nothing | Nothing | Nothing | Access to nearest replica in other site, or create a new replica | Go for some data and put them in the cache | Access the data |
| Computation performed in several sites | Check if all the replicas are consistent (same version) | Nothing (Assert validness of the data cached) | Nothing | Access to nearest **N** replicas, or create new **N** replicas. | Go for some data and put them in the cache | Access the data |

## 2.2  Working DataSet Phase

During the computing process the application could create new data, as temporal datasets, checkpointing, visualization data, etc. The working dataset size may be greater that the original data. For that reason, we could also want to use the DataGrid resource in order to store them temporarily. However, the usage of remote storage may not be a good idea because temporal data must be stored as nearest to the tasks as possible in order to achieve a high-performance. More complex issues may arise whether application's tasks run in several sites and a consistent view should be maintained.

Table 2 shows the problems that can arise when the application is in a local environment inside a DataGrid, and some techniques that could enhance performance by integrating several storage resources.

In order to select one of these solutions the working dataset size must be taken into account. For example, it is not recommendable to use local storage whether we are dealing with a huge amount of data or whether the data are shared among several nodes.

**Table 2.** Several processes of an application working with the same data

| | Data consistency must be maintained | | No data consistency must be maintained | |
|---|---|---|---|---|
| | Several tasks work with data | One task works with data | Several tasks work with data | One task works with data |
| All application's tasks run in one site | DFSs Parallel I/O RAID + Consistency Protocols | Local storage Parallel I/O RAID | DFS Parallel I/O RAID | Local storage Parallel I/O RAID |
| Application's tasks running in several sites | DFSs Parallel I/O + Consistency Protocols | | DFSs Parallel I/O | |

In addition to those techniques, some others can be used to provide high-performance I/O, as collective I/O [15], data sieving [16], etc. A great deal of work has been performed in this field considering homogeneous systems. In the DataGrid a great level of heterogeneity among storage nodes must also be faced.

Management of the resources is more complex if we consider that several applications may be also running simultaneously. This leads to heterogeneity not only in resources, but in the policies that each application needs to obtain high-performance I/O. For this reason we need some kind of informed/adaptive/intelligent mechanisms to guide data access policies used by the applications.

## 2.3    Result DataSet Phase

New resulting data may lead to update existing datasets or to create new ones. Creating new datasets does not cause many problems aside the usage of new storage resources, and the creation of replicas if needed. Major problems arrive whether existing data must be updated, especially if several replicas must be updated. Most Grid architectures put aside this problem indicating that replicas are read-only datasets.

**Table 3.** Treatment of the datasets generated by an application

| | Update dataset | | | New dataset | | |
|---|---|---|---|---|---|---|
| | Replica | Cache | Direct | Replica | Cache | Direct |
| Computation performed in one site | Update all the replicas | Update /Invalidate all the caches | Nothing Data already updated | Inform the replica service of new dataset | Write the data to permanent storage. | Nothing Dataset already created |
| Computation performed through several sites | Synchronize all the changes and update all the replicas | Synchronize all the data, and update/ invalidate cache | Nothing Data already updated | Put together all data, an create a new file, inform the replica service of new dataset | Put together all data. | Put together all data. If Parallel I/O is used, nothing to do (parallel file) |

Table 3 presents some possibilities in order to integrate the result datasets in the DataGrid based in the mechanisms used to access data.

The usage of replicas may lead to a huge data flow if all replicas must be updated, or whether the replicas have to be invalidated and created again. The problem increases if the application has been running through several sites and the results must be integrated in a single view.

The integration of results in one file might be the common solution, and requires the movement of data to some site. But, if the DataGrid support parallel files, all the available working datasets could be integrated in one result parallel file.

The usage of caches may alleviate the update/invalidate work because they only maintain a data subset near the clients and only must actualize a smaller amount of data in storage system.

### 2.4  Application to Our Grid Architecture Approach

Based on the study presented, we have selected different techniques to access data in each file (as shown in Table 4).

Table 4. Selected Techniques for each phase

| Initial Phase | -Read-Only Replica for some famous data.<br>-Cache by site with informed/intelligent prefetching<br>-Direct Access with Parallel I/O if data are not in the neighbourhood. |
|---|---|
| Working Phase | -Direct Access with Parallel I/O and other high performance I/O techniques.<br>-Emphasis in the use of local or nearest storage resources. |
| Result Phase | -Cache consistency protocols.<br>-Direct Access with Parallel I/O.<br>-Parallel files (easy integration of results across several sites.) |

Parallel I/O has been selected as a technique to increase data access bandwidth and load balancing. Also other techniques as collective I/O and data sieving can be used in order to achieve high performance I/O. The usage of replicas has been limited to famous data with read-only access, which alleviates most of the problems related to consistency. Cache by site is the mechanism chosen in order to performance increasing, but data consistency must be taken into account when caching data.

During the Working phase the decision taken is to maintain data as close to the application as possible, but using all the DataGrid resources. This issue is discussed in next sections, where the logical components of our grid storage model will be defined.

## 3  Storage Architecture

Independently of the data access phase, the infrastructure's features and the user data access pattern must be taken into account.

Access to data in a DataGrid storage infrastructure may involve several important factors: usage of one or several storage nodes, kind of network, server' performance, protocols, etc. According to them, the storage nodes may vary greatly from a central huge storage server to a homogeneous storage cluster. Each of these configurations may require different allocation, caching, prefetching, or replica policies.

## 3.1 Storage Infrastructure Concepts

To cope with the diversity of the Grid, different types of data partitions must be defined. A DataGrid partition $P$ is a set of storage nodes ($s_i$) that support a file. The features of a partition are derived from the storage infrastructure. A partition is defined by the storage nodes' location ($L_{s_i}$), the hardware characteristics of each storage node ($H_{s_i}$), and the network protocols used ($N_{s_i}$).

Taking into account physical resources across the DataGrid infrastructure, three possible kinds of partitions can be distinguished:

- **Server/Standalone:** Only one storage node is used to store data (which implies not parallel file access).
- **Intra-grid:** The data of a file are distributed inside an organization.
- **Inter-grid:** The data of a file are distributed through several organizations.

If the storage nodes features and network performance are taken into account two kinds of scenarios can be distinguished:

- **Homogeneous storage nodes:** The common example is a cluster.
- **Heterogeneous storage nodes:** Several PCs across a department.

Another feature that must be taken into account is the networking infrastructure and the set of protocols used to access data. So two scenarios can be distinguished:

- **Homogeneous set of protocols:** Only one network protocol is used to access to the storage nodes, for instance, GridFTP.
- **Heterogeneous set of protocols:** Several protocols are used to access to the storage nodes. For instance, in our storage infrastructure we may have a cluster with PVFS, a set of machines with NFS, and several GridFTP servers, all of them used in parallel to define a distributed partition.

Taking into account all the former features, a distributed partition may need different allocation, caching, prefetching or fault tolerant policies.

## 3.2 Data Access Policies

In order to enhance the access to data several factors related to infrastructure and applications must be taken into account: caching, prefetching, data allocation, degree of parallelism (number of servers), stride size, consistency, etc.

$$\text{PoliciesToBeUsed} = \{ \text{ prefetching, caching, data\_allocation, n\_servers,} \qquad (1)$$
$$\text{stride\_size, consistency, } \dots \}$$

For example, for the allocation policy of resources, several policies can be used: random selection of nodes, greedy algorithms, allocation in nearest nodes, etc. The policies to access a file by an application depend on the infrastructure and access patterns to data.

$$\text{Policy}_i = \text{PolicySelectionFunction}_i ( \text{ Infrastructure, App. access pattern } ) \qquad (2)$$

Thus, function per policy is needed in order to obtain high performance Grid I/O. The I/O policies have been an intensive field of research, but most of the times under a homogeneous system perspective, and most of them do not deal with the Infrastructure parameter. The Infrastructure parameter has been addressed in previous sections, but a deeper study is required. A Partition ($P_i$) has been defined as the set of storage nodes that support a file $i$:

$$P_i = \cup s_j \tag{3}$$

In most systems, a file is supported by a single storage node ( $P_i = s_i$ ). But in the model proposed in this paper, it must be supported by several storage nodes and several subfiles, in order to model parallel I/O.

$$File_i = \cup SubFile_i / \ Subfile_i \text{ stored in node } s_i \tag{4}$$

So, the *Infrastructure* used by a file is supported by the storage nodes that contain the subfiles. The infrastructure aspect of storage nodes can be modeled by the parameters presented in 3.1.

$$StorageNodeInfrastructure_i = s_i = ( \ Ls_i, Hs_i, Ns_i \ ) \tag{5}$$

Equation 2 can be expanded to:

$$Policy_{i\_for\_subfile_j} = PolicySelectionFunction_i(Ls_j, Hs_j, Ns_j , \text{App. access pattern } ) \tag{6}$$

As we have $n$ subfiles and $m$ policies, the policies for a file in our system are defined by a two dimensional matrix:

$$FilePolicy[i=1..n][j=1..m] = PolicySelectionFunction_i(Ls_j, Hs_j, Ns_j , \text{App. access pattern)} \tag{7}$$

And taking into account the data access phases defined in section 2, we obtain:

$$FilePolicy=[PI,PW,PR][i=1..n][j=1..m]=PolicySelectionFunction_i(Ls_j, Hs_j, Ns_j , \text{App. access pattern )} \tag{8}$$

This general system allows modeling the policies to be used in a huge distributed heterogeneous system, but it is also valid for other common environments.

### 3.3  Storage Infrastructure Entities

In order to facilitate the analysis and the application of existing mechanisms, an organization of the storage resources is performed. The main organization's element is the "I/O community".

I/O communities consist on one or several storage nodes in a LAN (see Fig. 2) that support the storage of nearby clients, but sometimes could serve clients in other I/O communities.

As the storage infrastructure grows, the apparition of new I/O communities must be organized. All the I/O communities in an enterprise or a university compose an element called a data intragrid (see Fig. 2). Usually, data intragrids connects I/O communities with a fast network infrastructure. The connection of several intragrids may lead to the apparition of what it is called an intergrid (see Fig. 2). The aim of this organization is to increase locally of data and applications in a Grid, and to facilitate the integration analysis of several sites through the entire DataGrid. As noted before the policies used in I/O communities, intragrid and intergrid could be different. Next sections develop the approach described and present an implementation of the concepts proposed in this paper.

### 3.3.1  I/O Communities

An I/O community is defined as a set of neighbour storage nodes that serve requests to clients, most of them in the neighbourhood. Our definition has some similarities with other [17]. Each I/O community has a resource broker and location services for I/O nodes. Three metrics have been defined in order to assist the creation of I/O communities and the selection of the storage nodes that clients of the I/O community are going to use.

- Distance metric ($\Delta$).
- Storage performance metric ($\Pi$).
- Network performance metric (N).

Those metrics are directly related to the *Infrastructure* parameters proposed in (5):

- $Ls_i$: Location of the Storage nodes → $\Delta(x, y)$: Distance metric between two nodes.
- $Hs_i$: Hardware characteristics → $\Pi(x)$: Performance metric for a node.
- $Ns_i$: Network protocols used to access data → $N(x, y)$: Network performance metric between two nodes.

Formula (8) can be rewritten taking into account these parameters:

$$\text{FilePolicy}[k=PI,PW,PR][i=1..n][i=1..m] = \text{PolicySelectionFunction}_i{'} \ (D(j,k), \qquad (9)$$
$$P (j), N(j,l) , \text{App. access pattern} )$$

The distance metric ($\Delta$) helps to cluster storage nodes in I/O communities. Each I/O community has a broker and location service that is called *Center (C)*. After those services are started the storage nodes try to locate these services and add themselves to the communities that are inside a defined radius, this threshold can be statically defined in the community initialization or extended dynamically to allow farther nodes to be added to the community.

$$\text{Community}_i = \cup s_j / \ s_j \in \text{DataGrid} \wedge \Delta(s_j, C) \leq \text{RadiusCommunity}_i \qquad (10)$$

If the node hosting the location and resource broker fails after the community is already formed, another node of the community starts those services and the I/O community remains.

The distance metric used take into account the IP number proximity, the ping time to the *Center* and whether the storage nodes are in the same Ethernet segment.

When clients desire to access data, the file policies must be defined taking into account the distance metric and a data performance metric. The network performance metric (N) is not taken into account if a high speed network is available through all the community.

For example, the default allocation policy in our infrastructure is that a client uses those nodes closest to it. When the client needs to create new files, it contacts with the broker service and asks for available storage nodes. If possible the service answers with storage nodes of its own I/O community.

The performance metric is used to rank the storage nodes. This allows the system to assign new storage tasks to those nodes than could cope with the new requests in a better way. The performance metric defined in our system is based on hardware characteristics of each storage node and free space in the node. As can be seen, the values for each storage node may vary, which implies that some times one node may be preferred, but other may be discarded to store new files.

It may occur that none of the storage servers in the I/O community have enough free resources for new data. In this case, two solutions are possible: adding storage servers or using storage servers in other communities. For the second solution we have defined a network performance metric (N) that, joined with information obtained from the distance metric (Δ), allows finding those I/O communities that better fit the needs of the former community clients.

The network performance metric takes into account the bandwidth and the latency among I/O communities (among centers).

### 3.3.2  Intragrid I/O

In the network of an enterprise or a university the existence of several I/O communities might be a common scenario; for example, one for each department. The aggregation of several I/O communities is defined as an *intragrid*.

$$\text{Intragrid}_i = \cup \text{Community}_j \ / \ \text{Community}_j \in \text{DataGridCommunities} \ \wedge \qquad (11)$$

$$\Delta(\text{Center}(\text{Community}_j), \ \text{Center}(\text{Community}_k)) \leq \text{RadiusIntraGrid}_i$$

$$\wedge \forall \text{Community}_k \in \text{DataGridCommunities}$$

As described before, an I/O community may request the service of storage nodes for new files. If a parallel distributed partition is used, the system may cope with a parallel partition in which the servers, protocols and network characteristics may differ from one subfile to another, and reside in several communities.

Other kind of interactions may appear among I/O communities. It is normal for a client to access data in its I/O community, but sometimes the client may need to access data in other I/O communities. For that reason, if the location system into an I/O community does not find the requested file in the community, it sends the request to the nearest (distance and network performance metric) I/O communities until the file is found. Currently, a simple protocol is used for location, but we do not discard the integration with Chord [18] or other location system.

### 3.3.3  Inter-grid I/O

In order to connect several organizations (intragrid), an intergrid can be defined.

Intergrids bring up new problems, such as security, network performance, network infrastructure and services interoperability that are research lines in Grids nowadays.

As indicated in previous sections, replication has been a common solution to solve the data access problem. But replication arises some new problems again, mainly consistency and replication management (replicating 1 TB each day may not be feasible). In the infrastructure proposed the replication is only used for read-only data and applicable to famous datasets. For other scenarios, a site cache called *Cache-Proxy* is defined.

Those Cache-Proxies reside in several nodes of an intra-grid an act as a cache for files or subfiles that reside in other intra-grids. Those Cache-Proxies contact with the I/O communities when they need to update, to request or to invalidate data. The usage of those Cache-Proxies is not always advisable; so, other solution is the direct access to remote storage nodes. The selection of one or other mechanisms is defined by the policies selected. Currently LAN protocols (NFS, CIFS, PVFS) are used in order to provide access to I/O communities and intra-grids, and WAN and grid protocols (GridFTP, WebDAV) for inter-grid data access.

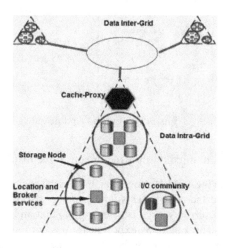

**Fig. 2.** Storage Infrastructure Architecture

## 4   GridExpand Storage System

In order to test some of the ideas proposed in this article, a DataGrid middleware was developed. The approach defined integrates all available data storage servers, organizes those resources and applies them necessary techniques based on the DataGrid infrastructure. This implementation is called GridExpand, being one of its basics the effective integration of existing protocols, services and existing solutions (See Fig. 3). GridExpand is an evolution of the Expand parallel file system [19] for Grids, which allows the system to scale and to continue providing high-performance I/O as the system grows from small clusters to DataGrids. It also provides a virtualization of the Grid Storage Infrastructure providing common I/O APIs and the possibility to define new ones that allows a high control over the application's environment and behavior of the application based on he data phases and the infrastructure.

GridExpand uses the available protocols in a network to communicate with the data servers without needing to install new and specialized storage servers. The former approach offers several advantages: no changes to the servers are required, parallel I/O middleware construction greatly simplified, usage of servers with different architectures and operating systems, usage of heterogeneous protocols, and fault-tolerance using a network RAID approach.

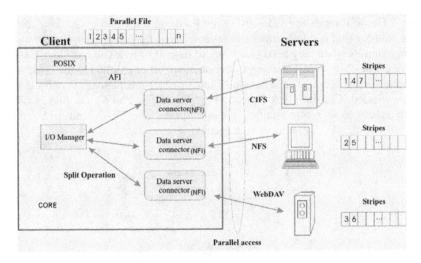

**Fig. 3.** GridExpand Architecture

The GridExpand client middleware structure has three major parts:

- **Abstract File Interface (AFI):** new user I/O interfaces can be implemented over an Abstract File Interface (AFI). This interface exports GridExpand core functions as well as some structures (Virtual file descriptor) that an I/O API can use to access to the middleware. The functions exported by the core system comprehend basic I/O functions (open, create, read, write, etc) and advanced functions (request splitting, prefetch policy, cache policy, fault tolerance, etc). This AFI also allows a differentiation in the different data phases, supporting different policies for each of them.
- **Network File Interface (NFI):** GridExpand uses the available protocols in a network to communicate with the data servers without needing specialized servers. In order to integrate existing protocols in the GridExpand system a Network File Interface (NFI) has been defined, similar to the ADIO [20] used in ROMIO. NFI allows the creation of specific protocol plug-in modules that allow the access to all existing network storage server. Those modules translate the internal representation of GridExpand to specific protocol requests and structures. At the moment, two modules have been developed: local storage and NFS2.
- **Core System:** The core system is the central part of the system; it allows applying different policies to each files and access to Grid services as the resource broker or the localization services in order to isolate the user from these issues. The core is designed in order to allow the easy substitutions of functions for each data access policy. It also abstracts the common structures and functions used in most file systems and creates an internal representation of them.

For each distributed file (a set of one or more subfiles), GridExpand store a small metadata file separated of the main file. This metadata file resides in databases that also support the resource broker and the localization system.

## 5 Evaluation

Using the presented middleware, we have made some test in order to evaluate the importance of the infrastructure and the policies used, with the aim to test some of the concepts presented here.

The test application is an image processing application that processes a set of 1000 images. This application reads an image, applies a mask and creates new processed image files. This application only has an initial data phase and a result data phase because it does not create temporal files, checkpointing or intermediate results.

Two I/O communities (in this case two university's classroom) located in two different locations are used. Each community is composed of 16 computers with the following features: AMD Athlon 1700, 512 MB SDRAM, 40 GB HD, Fast Ethernet, Linux Debian and NFS-Kernel-Server 1.0-2.

Each of the images is a parallel file supported by 8 storage nodes selected with a greedy algorithm from the 16 nodes in each community. The test has been performed with different number of parallel tasks, 2, 4, 8, 16 and 32.

In order to simulate the access to far communities, a delay (using *nanosleep*) has been introduced in each access to data (modifying the AFI layer). The tests that use some delays are indicated with the delay in millisecond.

Fig. 4 shows the performance for several infrastructure configurations: *same community* (the initial and result data resides in the community where the application is running), *close community* (the initial and result data resides in a close community, in the same intra-grid), *close community/same community* (the initial data resides in a close community and the results are stored in the community where the application is

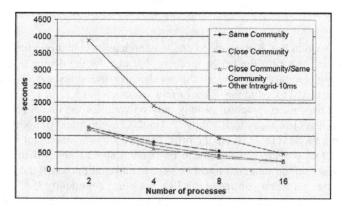

**Fig. 4.** Computation time results for close storage nodes

running), *other intragrid-10ms* (the initial and result data are stored in other community, in other intra-grid, with 10 ms of delay). As can be seen the infrastructure used play a great role in the application's performance, but this difference is decreased as the parallelism degree is increased; this fact benefits the access to data in remote places.

To corroborate that, the test has also been run with far communities (classrooms). A time comparison for several architectures is presented in Fig. 5: *close community* (the initial and result data resides in a close community, in the same intra-grid), *other intragrid-10ms* (the initial and result data are stored in other community, in other intra-grid, with 10 ms of delay), *other intragrid-20ms* (the initial and result data are stored in other community, in other intra-grid, with 20 ms of delay) and *other intra-grid-30ms* (the initial and result data are stored in other community, with 30 ms of delay).

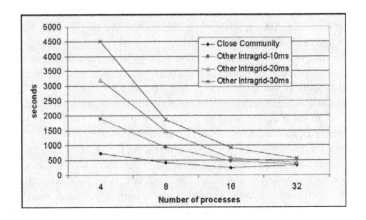

**Fig. 5.** Computation time results for far storage nodes

As can be seen in Fig. 5, the time to end the application is highly influenced by the infrastructure, in this case the network metric, but also by the degree of parallelism. So, for our application if we increase the number of parallel tasks we can access directly to the data and to avoid the usage of replicas or caches.

Of course, the former conclusions may only be valid for the image processing application, but it is clear that specific policies (in this case location of nodes) per application are an important issue where the infrastructure plays an important role.

Another effect observed in the image processing application is that computation and I/O are made in the same intra-grid (16 nodes make all the work) the performance is a little worst that when you make the I/O in a close community (See Fig. 4). The reason is that in the first case the nodes must cope with two charges, computation and I/O. In the second case, a community makes the computational work and the other provides data storage. Is also noticeable that the best policy is to maintain initial data in a close community and store the results in the community where the computation is made. From the results obtained we must emphasize the importance of the infrastructure, the differentiation of data in several classes (or phases), and the importance in the selection of the adequate policies.

# 6  Conclusions

Most works on Grid computing has taken an approach in which Grids are seen as a mixture of clusters and other resources. But a clear Grid model has not been defined, especially in the I/O field where the network and the heterogeneity of the infrastructure play a great role. We propose the definition of new concepts and the adaptation of old ones, as the differentiation made in the data used by the application that we call data I/O phases. This differentiation leads to the selection of appropriate policies for each particular case.

As the Grid environment is very dynamic, not only in the number of resources, but also in the heterogeneity and load of the resources, the policies selected must take into account the environment or infrastructure in which the applications are going to be run. A great deal of work has been made in the importance of the user pattern access to data in order to select adequate policies, but we think that in the DataGrid field the study of the infrastructure must complement the selection of this policies. The proposed model tries to cope with that importance and establish a base for this idea.

In the future we will develop that approach to provide a deeper study and model for the influence of the infrastructure and heterogeneous resources in the DataGrid field, and integrate the results with other works performed in the data access pattern in order to provide a deeper knowledge in the operations and basis of the data I/O in Grids.

# References

1. I. Foster, C. Kesselman, editors. *The Grid: Blueprint for a New Computing Infraestructure.* Morgan Kaufmann, 1999.
2. D.Patterson, G. Gibson and R. Katz. *A Case for Redundant arrays of Inexpensive Disks (RAID).* Proc. Of the ACM SIGMOD'88, (June), 109-116.
3. Sponsored by the European Union. *The Data Grid Project.* http://eu-datagrid.web.cern.ch/eu-datagrid.
4. Sponsored by the U.S. DOE Office of Science. *The Earth System Grid.* http:// www.earthsystemgrid.org
5. O. Wolfson, S. Jajodia and Y. Huang. *An Adaptive Data Replication Algorithm.* ACM Transaction on Database Systems, Vol. 22, NO. 2, June 1997, pages 255-314.
6. Esther Pacitti, Pascale Minet, and Eric Simon. *Fast algorithms for maintaining replica consistency in lazy master replicated databases.* In VLDB, pages 126--137, 1999.
7. Michael Dahlin, Randolph Wang, Thomas Anderson, David Patterson. *Cooperative Caching: Using Remote Client Memory to Improve File System Performance.* OSDI, November 1994.
8. Michael Dahlin, Clifford Mather, Randolph Wang, Thomas Anderson, David Patterson. *A Quantitative Analysis of Cache Policies for Scalable Network File Systems.* SIGMETRICS, 1994.
9. F. Garcia, J. Carretero, F. Perez, P. de Miguel, and L. Alonso. *High Performance Cache Management for Parallel File Systems.* Lecture Notes in Computer Science, vol. 1573, 1999.

10. Douglas Thain, Jim Basney, Se-Chang Son, Miron Livny. *The Kangaroo Approach to Data Movement on the Gr4id*. Proceedings of the Tenth IEEE Symposium on High Performance Distributed Computing.

11. Huseyin Simitci, Daniel A. Reed, Tyan Fox, Mario Medina, James Oly, Nancy Trand, and Guoyi Wang. *A Framework for Adaptive Storage Input/Output on Computational Grids*. Proceedings of the 3rd Workshop on Runtime Systems for Parallel Programming, April 1999.

12. Tara M. Madhyastha, Christopher L. Elford, Daniel A. Reed. *Optimizing Input/Output Using Adaptive File System Policies*. Proceedings of the Fifth Goddard Conference on Mass Storage Systems and Technologies, College Park, MD, September 1996, pp. 493-514.

13. Kavitha Ranganathan and Ian Foster. *Identifying Dynamic Replication Strategies for a High Performance Data Grid*. Proceedings of the International Grid Computing Workshop, Denve, November 2001.

14. Kavitha Ranganathan, Adriana Iamnitchi, Ian Foster. *Improving Data Availability through Dynamic Model-Driven Replication in Large Peer-to-Peer Communities*. Global and Peer-to-Peer Computing on Large Scale Distributed Systems Workshop, Berlin, May 2002.

15. Rajeev Thakur and Alok Choudhary. *An Extended Two-Phase Method for Accessing Sections of Out-of-Core Arrays*. Scientific Programming, (5)4:301-317, Winter 1996.

16. Rajeev Thakur, William Gropp, Ewing Lusk .*Data Sieving and Collective I/O in ROMIO*. Proceedings of the Seventh Symposium on the Frontiers of Massively Parallel Computation, 1998.

17. Douglas Thain, John Bent, Andrea Arpaci-Dusseau, Remzi Arpaci-Dusseau, an dMiron Libny. *Gathering at the Well: Creating Communities for Grid I/O*. Proceedings of Superconputing 2001, Denver, Colorado, November 2001.

18. Ion Stoica, Robert Morris, David Karger, M. Frans Kaashoek, Hari Balakrishnan. *Chord: A Scalable Peer-to-peer Lookup Service for Internet Applications*. Proceedings of the 2001 ACM SIGCOMM Conference, San Diego, California, USA.

19. F. Garcia, A. Calderon, J. Carretero, J.M. Perez, J. Fernandez. *The Design of the Expand Parallel File System*. International Journal of High Performance Computing Applications, 2003.

20. W. Gropp R. Takhur and E. Lusk. *An Abstract-Devide Interface for Implementing Portable Paralle-I/O Interfaces*. Proceedings of the 6th Symposium on the Frontiers of Massively Parallel Computation, Oct. 1996, pp. 180—187.

# Modelling a Protein Structure Comparison Application on the Grid Using PROTEUS

Mario Cannataro[1], Matteo Comin[2], Carlo Ferrari[2],
Concettina Guerra[2], Antonella Guzzo[3], and Pierangelo Veltri[1]

[1] University of Catanzaro
{cannataro, veltri}@unicz.it
[2] DEI - University of Padova
{comin, carlo, guerra}@dei.unipd.it
[3] DEIS - University of Calabria
guzzo@deis.unical.it

**Abstract.** Bioinformatics applications manage complex biological data stored into distributed and often heterogeneous databases and require large computing power. Among these, protein structure comparison applications exhibit complex workflow structure, access different databases, require high computing power. Thus they could benefit of semantic modelling and Grid infrastructure. We present the modelling and development of the PROuST structure comparison application on the Grid using PROTEUS, a Grid-based Problem Solving Environment.

## 1 Introduction

Research in biological and medical areas (also known as *biomedicine*), requires high performance computing power and sophisticated software tools to treat the increasing amount of data derived by always more accurate experiments in biomedicine [1]. The emerging bioinformatics area involves an increasing number of computer scientists studying new algorithms and designing powerful computational platforms to bring computer science in biomedical research.

Among the different interests, bioinformatics is focusing on the study of proteins and their biological functions. Proteins are sequences of *amino acids*, represented by strings. Amino acids sequences fold in three dimensional (3D) space assuming a variety of 3D structures. Since the structure of a protein is highly related to its functionality, knowing the amino acids sequence as well as its 3D space conformation helps biologist in predicting protein functionalities [11]. The high number of possible combinations of amino acids composing proteins, as well as the huge number of possible cell-mutations, require a huge effort in designing software environments and architectures able to manage the huge amount of data and to support protein studies. Proteins spatial structure prediction and folding are important issues for studying pathologies and to design new drugs.

For such reasons research communities are interested in studying existing proteins functionalities and in discovering new ones. Databases accessible to such

P. Herrero, M.S. Pérez, and V. Robles (Eds.): SAG 2004, LNCS 3458, pp. 75–85, 2005.

communities have been designed and populated (see Protein Database, PDB [8]) and algorithms for analyzing and comparing proteins have been designed. Such algorithms have to deal both with string representations, i.e. amino acids sequences, and with their 3D structures. In particular, the structural comparison problem plays an important role in the functional classification of known proteins and in the prediction of the function of new ones. Recently, a new approach, named PROuST [4] has been proposed. It combines and integrates different techniques for structure comparison operating at different levels of protein representation with different degrees of accuracy. Comparison techniques need to interact with huge amount of data, requiring high computational efforts. PROuST compares an input query protein with a data set of known proteins, to obtain the 3D protein shapes most similar to the query protein. It works in two phases. First it stores information about the existing proteins in a hash table indexed by invariant properties of the protein structures. These properties are the angles and distances of triplets of segments associated to the secondary structures of the proteins. Then, for a given query protein, the algorithm computes the same invariant features and uses them to access the hash table and retrieve similarity information with the existing proteins. This fist step of the processing generates a list of candidate similar proteins. Next a dynamic programming approach is used to align the query protein with each candidate protein of the obtained list. A snapshot of the protein structural comparison workflow is reported in Figure 1. The protein structures are obtained from publicly available databases, i.e. from the Protein Data Bank that currently contains over 27,000 different structures. Thus, building indexes and evaluating a set of candidate proteins is a computationally intensive problem.

Grid community [9] recognized bioinformatics as an opportunity for distributed high performance computing and collaborative applications. Computational Grids (or simply Grids) are geographically distributed environments for high performance computation [10]. In a Grid environment is possible to manage heterogeneous and independent computational resources offering powerful services able to manage huge volumes of data. Managing heterogeneous datasets (e.g., protein databases) or creating new datasets (e.g., mass spectrometry proteomic data [7]), may take advantages by Grid environment [12].

In this paper we present the modelling and the implementation of the PROuST protein structure comparison application on the Grid, using the PROTEUS [2] Grid-based Problem Solving Environment. Migrating PROuST on Grid platform has been proposed in [6]. PROTEUS allows to design and model bioinformatics applications on Grid, using ontologies for modelling, and workflow techniques for designing and scheduling. In particular PROTEUS embeds an ontology based workflow designer allowing ontology-based design of the application. Moreover, a set of workflow engines allows controlling and enacting different phases of activities.

The paper is organized as follows. Section 2 presents PROTEUS architecture focusing on workflow management and modelling. Section 3 describes the PROuST structure comparison method and Section 4 presents the definition of PROuST application on PROTEUS through workflow modeling. Section 5 concludes the paper and outlines future works.

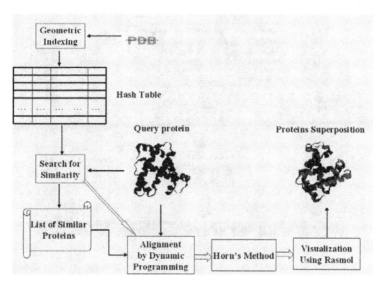

**Fig. 1.** PROuST Overall Workflow

## 2    Workflow Management in Proteus

Semantic modelling of Grid resources and workflow-based Grid programming are emergent trends in Grid community [3]. Along this direction, we developed PROTEUS, a Grid-based Problem Solving Environment allowing to model and execute Grid-aware bioinformatics applications through ontologies and workflows. Figure 2 shows main components of PROTEUS architecture.

The *Component and Application Library* contains software tools, databases, data sources, and user-defined bioinformatics applications, whose metadata are contained into the *Metadata Repository*. The *Ontology Repository* contains ontologies describing, respectively, biological concepts, bioinformatics tasks, and user-defined bioinformatics applications, represented as workflows. The *Ontology-based Workflow Designer* allows the design of a bioinformatics application as a workflow of software and data components selected by searching PROTEUS ontologies. It comprises the *Ontology-based Assistant*, that suggests available tools for a given bioinformatics problem, and the *Workflow User Interface*, used to produce workflow schema, stored into the *Workflow Metadata Repository*. Finally, the *WF-model Wrapper* maps an abstract workflow schema into a schedulable workflow, that in turn is scheduled (i.e. *enacted*) on the Grid by the *Workflow Engine*.

While deploying bioinformatics applications, particular attention should be devoted to the modelling phase; in this phase, in fact, the actors of the application as well as the way in which they operate to reach their goals must be described. From a conceptual point of view, such a description is equivalent to build a *workflow model*, i.e., a formal description of the tasks to be carried out, the dependencies/relationships among them (e.g. data flow, temporal prece-

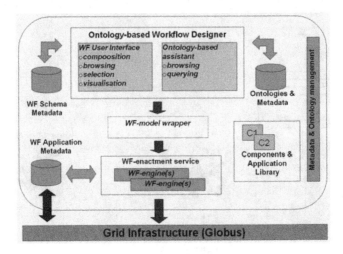

**Fig. 2.** Proteus Architecture

dences) and the entities involved in the application/process. Our proposal is to use workflow capabilities of PROTEUS in order to support users in the design of complex applications and in deploying experiments in an automatic manner. There are many reasons supporting this choice. First, as the design phase serves as the basis for the deployment, it is clear that correctness of the experiment specifications should be guarantied before the deployment phase, unless to bear the costs of doing so at implementation level. Workflow technology offers *Process definition tools* that allow the user to specify a process/application in a formal and unambiguous manner, according to some formal specification language.

Workflow technology offers several more intuitive graphical user-interfaces to specify bioinformatics applications, thus allowing the users to encode their knowledge without caring of implementation details.

Finally, it is generally recognized that supporting the design phase of an applications is a prerequisite for achieving the benefits with respect to maintainability, comprehensibility and reusability of the applications, which are crucial issues in the bioinformatic domain.

## 2.1    Basic Workflow Concepts

A *workflow* is a partial or total automation of a business/scientific process, in which a collection of *activities* must be executed by some *entities* (humans or machines), according to certain *procedural rules*. In this context, *Workflow Management Systems* (WfMSs) are well established technological infrastructures, aiming at facilitating the design of any workflow, and supporting its enactments, by scheduling different activities on available entities. According to the Workflow Management Coalition (WfMC) Reference Model (see http://www.wfmc.org), the two most relevant components of WfMSs are: *Buildtime component* and *Runtime component*.

**Buildtime Component** allows the definition of the workflow by means of some formal description such as the workflow schema, and ensures its persistent storage. It includes two level of specification: (i) *control flow* level, specifying the dependencies among tasks and their execution requirements, through language constructs (e.g. sequencing, synchronization, choice, etc); (ii) *data flow* level, specifying the information about processing entities, such as activity assignment, input and output parameters, etc.

**Runtime Component** consists of a workflow engine (often called workflow scheduler) responsible of the enactments, by controlling and coordinating execution of activities. Moreover, it stores log files about workflow executions and provides monitoring tools that keep track of execution progress.

### 2.2   Conceptual Workflow Modelling by Using UML

Many research works deal with the modeling of workflow schemes and currently there are many existing workflow languages, such as Xlang, WSFL, and BPEL from Microsoft and IBM; XPDL from the workflow management coalition; UML extensions and EDOC from the OMG; and WSCI, which is under the umbrella of the W3C, since no such languages is considered the "best" standard. In PROTEUS we use the UML activity diagrams as a workflow language specification. The Unified Modelling Language (UML) is a de-facto industry standard consisting of several graphical languages for representing software system designs and it is frequently used to illustrate processes in software applications. Recently, the activity diagrams are useful for modelling workflow specifications [5]. In particular, several works have demonstrated that UML supports the majority of the control flow constructs and is suitable to modelling the most of recurring situations related to the workflow execution.

Activity diagrams notation describes *activities* and the flow between them, which is determined by *transitions, forking, synchronization* elements, and flow directions notations, such *decision diamonds*. Figure 3 shows the basic notation for activities nodes; solid arrows represent control flow transitions; decisions are diamonds and forks and synchronization are expressed by solid bars.

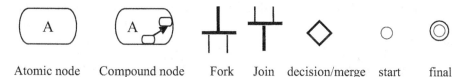

| Atomic node | Compound node | Fork | Join | decision/merge | start | final |

**Fig. 3.** Graphical Notation for UML Activity Diagrams

## 3   Protein Structure Comparison: The PRoUST Approach

The structural comparison problem plays an important role in the functional classification of known proteins and in the prediction of the function of new ones. This problem has been studied by several research groups using a variety of techniques including dynamic programming, graph algorithms, minimization of distance matrices, etc. Moreover some approaches have led to the design and implementation of web servers, such as DALI, CE, SSAP and VAST (see http://www.ebi.ac.uk/dali, http://cl.sdc.ede/ce.html, http://www.biochem.ucl. ac.uk/orengo/ssap.html, and www. ncbi.nlm.nih.gov). Recently, a new approach, namely PROuST, has been proposed [4], that combines and integrates different techniques to structure comparison operating at different levels of protein representation with different degrees of accuracy. PROuST consists of many computational components. The computational modules that can be arranged in various ways depending on the specific type of the requested task: a protein can be matched against all the proteins in PDB, or against a list of representative proteins selected from PDB (for instance, choosing only proteins with low degree of sequence similarity), or it can be compared with another protein to obtain an alignment of their structural elements. Moreover, a display of the aligned proteins can be obtained at the level of the secondary structures only, or extended to a subset of the atoms, the Cα backbone atoms or to all atoms.

Basically, PROuST design relies on two main techniques: it uses indexing for a fast retrieval of similarity information from a database of protein substructure features, followed by dynamic programming to obtain an accurate comparison and alignment between the query protein and each of the proteins extracted from the database by the fast index-based search. Indexes are derived from the segments associated to the secondary structure of Proteins, i.e. α-helices and β-strands. Recent comparisons of PROuST with stand alone procedures have demonstrated its efficiency. Moreover in [6] a possible immersion of PROuST on a Grid based environment has been proposed. Since PROTEUS offers a workflow management platform for workflow design and execution on Grid (see Figure 2), after presenting the overall PROuST workflow, we describe its design on PROTEUS.

We now review how PROuST works. More details can be found in [4]. Besides its atomic representation (as a list of 3D coordinates of all its atoms), a protein can be described in terms of its secondary structures (α-helices and β-strands). Our approach represents each protein as a set of vectors associated to secondary structures; the vectors are the best fit line segments for β-strands and the axes of α-helices. PROuST is based on indexing techniques for database access and fast similarity search. It computes angular features of triplets of segments associated to secondary structures. These features generate triplets of numbers that provide indexes to specific locations in an Hash Table (HT). Each table cell (bucket) consists of a list of records corresponding to proteins with one or more triplets of secondary structures that index into that cell. The Hash Table is built in a **pre-processing** phase that inserts all proteins and takes $O(n^3)$ time for the insertion of a protein with $n$ secondary structures.

The **similarity search** problem involves a query protein Q and all the other proteins represented in the hash table. The search procedure accesses the database looking for triplets of secondary structures that are similar to those of Q, that is triplets with similar angles and distances between their vectors.

Proteins similar to Q are selected according to a similarity measure that takes into account the number of similar triplets between the two proteins. For each triplet of segments associated to the secondary structures of Q, the related three dihedral angles are computed and used as indexes to a table cell. All similar triplets of all stored proteins are stored in either that same cell or in adjacent cells. For each protein in the database, the search procedure keeps track of the number of triplets that are found similar to triplets of the query protein Q by incrementing for each access in a given cell a proper counter associated to that protein. After all triplets of Q have been examined, the proteins with the largest value of such counter are selected as the ones most similar to Q. The indexing method described above returns a ranking of candidate similar proteins but does not generate an alignment of secondary structures and atoms of the query protein with each of the candidate proteins.

The **structural alignment** procedure based on dynamic programming generates pairs of corresponding secondary structures and atoms of the two proteins that satisfy the continuity constraint given by the order of secondary structures along the sequence. The alignment optimizes a function based on the score between two secondary structures defined in terms of the number of similar triplets. The score is derived from the Hash Table (HT).

The final stage of the protein structure comparison is the superposition of the two proteins, that is the determination of the rigid transformation that results in the "best" overlap of the two proteins. Horn's algorithm is used to determine the optimal transformation that minimizes the Root Mean Square deviation (RMSD) distance between sets of atoms (pairs of corresponding points of two proteins).

## 4    Designing PROuST Application on PROTEUS

Currently PROuST is implemented as a stand alone application, so we wish to implement it by using a service-oriented approach. The main phases of the application have to be made independent by each others and implemented as autonomous software components, able to fulfill requests coming by different users, or triggered by external events.

Taking a bottom-up approach, we first model with PROTEUS the inner workflow schema of each PROuST phase (that represents a service), such sub-workflows are then combined to obtain the overall application. The description of workflows is carried out by means of the UML syntax introduced before. Note that activity diagrams specify not only the control flow, but also the data flow. This is an important feature because to enact a process, a WfMS needs to know which activity to call next and what data the activity needs. UML class diagrams can be used to describe the internal structure of data objects. In the following, the main phases of the PROuST application (Pre-processing, Similarity search and Structural alignment) are described as UML activity diagrams.

***Pre-processing.*** This phase is represented as the activity diagram of Figure 4 where UML data flow (dashed arrows) is the connection of data objects with activities that require them as input and/or produce them as output. The input of this phase, the *PDB* file, is processed to obtain an internal protein representation allowing an accurate and efficient protein comparison. In some cases the *DSSP* database can be queried to obtain information about the secondary structures of a protein if it is not present in the PDB file. The output of this phase is the *Hash Table* (*HT*) introduced above. This phase is executed once, when the system starts up and whenever updates affect the PDB. From a computational point of view, Pre-processing is triggered by relevant updates in PDB, or by timeout expiration (e.g. each month), or by user action. Hash Table updating can be obtained by (incrementally) applying the Pre-processing phase on a local copy of the updated PDB file, or by using an agent-based system to periodically report PDB updating. A structured relational database allows to enhance the Pre-processing phase. In summary the Pre-processing phase has INPUT={*PDB, DSSP*}, OUTPUT={*HT*}.

As reported in the workflow of Figure 4, the preprocessing phase starts by accessing the PDB file (*"PDB access"* task). If PDB contains the secondary structure of a protein the task *"Compute SS from PDB"* is executed; otherwise, the DSSP file is used for its extraction (*"Compute SS from DSSP"* task). However, if the secondary structure is not available in any databases, the current PDB file is no more processed and the workflow returns in the starting activity. The secondary structure of a protein results in a couple of files representing its starting and ending residua (file .sec) and the coordinates of the carbon atoms (file .ca). They are the input of the task *"Vectorial representation"* that computes a representation (file .fit) of the secondary structure stored in the Hash Table (task *"Hash table update"*). Specifically, two possible updates might occur: (1) the insertion of a new protein, and (2) the insertion of a new version of an existing protein.

***Similarity Search.*** In this phase (Figure 5), a target protein $P$, identified through its PDB identifier (e.g. 1tim is the <pdbID> of the protein Tim barrel), is compared against **all** the proteins contained in $HT$ to obtain a list of similar proteins $L_S$, according to a similarity measure $S$.

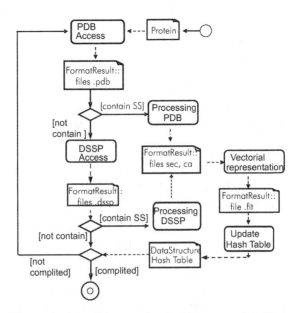

**Fig. 4.** Activity Diagram for the Pre-processing Phase

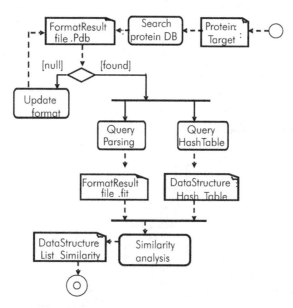

**Fig. 5.** Activity Diagram for the Similarity Search Phase

Each element of $L_S$ contains a similar protein identified through its <pdbID>, and a value representing the similarity measure $S$ with respect to the target protein $P$. Without loss of generality we can order the list $L_S$ according to the similarity measure, and choose the sub list $L_S^k$ containing the first $k$ similar proteins, where $k$ is a parameter provided by the user on the basis of his/her experience. Notice that similarity search is conducted against all the proteins stored in $HT$, so the parameter $k$ is only a way to select the useful output for this phase but does not affect complexity or efficiency of the similarity search phase. The value of $k$ may eventually be determined dynamically on the basis of a required minimum similarity threshold $t$, i.e. we could search for the first $k = k(t)$ similar proteins whose similarity measure is greater than $t$. Finally, since similarity search is conducted comparing vector-based representation of proteins, the target protein P has to be pre-processed by a parser module. In summary, Similarity search phase has INPUT={$P$, $HT$}, PARAMETERS={$k$}, OUTPUT={$L_S^K$ }.

As reported in the workflow of Figure 5, this phase starts by supplying a target protein P= <pdbID> used to query the PDB file to obtain the secondary structure protein information (task *"Search protein"*). In case the target protein is not stored in a PDB format, the task *"Update format"* is responsible of deriving the PDB information. Then, in the *"Query parsing"* task the file .fit is generated. Such file is needed for the *"Similarity analysis"* task. Which, in fact, computes a list of proteins sorted according to their degree of secondary structural similarity with the target protein.

***Structural Alignment.*** In this phase (Figure 6) a detailed similarity analysis is performed by considering the position of atoms of target and similar proteins. The user chooses a protein $L_i$ ($i=1,...,k$) from the similarity list $L_S^k$, then a

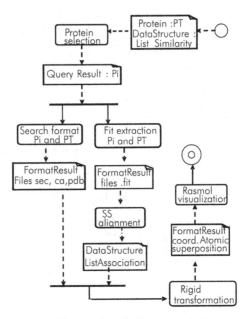

**Fig. 6.** Activity Diagram for the Structural Alignment Phase

*structural alignment* between $L_i$ and the target $P$ is performed. Next an *atomic superimposition* of these two proteins, based on a rigid transformation composed by roto-translation movements, is performed.

Finally, this superimposition can be eventually visualized using a 3D *visualization* tool such as Rasmol ( see http://www.umass.edu/microbio/rasmol/). It should be noted that both $Li$ and $P$ are visualized with respect to the same point of reference. After visualization the user can choose another similar protein $Lj$, to conduct a new Similarity analysis, or he/she can stop the process. In summary the Similarity analysis phase has INPUT=$\{P, L_i\}$, OUTPUT=$\{superimposition\ (P, L_i)\}$.

As reported in the workflow of Figure 6, a protein occurring in the similarity list is selected (task *"Protein selection"*) for testing its actual structural similarity with the target protein on the basis of the degree of atoms overlapping. This measure is obtained by computing the rigid transformation of the proteins that makes their structures overlap as much as possible.

This task can be performed by analyzing not only the PDB, .sec, .ca files (task *"Files extraction"*) associated to both proteins, but also an association list between the secondary structures. This list is computed from the .fit files (obtained by means of the task *"Fit extraction"*), by means of the task (*"SS alignment"*).

Notice that the tasks *"SS alignment"* and *"Files extraction"* are synchronized in a way that the *"Rigid Transformation"* task can be executed only after their proper termination. Finally, the overlapping can be visualized by means of a visualization tool, such as Rasmol.

After the application modelling phase, the workflows designed so far, stored into the Workflow Metadata Repository of PROTEUS, are combined together to form the overall Grid-aware PROuST application. Using the PROTEUS workflow-enactment service, the application is then executed on the Grid. On the other hand, some of the designed workflows represent self-contained services that can be reused for further applications.

## 5    Conclusions and Future Work

Bioinformatics applications, such as structure comparison, present complex workflows that involve different data sources and software components, and often require high computing power. The deployment of such applications on the Grid can benefit from semantic modelling of both the elementary tasks and the overall application through workflow. We described the modelling and implementation of the PROuST structure comparison application through PROTEUS, a Grid-based Problem Solving Environment. Detailed descriptions of PROuST phases and related PROTEUS workflows have been presented.

Future work regards the completion of the PROTEUS workflow-enactment service and its use to evaluate the Grid-aware PROuST application. Moreover, PROuST workflow shows various sources of parallelism that can further benefit of Grid deployment, such as Hash Table construction and querying, and parallel execution of PROuST phases in a multi-user setting.

## References

1. P. Baldi and S. Brunak. *Bioinformatics: The Machine Learning Approach*. MIT Press, 2001.
2. M. Cannataro, C. Comito, F. Lo Schiavo, and P. Veltri. Proteus, a grid-based problem solving environment for bioinformatics: Architecture and experiments. *IEEE Computational Intelligence Bulletin*, 3(1):7–18, February 2004.
3. M. Cannataro and D. Talia. Semantic and Knowledge Grids: Building the Next-Generation Grid. *IEEE Intelligent Systems*, 19(1):56–63, January-February 2004.
4. M. Comin, C. Guerra, and G. Zanotti. PROuST: A comparison method of three-dimensional structures of proteins using indexing techniques. *J. of Computational Biology*, 11:1061–1072, 2004.
5. Marlon Dumas and Arthur H. M. ter Hofstede. UML Activity Diagrams as a Workflow Specification Language. *UML01, Lecture Notes in Computer Science*, 2185, 2001.
6. C. Ferrari, C. Guerra, and G. Zanotti. A grid-aware approach to protein structure comparison. *Jounal of. Parallel and Distributed Computing Special issue on High Performance Bionformatics*, 63, 2003.
7. NCBI-National Cancer for Biotechnology Information. Genbank dna sequences. http://www.ncbi.nlm.nih.gov/.
8. Research Collaboratory for Structural Bioinformatics (RCSB). The protein data bank. www.rcsb.org/pdb.
9. Global Grid Forum. Life science grid - research group. http://www.ggf.org/7_APM/LSG_b.htm.
10. I. Foster and C. Kesselman. *The Grid: Blueprint for a Future Computing Infrastructure*. Morgan Kaufmann Publishers, 1999.
11. C. Guerra and S. Istrail. *Mathematical Methods for Protein Structure Analysis and Design*. LNBI, Springer, 2000.
12. University of Manchester. Mygrid. http://mygrid.man.ac.uk/.

# Grid Services Complemented by Domain Ontology Supporting Biomedical Community

Maja Hadzic and Elizabeth Chang

Curtin University of Technology, School of Information Systems,
GPO Box U1987 Perth,
Western Australia 6845, Australia
{hadzicm, change}@cbs.curtin.edu.au

**Abstract.** This paper describes the increasing role of ontologies in the context of Grid computing for obtaining, comparing and analyzing distributed heterogeneous scientific data. In the communities of people committed to a common goal, the management of resources and services becomes very important. We chose the application domain of human disease research and control. A characteristic of the domain is that trusted databases exist but their schemas are often poorly or not documented. The network of biomedical databases forms a loose federation of autonomous, distributed, heterogeneous data repositories ripe for information integration. Grid services will provide a dynamic way to use resources in such a large distributed scientific environment while the use of ontology enables the system to carryout reasoning at 3 levels: a) available information in all Bio-Databases (Grid nodes) worldwide, b) reasoning about the retrievable information from each node, c) reasoning about the retrieved information and presenting it in a meaningful format for users. We adopted the ontology design methodology of DOGMA and developed Generic Human Disease Ontology (GenDO) that contains common general information regarding human diseases. The information is represented in 4 "dimensions": (a) disease types, (b) causes (c) symptoms and (d) treatments. We illustrate how this GenDO helps to produce Specific Human Disease Ontologies (SpeDO) on request. We show how the combination of two different but complementary techniques, namely Grid computing and ontology, results in a dynamic and intelligent information system. The two approaches together, being complementary, enable the system as a whole.

## 1 Introduction

Recent developments in integrating parallel and distributed computing, combined with improvements in overall network bandwidth have made it possible to add a new dimension to distributed computing: the Grid. Grid offers data management facilities and access to distributed resources by providing cross-institutional integration of information and resources in an environment. Grid means resource integration and collaboration [13].

P. Herrero, M.S. Pérez, and V. Robles (Eds.): SAG 2004, LNCS 3458, pp. 86–98, 2005.
© Springer-Verlag Berlin Heidelberg 2005

The biomedical community is a distributed one and involves the storage and analysis of experimental and observational data. A large body of knowledge has become available through the Internet. The information sources have complete autonomy and they are continually extending their content. Also, each area of biomedical research generates its own databases. In this community, sharing of information inside an area as well as between different research areas is essential and data from one source often must be combined with data from other sources to give users the information they desire. This network of biomedical databases forms a loose federation of autonomous, distributed, heterogeneous data repositories ripe for information integration.

The systematic growth of research efforts in biomedicine resulted in vast amounts of observational, experimental and theoretical data being scattered  around the world. Two fundamental challenges in biomedical science are the management of the available information and the extraction of useful information from large data sets. There is also a need for cooperation of multi-disciplinary teams located at geographically dispersed sites on a single experimental level as well as on a higher level. Sometimes, on a higher level, information from one area in biomedicine must be linked with information from other areas (e.g. to link information about genetic causes with the information about environmental causes in order to get an overall picture of all causes responsible for a particular human disease) in order to form a network of evidence. We support a collaboratory effort in which biomedical scientists and researchers may utilize distributed computing resources to discover, access, select, and analyze data from information resources worldwide.

Classical techniques and methodologies are largely inadequate because of the inherently autonomous and heterogeneous nature of the information resources, which forces applications to share data, respectively services, often without prior knowledge of their structure respectively functionality.

Grid services will provide a dynamic way to use resources in such a large distributed scientific environment. It will constitute a distributed, collaborative, and high-volume computing environment that poses particular new challenges to the efficient and effective design of data and transactions. Another major advantage Grid offers is the freedom of information resources. In a Grid environment the resources may come and go, may belong to different institutions, have different usage policies and pose different requirements on acceptable requests. Grid applications, at the same time, may have different constraints that can only be satisfied by certain types of resources with specific capabilities.

Computer based ontologies may be seen as shared formal conceptualization of domain knowledge and therefore constitute an essential resource for enabling interoperation in an open environment such as the Web on the Grid. We illustrate how ontologies can be developed for the knowledge domain of biomedical and bio-engineering research. We chose the application domain of human disease research and control since it necessarily involves resources of medical, genetic, environmental and treatment data. A characteristic of the domain is that trusted databases exist but their schemas are often poorly or not documented for outsiders, and explicit agreement about their contents is therefore rare.

In a Grid environment, information structured in ontologies may become crucial to many of the operations necessary to obtain and analyze desired data. For example, a user may want to make a collection of data files regarding only symptoms of a human disease, but the user may not know the physical location, the name of each individual file etc. At a higher level of interoperability, shared ontologies between different systems, and mappings of a domain ontology onto a service, are important components of a service-based open architecture and re-use of tools on a semantic basis.

In the Section 2 (Related Work), we discuss related work. In the Section 3 (Ontology Data Repository on Grid for Human Disease Study) we describe extraction of the relevant information used to build the ontology. Section 4 (Principles of Building Generic Human Disease Ontology) describes the four main branches of Generic Human Disease Ontology made by using DOGMA Modeler. Section 5 (From Generic to Specific Human Disease Ontologies) illustrates on the examples the ontology as a tool for physicians (section 5.1.) and for researchers (section 5.2.). In the Section 6 (Comparisons, Discussion and Conclusions) we discuss the combination of the two complementary techniques and give final remarks.

## 2 Related Work

Ontology based bioinformatic work includes the Riboweb ontology[1], the Gene Ontology (GO) [6] and the TAMBIS Ontology while L&C's LinkBase® and UMLS are designed to support human disease studies.

The TAMBIS Ontology, Transparent Access to Multiple Bioinformatics Information Sources [15], uses ontology to enable biologists to ask questions over multiple external databases using a common query interface. The RiboWeb Ontology can be helpful for scientists studying ribosome related diseases, but it doesn't support study of other much more numerous diseases. Gene Ontology provides us with information about all genes within an organism and the TAMBIS Ontology represents all nucleic acids and proteins, but scientists studying a particular disease are only interested in genes and proteins responsible for that particular disease.

LinKBase® by L&C incorporates recent results involving a very large commercially available formal domain ontology. It is reported [12] to currently contain over 5.000.000 knowledge entities of various types: concepts, relationships, terms etc. These entities represent medicine in a way that can be understood by algorithms. Consistency is maintained through a description-logic based knowledge system called LinKFactory®.

The Unified Medical Language System (UMLS) [3] project develops and distributes multi-purpose, electronic "Knowledge Sources" and associated lexical programs. System developers can use the UMLS products to enhance their applications in systems focused on patient data, digital libraries, Web and bibliographic retrieval, natural language processing, and decision support. Researchers will find the UMLS products useful in investigating knowledge representation and retrieval questions.

None of the above mentioned ontologies make use of Grid services to access and retrieve the significant information. In this paper, we show how the combination of the Grid computing and ontology can be very useful for the biomedical community.

The Grid is proposed as the new distributed computing. Originally conceived as a means of sharing resources on demand, the Grid's vision and reach has rapidly evolved to intelligent middleware for flexible, secure, coordinated resource sharing among dynamic collections of individuals, institutions, and resources. These kinds of services enable our system to make Specific Human Disease Ontologies on request. Inter-community technology exchange and inter-disciplinary research can generate inspirational innovations. The inter-community and inter-disciplinary information exchange is important for us when constructing the Generic Human Disease Ontologies in 4 "dimensions". For example, medical researchers examining causes of a specific human disease need to exchange the information with medical researchers working on drug design to prevent or cure that particular disease. The Grid and Semantic Web are now drawing closer together through Web Services and have a new off-spring "the Semantic Grid", the application of knowledge technologies from the Semantic Web to both Grid applications and deep Grid infrastructure [13].

MyGrid is a project targeted at developing open source high-level middleware to support personalised in silico experiments in biology on a Grid. A number of BioGrid projects are underway, including the Asia Pacific BioGrid, the North Carolina BioGrid, the Canadian BioGrid, the EUROGRID project and the Biomedical Informatics Research Network. MyGrid is building services for integration such as resource discovery, workflow enactment and distributed query processing. The target users of myGrid are tool and service providers who build applications for a community of biologists. Early prototypes of myGrid services were developed and tested with use cases based on the functional analysis of clusters of proteins, identified in a microarray study of genes showing circadian rhythms in Drosophila melanogaster (fruit fly). Following this, a distributed system has been developed to meet the requirements of researchers studying the genetics of Graves' disease [16]. On the contrary, our intelligent computer system is constructed that way so that it supports research, study and control of all human disease.

## 3   Ontology Data Repository on Grid for Human Disease Studies

Central to the Grid concept are communities of people committed to a common information-dependent goal. Medical researchers consist of teams with heterogeneous members with different capabilities. There does not exists a unique organization that has all the required resources or skills and team members to be distributed around the globe. Hence, the Grid should enable resources sharing and usage co-ordination in dynamic, virtual, multi-institutional organizations.

Grid computing is not only about accessing computing resources, but more about accessing remote data sources like stored medical and biological information in large quantities. But it would be very time consuming to figure out for each database one may need, what is in it, what is the value of the information, where it fits into the whole knowledge world and how one can access it. This is where ontologies are needed: a way to capture and present in the computer, knowledge all people in a certain community share. For instance, one could want to combine a medical data source in Europe with a biological data source in China in order to perform an analysis. Firstly, we need Grid services to provide a dynamic way to use resources and services in such a large distributed scientific environment. Secondly, we need domain ontology to describe data and resources in a way that is understandable and usable by the target community.

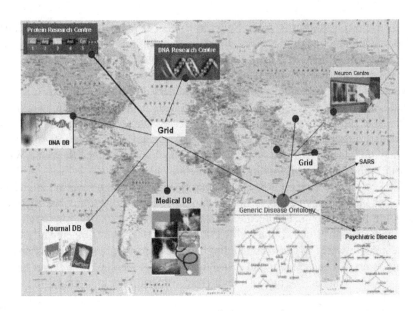

**Fig. 1.** Information from different databases worldwide used to create Generic Disease Ontology. Specific Ontologies such as Psychiatric Disease or SARS Ontology, derived from Generic Disease Ontology

Ontologies can effectively integrate distributed world wide research in the area of disease by aligning and merging relevant information from publication and medical databases, DNA and protein databases, research institutes, health departments, hospitals etc. [5]. Grid middleware can provide the required distributed collaborative platform as well as easy access to resources. Another major advantage of using the Grid is that it respects complete autonomy of the existing ontology nodes. Each of the existing nodes can withdraw or join the Grid whenever it is necessary. This is very important when generating on request Specific Human Disease Ontologies as we show in Section 5.

A grid-computing-based middleware system helps extracting relevant available information related to disease research from around the world . After analysis, combination and interpretation of the information according to an agreed structured representation of domain knowledge by using ontology, the result is presented in a way that makes it easier for the user to have an overview of the up-to-date knowledge about a specific disorder. Generic and Specific Human Disease Ontologies (see models in Fig. 1.) make it possible for researchers to carry out integrated studies involving in general multiple factors to be considered. The proposed solution provides a real-time information resource that assists researchers and physicians to analyze the different factors and the relationships between them  as well as different types of diseases. Figure 1 shows a pictorial presentation of the Human Disease Ontologies deployed on a Computing Grid.

## 4  Principles of Building Generic Human Disease Ontology

A body of formally represented knowledge is based on conceptualisation. Conceptualisation is an abstract, simplified view of the world that we wish to represent for some purpose, usually involving computers. It consists of a set of objects, concepts and other entities about which knowledge is being expressed (often called the *universe of discourse*) and of relationships that hold among them. Every formal knowledge model is committed to some conceptualisation, implicitly or explicitly. An explicit specification of this agreed conceptualisation is called an ontology [7]. In the sequel we shall adopt the DOGMA formalism [11], [14] for the description and terminology involving ontologies.

*Ontological commitments* are formal agreements (expressed in DOGMA as views, rules, and constraints) to use the shared vocabulary in coherent and consistent manner. Shared vocabulary is different for different knowledge domains. Our knowledge domain is going to have its own vocabulary written in an ontological lexicon. An *ontology base* consists of *lexons*, expressing *facts* between *terms*. Terms are often organized hierarchically in taxonomy. Facts in DOGMA are always true only within a *context*. A lexicon L consists of a finite set of semantically meaningful concepts, denoted by C and a finite set of Relationships R (L = C ∪ R). An ontology is a formal specification of a shared conceptualization, that is, the knowledge structure that describes the semantics of an information source by commitment to a lexicon L.

The conceptual framework of our GenDO methodology and prototype will be based on such a formal theory of ontology. Indeed, we will extract relevant information from publication and medical databases, DNA and protein databases, research institutes, health departments, hospitals etc. Upon the analysis and combination of the

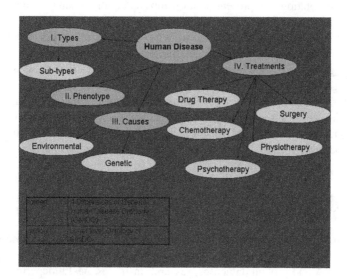

**Fig. 2.** Generic Human Disease Ontology and its four main subontologies: type, phenotype (symptoms), cause and treatment

information, the result will be presented in a way that makes it easier for the user to have an overview of the up-to-date knowledge about a specific disorder. Use of ontologies provides us with a more controlled and systematic way to perform information retrieval. Moreover, the inherited organisation of ontologies adds taxonomical context to search results, making it easier for the researcher to spot conceptual relationships in data. The latter fact is important for instance in the case of complex human disorders where one looks for relationships between different factors that are simultaneously responsible for each of the many types of disorders.

The GenDO has four main branches: (1) types, describing different types of a disorder; (2) causes responsible for that disorder which can be environmental and/or genetical; (3) phenotype, describing symptoms of a disease; (4) treatments, giving an overview of all treatments possible for that particular disease as well as treatments efficiency. This ontology helps to produce SpeDO as illustrated in Section 5. In the Fig. 2. we show four main branches of the GHDO. Terms within GHDO are much more numerous than shown and are validated for existence against concepts from a biomedical lexicon such as UMLS Metathesaurus [3].

Consider a vocabulary $V = (T, R)$ where $T$ is a set of terms denoting concepts, and $R$ is a set of relationship names. As a simple example, we develop a small generic ontology representing the main concepts, identified in a given (implicit) context. Let $T$ = {disease, type, subtype, sub-subtype, phenotype, treatment, drug therapy, chemotherapy, physiotherapy, surgery, psychotherapy, cause, genotype, gene, gene complex, DNA region of interest, environment, stress, climate, family conditions, drugs, microorganism, bacteria, virus} that represent the lexicon of user's world of diseases, and $R$ = {has, isof, isa, is caused by, is responsible for, is cured by, cures, shows, characterizes} that represent relationships (roles) for this domain. The DOGMA Modeler uses ORM [8] notation to represent relationships and commitments such as "each disease is caused by at least one cause" and "each disease shows at least one phenotype".

The ontology explains that a disease may have (1) different types which also may be further divided into subtypes etc. Each disease is caused by (2) cause(s) which can be genetic (genotype) or environmental. Genetic causes can be a mutated gene, a complex of genes or a region in the DNA sequence that potentially contains a gene responsible for the disease and needs to be further examined. Environmental causes can be stress, climate, drugs or family conditions. For each disease, there is (3) corresponding phenotype namely, observable characteristics of an ill individual and (4) treatments possible for the disorder that can be drug therapy, chemotherapy, surgery, psychotherapy or physiotherapy.

## 5   From Generic to Specific Human Disease Ontologies

By combining grid services with a prototype of Generic Human Disease Ontology (GenDO), we extract and align the relevant information from publication and medical databases, DNA and protein databases, research institutes, health departments, hospitals etc. The Specific Human Disease Ontologies (SpeDOs) are specified and generated when a user queries the system. The GenDO stands here central as a link between multiple heterogeneous information resources on one side and the users on the other side. With its four main branches (types, causes, phenotypes and treatments of a disorder) it serves as a template. Grid services then "feed" applications committed to this GenDO ontology with relevant data required by a user which results in SpeDOs.

The source information covers different areas of interest with respect to human diseases in order to allow different user categories, each having specific intentions, to query the system. This has been illustrated on the following examples. The examples are intended to show typical, common problems researchers and physicians encounter. Researchers are constantly searching for and adding more information to the already existing pool of knowledge regarding a particular disorder. Physicians are directly in contact with patients and are using all significant information to help and treat the patients. Researchers and physicians are strongly connected because they are working towards the same goal, but on different knowledge levels.

### 5.1  Ontology as Support Tool for Physicians

If a medical professional queries the system, she/he will mainly be interested in two of the four components of our system, namely symptoms and possible treatments of a particular disorder. There are some exceptions to this rule, such as in the next use case.

**Use case one: Physician cannot identify the disease.** A physician may have a patient showing some symptoms of a disease but he may not be able to say what kind of disease it is. At this stage, it is recommended to keep three components involved in the search (symptoms (phenotype), causes and treatments). In this case, the derived SpeDOs have the "phenotype", "cause" and "treatment" branches.

By entering the symptoms into the system, she/he may be able to retrieve the information regarding that disease. It is also possible that different diseases are showing the same or similar symptoms, so that the physician retrieves more than one SpeDO (in Fig. 3. we show two different SpeDOs). In that case, it may become useful to look for some significance in the causes of the disorders.

For example, in case of disease_1, gene_1 is mutated and thus causes this disorder. And disease_2 is caused by mutation of gene_2. The physician can do the screening of the patients DNA to check if gene_1 or gene_2 is mutated. If mutation found in gene_1, the patient has disease_1 and if gene_2 mutated the patient suffers from disease_2. Only when the patient is correctly diagnosed, the physician may consider possible treatments for the patient. Our information system therefore also reduces the risk of misdiagnosis.

**Use case two: Physician can identify the disease and wants to consider possible treatments.** It is common that there is more than one (drug) treatments possible for a particular disease (see Fig. 4. ). A physician will wish to look at all the options possible before choosing one. Choosing medication is also a personal thing because not all the people respond in the same way to same medication. At this point a medical professional might for instance consult our ontology-based information system to do a one-component search (treatments). In this case, the derived Specific Ontology has only the "treatment" branch.

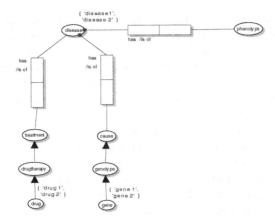

**Fig. 3.** Two different diseases caused by mutations of different genes and treated by different drugs showing same symptoms

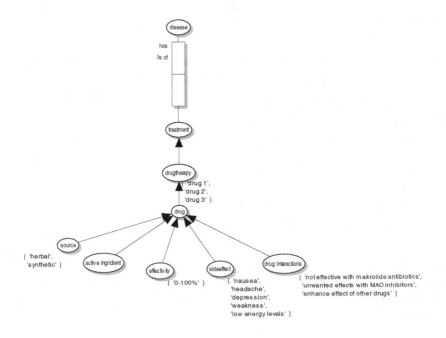

**Fig. 4.** Different drugs target same disease

## 5.2 Ontologies as Tools for Researchers

When a biomedical researcher uses our system, she/he will in general mainly be interested in one specific of the four possible components of our system, namely causes or treatments depending of her/his research area. Researcher working on drug discovery would be more interested in the "treatment" branch. We show another example where the derived Specific Human Disease Ontology has only the "cause" branch.

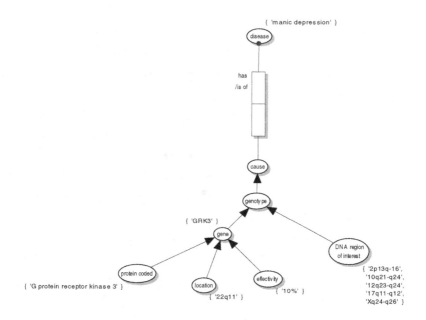

**Fig. 5.** Genetical causes of manic-depression, current research

**Use Case Three: Researcher examines possible causes of a disorder.** Often not all the causes responsible for a particular disorder are known, e.g. in the case of manic-depression.

By querying our system and getting back significant information systematically represented (see Fig. 5.), the researcher is able to identify some regions of interest in the DNA sequence such as regions 2p13-16, 10q21-24, 12q23-24, 17q11-12 and Xq24-26 on chromosomes 2, 10, 12, 17 and X respectively [2], [4], [9], [10]. Those regions need to be further examined in order to find a gene and a mutation inside that gene.

If a new gene is found on one of the already identified DNA regions of interest, our model will now have four instead of five instances of the term "DNA region of interest" and one more instance of the term "gene" (see Fig. 6.). Because of the length of DNA sequence it obviously is much easier for a researcher to target a specific area of a chromosome such as 2p13-16 than the whole chromosome 2. Further research, may allow her/him to narrow down the region of interest to, for example 2p14-15. Because of the agreed semantics in a shared ontology it will be easier for the next person to continue the research in the same direction and possibly to locate the gene of interest.

This aspect of cooperation between different teams increases productivity by saving time and research resources.

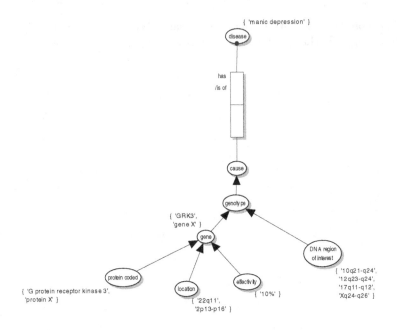

**Fig. 6.** Genetical causes of manic-depression, future research if gene of interest found on chromosome 2

## 6   Comparisons, Discussion and Conclusions

The development of an integrated Ontology deployed on Grid for the purpose of accessing, retrieving and representing the active knowledge about human disorders has a number of obvious but quite important advantages:

- it supports the work of scientists in gathering information on highly specific research topics of human disorders, and allows users on a world-wide basis to intelligently access new scientific information much more quickly;
- shared knowledge improves research efficiency and effectiveness, as it helps (a) to avoid unnecessary redundancy in doing the same experiments, such as the examination of the same region of a DNA sequence, and (b) to direct future work, such as the determination which part of DNA sequence needs to be further examined in order to find the gene responsible for a disease;
- it forms the basis of interoperation, by allowing distributed but autonomous and heterogeneous resources to function in a world-wide cooperative environment: this makes it possible to split effectively a big task between different research teams;
- constructing the data patterns combining different genetic and environmental causes and different disease types, will facilitate the sorting out of the exact combinations of the genetic and environmental factors involved as well as their individual influences on a specific complex disease type such as e.g. depression, thereby assisting medical professionals to diagnose, treat and possibly prevent the disorder.

The four "dimensions" (phenotype, cause, treatment and type) are built for a different purpose and are orthogonal to each other. The "Types" sub-ontology is more a classifying ontology and is strongly hierarchically supported. It does not provide a user with much scientific information. This ontology is based on classification. The "Phenotype" sub-ontology is more descriptive than the others and is based on observation and diagnosing characteristics of ill individual. The "Cause" sub-ontology is providing a user with scientifically proven facts and is strongly based on scientific research. The "Treatment" sub-ontology is a combination of classifying and research ontology. Modeling available treatments is research work but, for example all the discovered drugs can be further hierarchically classified. All four "dimensions" are different from each other and each "dimension" is unique. But jointly they give an overall picture and a good overview of knowledge on a human disorder.

In this paper we show how the combination of two different but complementary techniques, namely Grid computing and ontology, results in a dynamic and intelligent information system. This is especially important in the communities of people committed to a common goal such as medical researchers and physicians. The Grid enables resources sharing and usage co-ordination in dynamic, virtual, multi-institutional organizations. The ontologies provide a way to describe data and resources in a way that is understandable and usable by the target community. The two approaches together, being complementary, enable the system as a whole.

## Acknowledgments

This paper has been finalized during Maja Hadzic's research visit at the VUB STAR-Lab in Brussels. The authors would like to thank Prof. Robert Meersman, Sven Van Acker, Andriy Lisovoy and other research team members of VUB STARLab for helpful discussions and useful suggestions.

## References

1. Altman R., Bada M., Chai X.J., Whirl Carillo M., Chen R.O., Abernethy N.F., "Riboweb: An Ontology Based System for Collaborative Molecular Biology", *IEEE Intelligent Systems*, vol. 14, no. 5, pp.68-76, 1999.
2. Barrett T.B., Hauger R.L., Kennedy J.L., Sadovnick A.D., Remick R.A., Keck P.E., McElroy S.L., Alexander M., Shaw S.H., Kelsoe J.R., "Evidence that a single nucleotide polymorphism in the promoter of the G protein receptor kinase 3 gene is associated with bipolar disorder", *Molecular Psychiatry*, vol. 8, pp.546-557, 2003.
3. Bodenreider O., "The Unified Medical language System (UMLS): integrating biomedical terminology", *Nucleic Acids Res*, vol. 32, no. 1, pp.267-270, 2004.
4. Craddock N, Jones I., "Molecular genetics of bipolar disorder", *The British Journal of Psychiatry*, vol. 178, no. 41, pp.128-133, 2001.
5. Deray T., Verheyden P., "Towards a semantic integration of medical relational databases by using ontologies: a case study", *Proceedings of the ISMIS 99 Conference*, Lecture Notes in Computer Science vol. 1609, Springer-Verlag Heidelberg, pp.30-45, 1999.
6. Gene Ontology Consortium, "Gene Ontology: tool for the unification of biology", *Nat Genet*, vol. 25, pp.25-29, 2002.

7. Gruber, T. R., "A Translation Approach to Portable Ontology Specifications", *Knowledge Acquisition*, vol. 5, no. 2, pp. 199-220, 1993.

8. Halpin T.: Information modeling and relational databases, 3rd edition, Morgan-Kaufmann (2001).

9. Hattori E., Liu C., Badner J.A., Bonner T.I., Christian S.L., Maheshwari M., Detera-Wadleigh S.D., Gibbs R.A., Gershon E.S., "Polymorphisms at the G72/G30 gene locus, on 13q33, are associated with bipolar disorder in two independent pedigree series", *American Journal of Human Genetics*, vol. 72, no. 5, pp.1131-1140, 2003.

10. Liu J., Juo S.H., Dewan A., Grunn A., Tong X., Brito M., Park N., Loth J.E., Kanyas K., Lerer B., Endicott J., Penchaszadeh G., Knowles J.A., Ott J., Gilliam T.C., Baron M., "Evidence for a putative bipolar disorder locus on 2p13-16 and other potential loci on 4q31, 7q34, 8q13, 9q31, 10q21-24, 13q32, 14q21 and 17q11-12", *Mol Psychiatry*, vol. 8, no. 3, pp. 333-342, 2003.

11. Meersman R., "Semantic Ontology Tools in Information System Design", *Proceedings of the ISMIS 99 Conference*, Lecture Notes in Computer Science, vol. 1609, Springer-Verlag Heidelberg, pp.30-45, 1999.

12. Montyne Frank, "The importance of formal ontologies: A case study in occupational health", *Proceedings of the OES-SEO 2001 Rome Workshop*, Luiss Publications, 2001.

13. Carole Goble, "The Grid Needs you! Enlist Now", *Confederated International Conferences DOA, CoopIS and ODBASE 2002 Proceedings*. Lecture Notes in Computer Science, Springer-Verlag Heidelberg, ISBN 3-540-20498-9, pp.589-600, 2003.

14. Spyns P., Meersman R., Jarrar M., "Data modelling versus Ontology engineering", *SIGMOD Record*, vol. 31, no. 4, pp.12-17, 2002.

15. Stevens R., Baker P., Bechhofer S., Ng G., Jacoby A., Paton N.W., Goble C.A., and Brass A., "TAMBIS: Transparent Access to Multiple Bioinformatics Information Sources", *Bioinformatics*, vol. 16, no. 2, pp.184-186, 2002.

16. Stevens R. D., Robinson A. J. and Goble C. A., "MyGrid: personalised bioinformatics on the information grid", Bioinformatics, vol.19, pp.302–304, 2003.

# A Generic Architecture for Sensor Data Integration with the Grid

Jan Humble[1], Chris Greenhalgh[1], Alastair Hamsphire[1], Henk L. Muller[2],
and Stefan Rennick Egglestone[1]

[1] University of Nottingham, Department of Computer Science
{jch, cmg, axh, sre}@cs.nott.ac.uk
[2] University of Bristol, Department of Computer Science
henkm@cs.bris.ac.uk

**Abstract.** This paper describes the design and implementation of a model of
how to integrate sensors and devices into a Grid infrastructure. We describe its
proxy-based approach, the port-type requirements and the set of tools implemented to facilitate configuration of experimental scenarios. Two real world
devices, a wearable medical jacket and an Antarctic lake probe, deployed out in
the field using this architecture are described, along with their relevance in scientific research.

## 1 Introduction

The Grid platform provides great potential for delivering tools for computation, management of resources, and data storage for scientists [1, 2]. A substantial amount of
funding has concentrated on the requirements for post-processing of gathered scientific data. Our interest, however, lies beyond the lab and its suite of software tools.
We wish to accommodate the integration of data collected from remotely located
hardware sensors and devices into the Grid infrastructure and the Open Grid Services
Architecture (OGSA) [3] as we know it today.

Experimental scenarios often require a contextual analysis of the gathered data,
usually from a range of sensors attached to a particular device. Correlation of the data
from different sources and sensors (e.g. time, location and activity of a medical subject) is useful in explaining patterns and a requirement of both clinicians and "in the
field" scientists. We wish to facilitate the management of such experimental scenarios and provide easy access to historical or real-time data for further analysis. In some
cases it becomes necessary not only to make Grid facilities available to remote users,
but also to allow users of Grid services to directly interact with remote devices (e.g.
remote configuration).

Our architecture, constructed using the Globus Toolkit 3 [4], and a set of tools facilitate the publishing and processing of data by scientists without the need of extensive knowledge of Grid-based development. The devices and sensors that we are
dealing with typically have limited computational power, limited memory and limited
network connectivity (e.g. intermittent or occasional). As such, they are not suitable
for directly hosting Grid Services given current technologies. However, in some cases
they are capable of hosting Grid Services directly, while in others we might anticipate

P. Herrero, M.S. Pérez, and V. Robles (Eds.): SAG 2004, LNCS 3458, pp. 99–107, 2005.

improvements in underlying technologies that would make this possible. Our proxy-based approach will nonetheless guarantee communication with a device representative at all times, providing notification on current device and connection state.

Two real world sensor devices were already available as part of focused research by collaborating institutions: the CyberJacket [5, 6] from Bristol University, which collects data from patient life signals and ambient data, and the eScience Antarctic lake probe [7] from the University of Nottingham, which records data from a lake in the Antarctic. In detailing these, we will demonstrate how they were integrated into the sensor architecture and their role in future research together with Grid technologies.

## 2  Background

A common and generic architecture for monitoring devices is motivated by the prolific and long-standing research programmes in both health care and environmental research.

In the UK, there has been a rising trend in Telemedicine and Telecare clinical trials such as those carried out by the Oxford centre for e-health [8], the Biomedical Informatics group at Nottingham University [9] and the Glasgow Royal Infirmary and Glasgow University [10]. These required custom built sensors and infrastructures despite being of relatively small scale.

Our research partners have a long-standing interest in the recording of physiological data for clinical diagnosis [11, 12, 13, 14, 15] through sophisticated bio-signal processing strategies [16, 17]. We also have extensive experience in wearable devices and means of extracting, archiving and manipulating context driven data. Combining the various interests from the Science community and wireless networking is a UK government funded project entitled "Grid Based Medical Devices for Everyday Health" [13]. It aims to create tools and exercise strategies for unobtrusive medical monitoring.

Professor Laybourn-Parry and her colleagues have been studying the ecology of freshwater Antarctic lakes for 12 years and in particular the cycling of carbon through the ecosystem [7]. It is a well preserved and unique of environment and an immensely valuable resource of information, but its isolated location and harsh environment make it very difficult to study. A monitoring device with a range of sensors has taken over most of the labour-intensive manual work of the past; however work still needs to be done on exposing the data to the emerging Grid scientific tools for the scientists "back home".

## 3  Architecture

Our approach is, wherever possible, to make devices and sensors available on the Grid as if they were first class Grid Services. To this end we have devised a proxy-based approach and defined two new application-independent port types: one for a generic sensor, and one for a generic device (which is assumed to host a number of sensors). These port types can be supported directly by sensors and devices of sufficient capability and reliability of communication. However, all of the devices and sensors that we are working with at the moment depend on proxy Grid Services to implement these interfaces on their behalf. The – low capability and/or intermittently connected – devices then communicate with their respective proxies using whatever protocol is appropriate, as and when communication channels are available.

## 3.1 Device and Sensor Proxies

In our architecture, device proxies are used to expose sensing devices as Grid services and sensor proxies are used to expose individual sensors as Grid services. A physical sensing device may have several individual sensors attached to it. To model this, a device proxy is therefore a service group (which is a standard OGSI service grouping interface), with a number of sensor proxies as service group entries. This allows client applications to perform operations on the device as a whole (e.g. to configure the device) or to interact with individual sensors (e.g. to collect the latest data).

To expose a physical device and its sensors as Grid services, a client (which could be the device itself) interacts with a DeviceProxyFacoryService, passing it an XML configuration file. The file specifies the initial configuration of the device and its sensors. The DeviceProxyFactoryService creates a DeviceProxyService instance, which in turn creates a SensorProxyService instance for each physical sensor speci-fied in the configuration file (see figure 1). This factory idiom is typical for OGSI.

A client application is able to contact the device proxy to retrieve, among other things, a list of available sensors. The client is then able to contact some or all of the sensors to, for example, retrieve the latest readings. Sensor proxies can also provide other methods to interact with or reconfigure the physical sensor (such as changing the sampling rate of the sensor or monitoring battery life).

Sensor data produced by a physical sensor is sent to an instance of a sensor proxy service, where it is stored until downloaded or discarded. The duration for which the data is stored at the proxy is determined by a measurement discard policy dependent on the sensor. For example, because one of our portable devices in the wearable medical devices project has limited memory, stored data is discarded regularly. Storage of data at the proxy is only intended as temporary storage.

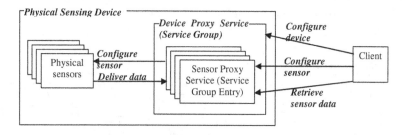

**Fig. 1.** Representing sensing devices as Grid devices

The sensor proxy stores an internal list of all un-discarded sensor data alongside a sequence number. Client applications are able to request a subset of the currently held sensor data (bound by min and max sequence number values), by requesting the MeasurementByCountQueryMinMax service data element (a dynamic property of the sensor service interface). Measurements returned are represented in XSIL format [19] in compliance with standardized databases, but with some straightforward modifications. A typical output might look like this …

```
<Table>
  <ColumnName="wind speed" Type="float" Unit="ms-1"/>
  <Column Name="wind direction" Type="float"/>
  <Stream Type="Local" Delimeter=",">
      10, 23
      12, 45
  </Stream>
</Table>
```

Different kinds of sensors may take measurements at widely varying rates, and each measurement may represent differing quantities of data. A measurement publishing policy allows the way in which the sensor reveals (publishes) new measurements to be controlled. For example, a very rapidly sampling sensor might be configured to announce new measurements no more than 5 times per second (even if it is taking and making available 5000 measurements during this period).

### 3.2  Managing Trial Scenarios

We use an application called a *trial manager* to pump data from the proxies into a persistent database. The user is presented with a list of devices with available sensors, and selects sensors to store data from. The trial manager uses the database Grid interface to configure the database to store data from the sensors, and a *sensor data pump* is then instantiated to deliver data produced by the sensor to the database.

The *sensor data pump* registers for notification of changes in the Measurement-Counter service data element in the proxy of the sensor for which it has been instantiated (this property counts the total number of measurements made by that sensor). The notification interface and style are again typical of OGSI. When notified the data pump fetches new data in the proxy's *measurement queue* and stores it in the database. For sensors with a high sampling rate, it can register for a notification after a number of new items of data, and can then retrieve the last posted items of data using the MeasurementByCountQueryMinMax service data element already described (see figure 2).

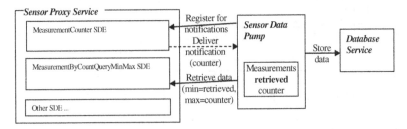

**Fig. 2.** Transferring sensor data to a database

Once data is stored in the database, methods on its Grid service interface can be used to access data and metadata. These include:

- getListOfDevices(): returns a list of device Ids stored in the database.
- getListOfSensorsPerDevice(deviceID): returns a list of sensor Ids for sensors attached to a device specified by a given device Id.
- queryBySensorIDandExpression(sensorID, where): this method returns an XSIL string containing sensor readings for the sensor specified by sensorID and conforming to the given where clause. For example, the where clause might indicate a date range, between which readings should be returned.

Other convenience methods are available to, for example, return data from several sensors of the same type. Further, the interface could easily be extended to provide more advanced querying mechanisms.

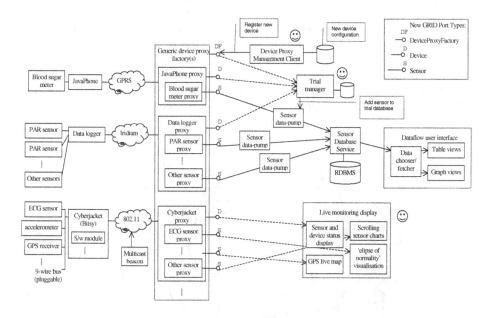

**Fig. 3.** Overview of architecture diagram

## 3.3  Tools

We have developed two main data viewing tools. The first supports a live device and sensor monitoring display. Since devices are self-describing they provide information about their own data output format. We take advantage of this property to automatically plot views of live data. A modifiable template plot window is easily summoned for quick monitoring, and is used as a base library for more complex monitoring applications.

The second data viewing tool works with archived data in the database and allows users to deal with larger blocks of data and do more complex processing and visualisation. Users can also specify a dataflow computation by creating a dataflow graph.

They then perform the computation by invoking a scheduling algorithm on the graph. The scheduling algorithm examines processing units in the graph, and executes a processing unit only when it has sufficient new input data and when it has an output that is clear onto which data can be placed.

The dataflow methodology was chosen as a potential way of offering easy access to data on an instance of the Grid database, because all the complexity of accessing the database can be hidden in the simple visual representation of a processing unit. Figure 3 shows a representative deployment of the overall architecture including proxies, management elements and data viewing tools.

## 4  Wearable Medical Devices

The wearable medical devices project aims to allow patients to be monitored remotely, allowing short-term clinical exercises without restricting the patient's movements. This would, for example, allow patients to walk about the hospital, clinical office or home whilst being monitored, subject to them being within range of total or partial wireless network connectivity.

Patients wear a jacket containing a small computer (bitsy), attached to which are several sensing devices through a 9-wire bus [6]. Each sensor takes a reading at a predefined interval and sends the reading to the wearable computer (see figure 4).

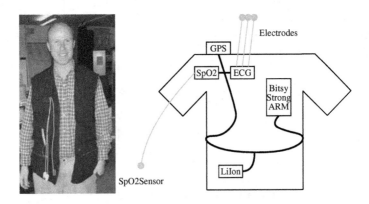

**Fig. 4.** Bristol Lifejacket and modular design

A Wavelan card attached to the bitsy allows the sensor readings to be transferred to network services for analysis and storage. Should the analysis suggest the patient is in immediate physiological danger, a clinician could be alerted. Additionally, data collection from a patient over a long period of time could be further analysed to reveal long term health problems.

In a Wavelan setting readings are produced regularly and continuously, so it was decided that individual readings would be reported. The bitsy has a lightweight implementation of SOAP called GSOAP [20], and this was used to add readings to individual sensor proxy measurements queues as they were produced. This data was used through the live monitoring application and/or pumped into the database as described.

Typically, information is gathered from multiple sensor types in order to accurately track and diagnose a given disease state. The combination of electro-physiological and other medical parameters that must be monitored for a specific medical condition varies widely; subsequently the sensors used in this study are designed to ease their introduction and withdrawal from the monitoring exercise as necessary. At the time of writing, the sensors integrated include:

**Blood Oxygen Saturation Sensor (SpO2):** derives the level of oxygen present in arterial blood via a calculation on the ratio of light absorption resulting from oxygenated and reduced haemoglobin through a well-perfused body part (e. g. the finger).

**Electrocardiogram (ECG):** signal produced on the surface of the skin by the electrical activity of the heart.

**Skin Temperature:** monitored using clinical grade thermistors.

**GPS:** Satellite positioning while outdoor.

Live monitoring of a patient's life signals can be achieved by requesting notification when new data becomes available (as described in section 3.2). The origin of such notifications can be directly from the devices (via the proxy), after a midway post-process, via notification from database updates, or from computation services. In this manner, clinicians are not only capable of accessing the raw patient data, but the data after a predetermined filtering mechanism or data as output from real-time computations making use of a window of historical data (e. g. to detect immediate health risk warnings).

## 5  The Antarctic Device

The Antarctic device (see figure 5) is deployed on the ice of a frozen lake and monitors local conditions. The body of the Antarctic device contains a commercial scientific data logger, facilities to communicate via Iridium satellite modem, a battery, and solar panels to augment the power available from the battery. It is only deployed when the ice is thick enough to support its weight. Various sensors are attached to the data logger, including light (Photosynthetically Active Radiation, PAR), air temperature (both above the ice and at various depths in the water column), and wind speed and direction.

Without the Grid this logged data is collected every few days, either via the satellite link or in person using a serial cable connected to the device. Each data file collected is post-processed to add units, and to generate correctly calibrated values. This file is then emailed to scientists in Nottingham for analysis.

Scientists in Nottingham are using data collected from the device to develop a physical model of the lake environment, which is used to help develop models of carbon cycling in the lake.

It was decided not to maintain a continuous connection to the Antarctic device over Iridium satellite connection due to expense. Therefore, a table of data containing hundreds of sets of readings is downloaded from the device and is then processed by the device proxy. For each sensor attached to the device, the device proxy extracts individual readings from the table and appends them to the sensor proxy's measure-ment queue. Data can then be pumped into an instance of the Grid database to be made available.

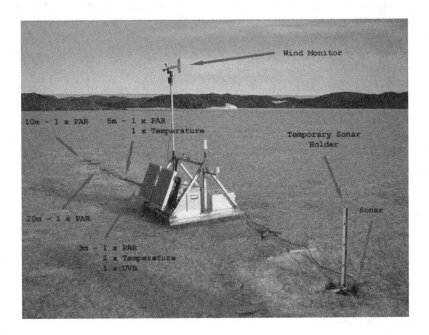

**Fig. 5.** The Antarctic device and connected sensors, which is currently deployed on Crooked Lake in the Vestfold Hills

## 6  Summary

We have described an architecture around Globus Toolkit 3 to integrate devices and sensors into the Grid. A proxy model intermediates between remotely connected devices and the local network and acts as an always-available first class Grid service. This facilitates as seamless as possible integration of collected data for immediate post-processing by available resources. We presented two examples with different methods and issues of connectivity utilizing an implementation of the architecture.

## References

1.  I. Foster, C. Kesselman, J. Nick, S. Tuecke, "The Physiology of the Grid: An Open Grid Services Architecture for Distributed Systems Integration", Open Grid Service Infrastruc-ture WG, Global Grid Forum, June 22, 2002.
2.  de Roure, D., Jennings, N., Shadbolt, N "Research Agenda for the Semantic Grid: A future e-Science infrastructure". http://dcs.gla.ac.uk/Nesc/general/technicalpapers/ DavidDeRoure.etal.SemanticGrid. pdf
3.  The Open Grid Services Architecture (OGSA) http://www.globus.org/ogsa

4.  GLOBUS. The globus toolkit. http://www.globus.org/toolkit/, April 2003.
5.  Barratt, C, et al, "Extending the Grid to Support Remote Medical Monitoring", Proceedings of the 2nd UK e-Science All Hands Meeting 2003
6.  J. Crowe, B. Hayes-Gill, M. Sumner, C. Barratt, B. Palethorpe, C. Greenhalgh, O. Storz, A. Friday, J. Humble, C. Setchell, C. Randell, H. L Muller, "Modular Sensor Architecture for Unobtrusive Routine Clinical Diagnosis", 24th International Conference on Distributed Computing Systems Workshops - W3: IWSAWC (ICDCSW'04), March 23 - 24, 2004, Hachioji, Tokyo, Japan.
7.  S. Benford, N. Crout, J. Crowe, S. Egglestone, M. Foster, C. Greenhalgh, A. Hampshire, B. Hayes-Gill, J. Humble, A. Irune, J. Laybourn-Parry, B. Palethorpe, T. Reid, and M. Sumner. e-Science from the antarctic to the Grid. Escience All Hands Meeting 2003.
8.  The Oxford Centre for e-health http://www.medicine.ox.ac.uk/ndog/tmr/
9.  The Biomedical Informatics Group at Nottingham University http://www.eee.nott.ac.uk/medical/
10. Computer Assisted Reporting of Electrocardiograms, Glasgow University http://www.gla.ac.uk/departments/medicalcardiology/research/care.html
11. C. Barratt, B. Hayes-Gill, H. Vyas, and J. Crowe. Selection of pulse oximetry equipment for ambulatory monitoring. Journal Medical Eng & Tech, 21(1):17–24, 2001.
12. J. Crowe, A. Harrison, and B. Hayes-Gill. The feasibility of long-term fatal heart rate monitoring in the home environment using maternal abdominal electrodes. Physiol. Meas, 16:195–202, 1995.
13. J. Crowe, B. Hayes-Gill, B. Francon, L. Hardebecke, D. Rogers, Y. Thong, P. Dimmock, K.Wyatt, and P. O'Brien. Customisation of a personal digital assistant for logging premenstrual syndrome symptoms. British Journal of Healthcare Computing & Information Management, 17(4):33–35, 2000.
14. A. Harrison, B. Hayes-Gill, J. Crowe, and S. Chang. The application of an Actel field programmable gate array in the design of an ecg rr interval recorder. Journal Medical Eng. and Tech, 19(6):198–204, 1995.
15. J. Pieri, J. Crowe, B. Hayes-Gill, C. Spencer, K. Bhogal, and D. James. Compact longterm recorder of the transabdominal foetal and maternal electrocardiogram. Med.Biol.Eng. & Comp., 39(1):118–125, 2001.
16. J. Hall and J. Crowe. Ambulatory electrocardiogram compression using wavelet packets to approximate the Karhunen-Loeve transform. Applied Signal Processing, 3:25–36, 1996.
17. A. Harrison, B. Hayes-Gill, J. Crowe, and S. Chang. The application of an Actel field programmable gate array in the design of an ecg rr interval recorder. Journal Medical Eng. and Tech, 19(6):198–204, 1995.
18. Grid based medical devices for everyday health. http://www.gridoutreach.org.uk/docs/pilots/meddev.htm, 2002.
19. XSIL Specification, http://www.cacr.caltech.edu/projects/xsil
20. gSOAP: Generator Tools for Coding SOAP/XML Web Services in C and C++. http://www.cs.fsu.edu/~engelen/soap.html

# Embarrassingly Distributed and Master-Worker Paradigms on the Grid*

J. Herrera[1], E. Huedo[2], R.S. Montero[1], and I.M. Llorente[1,2]

[1] Departamento de Arquitectura de Computadores y Automática,
Facultad de Informática, Universidad Complutense de Madrid,
28040 Madrid, Spain
[2] Laboratorio de Computación Avanzada, Simulación y Aplicaciones Telemáticas,
Centro de Astrobiología (CSIC-INTA), 28850 Torrejón de Ardoz, Spain

**Abstract.** Grids constitute a promising platform to execute loosely coupled applications, which arise naturally in many scientific and engineering fields like bioinformatics, computational fluid dynamics, particle physics, etc. In this paper, we describe our experiences in porting three scientific production codes to the Grid. Those codes follow typical computational models, namely: embarrassingly distributed and master-worker. In spite of their relatively simple computational structure, consisting of many "independent" tasks, their reliable and efficient execution on computational Grids involves several issues, due to both the dynamic nature of the Grid itself and the execution and programming requirements of the applications. The applications have been developed by using the DRMAA (Distributed Resource Management Application API) interface. DRMAA routines are supported by the functionality offered by the Grid*W*ay framework, that provides the runtime mechanisms needed for transparently executing jobs on a dynamic Grid environment. The experiments have been performed on Globus-based research testbeds that span heterogeneous resources in different institutions.

## 1   Introduction

It is becoming evident that the traditional concept of computing based on a homogeneous and centrally managed environment is being displaced by a new model based on the exchange of information and the sharing of distributed resources [1]. However, applications often involve large amounts of data and/or computing elements that are not easily handled by today's Internet and web infrastructures. Grid technologies attempt to provide the support needed for such an infrastructure, enabling applications to use remote resources managed by widespread "virtual organizations".

* This research was supported by Ministerio de Ciencia y Tecnología, through the research grant TIC 2003-01321 and 2002-12422-E, and by Instituto Nacional de Técnica Aeroespacial "Esteban Terradas" (INTA) – Centro de Astrobiología.

P. Herrero, M.S. Pérez, and V. Robles (Eds.): SAG 2004, LNCS 3458, pp. 108–119, 2005.

The Globus project [2] has constructed an open-source toolkit to build Computational Grids, implementing a set of non-proprietary protocols for securely identifying, allocating and releasing resources from the Grid. Due to its open-source nature and its increasing popularity, the Globus toolkit has become a *de facto* standard in Grid computing. Globus is a core Grid middleware that provides the following components, which can be used separately or altogether, to support Grid applications: GRAM (Globus Resource Allocation Manager), GASS (Global Access to Secondary Storage), GSI (Grid Security Infrastructure), MDS (Monitoring and Discovery Service), and GridFTP. These services allow secure and transparent access to resources across multiple administrative domains, and serve as building blocks to implement the stages of Grid scheduling [3].

Probably, one of the most challenging problems that the Grid computing community has to deal with is the fact that Grids are highly dynamic and faulty environments. *Adaptive scheduling* has been widely studied in the literature [4, 5, 6], and it has been demonstrated that periodic re-evaluation of the schedule can result in significant improvements in both performance and fault tolerance. On the other hand, *Adaptive execution* can improve application performance by adapting it to the dynamic availability, capacity and cost of Grid resources. Moreover, an application should be able to migrate to a new resource to satisfy its new requirements or preferences *(self-adaptation)*.

In a previous work [7], we have presented a new Globus experimental framework that allows an easier and more efficient execution of jobs on a dynamic Grid environment in a "submit and forget" fashion. The Grid*W*ay framework provides resource selection, job scheduling, reliable job execution, and automatic job migration to allow a robust and efficient execution of jobs in dynamic and heterogeneous Grid environments based on the Globus toolkit [2]. Moreover, Grid*W*ay provides support for the Distributed Resource Management Application API (DRMAA)[8].

The aim of this paper is to present our experiences on using the Grid to execute three real applications belonging to the bioinformatics, planetary geology and optimization research areas. These applications follow typical loosely coupled models: embarrassingly distributed and master-worker. We also show that DRMAA is a suitable and portable framework to express those distributed communicating paradigms. The tasks that made up the above computing models could require different complexity or instruction streams. Therefore, adaptive scheduling is again required to deal with their asynchronous temporal structure.

The main features of the Grid*W*ay framework and its code porting support are described in Section 2 and 3 respectively. The synchronous and asynchronous embarrassingly distributed models in the context of a bioinformatics and a planetary geology applications are analyzed in Section 4 and 5. Section 6 deals with the master-worker paradigm using a grid-oriented genetic algorithm as case of study. At last, the main conclusions and acknowledgments of this research are summarized in Section 7.

## 2    Main Features of the GridWay Framework

GridWay [7] is a Globus-based submission loosely-coupled framework that achieves an efficient execution of applications by combining:

- *Adaptive scheduling*: Reliable schedules can only be issued considering the dynamic characteristics of the available Grid resources [5]. In general, adaptive scheduling can consider factors such as availability, performance, load or proximity, which must be properly scaled according to the application needs and preferences. GridWay periodically gathers information from the Grid and from the running or completed jobs to adaptively schedule pending tasks according to the application demands and Grid resource status.
- *Adaptive execution*: In order to obtain a reasonable degree of both application performance and fault tolerance, a job must be able to migrate among the Grid resources adapting itself to events dynamically generated by both the Grid and the running application [9]. GridWay evaluates each *rescheduling event* to decide if a migration is feasible and worthwhile.
- *Reuse of common files*: Efficient execution of some applications profiles, like parameters sweep, can only be achieved by re-using shared files between tasks [10]. This is specially important not only to reduce the file transfer overhead, but also to prevent the saturation of the file server where these files are stored. Reuse of common files between tasks simultaneously submitted to the same resource is achieved by storing some files declared as *shared* in the GASS cache [11].
- *Fault tolerance*: The failures that may occur in a Grid can fall in a wide range of categories such as execution faults, network errors, hardware faults, configuration problems, etc [12]. Fault detection and recovery depends on the nature of the failure, and it may involve retrying, migrating or restarting the execution of an application.

## 3    GridWay Code Porting Support

The Distributed Resource Management Application API (DRMAA) Working Group[1], within the Global Grid Forum (GGF)[2], has developed an API specification that allows a high-level interaction with Distributed Resource Management Systems (DRMS). The DRMAA standard constitutes a homogeneous interface to different DRMS to handle job submission, monitoring and control, and retrieval of finished job status.

DRMAA allows scientists and engineers to express their computational problems in a Grid environment. The capture of the job exit code allow users to define complex jobs, where each depends on the output and exit code from the

---

[1] http://www.drmaa.org (2004)
[2] http://www.gridforum.org (2004)

previous job. They may even involve branching, looping and spawning of sub-tasks, allowing the exploitation of the parallelism on the work flow of certain type of applications.

The target application source code does not have to be modified. However, due to the high fault rate and the dynamic rescheduling, the application should generate **restart files** in order to restart the execution from a given point. If these files are not provided, the job is restarted from the beginning. User-level checkpointing managed by the programmer must be implemented because system-level checkpointing is not currently possible among heterogeneous resources. In order to adapt the execution of a job to its dynamic demands, the application can specify its host requirements through a **requirement expression**. Also, in order to prioritize the resources that fulfill the requirements according to its runtime needs, the application must specify its hosts preferences through a **ranking expression**. The **ranking expression** uses a performance model to estimate the job turnaround time as the sum of execution and transfer time, derived from the performance and proximity of the candidate resources [13].

In this work we will analyze the following loosely coupled paradigm:

- Embarrassingly distributed: Applications that can be obviously divided into a number of independent tasks. The application is asynchronous when require distinct instruction streams and so different execution times. A sample of this schema with its DRMAA implementation is showed in the figure1.

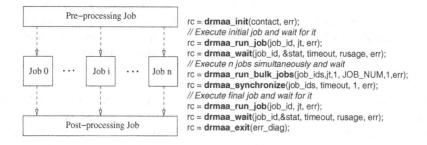

**Fig. 1.** Embarrassingly distributed paradigm and its codification using the DRMAA standard

- Master-worker: A Master task assigns a description (input files) of the task to be performed by each Worker. Once all the Workers are completed, the Master task performs some computations in order to evaluate a stop criterion or to assign new tasks to more workers. Again, it could be synchronous or asynchronous. Figure 2 shows a example of Master-worker optimization loop and a DRMAA implementation sample.

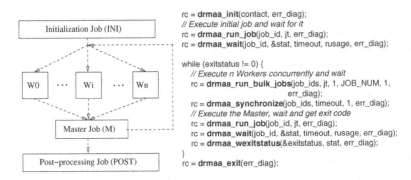

**Fig. 2.** Master-Worker paradigm and its codification using the DRMAA standard

# 4   Synchronous Embarrassingly Distributed Paradigm

## 4.1   A Protein Structure Prediction Application

Bioinformatics, which has to do with the management and analysis of huge amounts of biological data, could enormously benefit from the suitability of the Grid to execute high-throughput applications. In the context of this paper, we consider a bioinformatics application aimed at predicting the structure and thermodynamic properties of a target protein from its amino acid sequences. The algorithm, tested in the 5th round of Critical Assessment of techniques for protein Structure Prediction (CASP5), aligns with gaps the target sequence with all the 6150 non-redundant structures in the Protein Data Bank (PDB), and evaluates the match between sequence and structure based on a simplified free energy function plus a gap penalty term. The lowest scoring alignment found is regarded as the prediction if it satisfies some quality requirements. In such cases, the algorithm can be used to estimate thermodynamic parameters of the target sequence, such as the folding free energy and the normalized energy gap [14].

To speed up the analysis and reduce the data needed, the PDB files are preprocessed to extract the contact matrices, which provide a reduced representation of protein structures. The algorithm is then applied twice, the first time as a fast search, in order to select the 100 best candidate structures, the second time with parameters allowing a more accurate search of the optimal alignment.We have applied the algorithm to the prediction of thermodynamic properties of families of orthologous proteins, i.e. proteins performing the same function in different organisms. If a representative structure of this set is known, the algorithm predicts it as the correct structure.

## 4.2   Results

The experiments presented in this section were conducted on a research testbed based on the Globus Toolkit described in table 1. This testbed is highly heterogeneous and it is made up of resources belonging to two different sites interconnected by a "public" non-dedicated network.

**Table 1.** Research testbed for the protein structure prediction application

| Name | Site | Architecture | Speed | Mem. | OS | DRMS |
|------|------|--------------|-------|------|-----|------|
| ursa | DACYA-UCM | 1×UltraSPARC-IIe | 500MHz | 256MB | Solaris | fork |
| draco | DACYA-UCM | 1×UltraSPARC-I | 167MHz | 128MB | Solaris | fork |
| pegasus | DACYA-UCM | 1×Pentium 4 | 2.4GHz | 1GB | Linux 2.4 | fork |
| solea | DACYA-UCM | 2×UltraSPARC-II | 296MHz | 256MB | Solaris | fork |
| babieca | LCASAT-CAB | 5×Alpha EV67 | 450MHz | 256MB | Linux 2.2 | PBS |

The following set of experiments shows how adaptive scheduling improves the performance and adaptive execution provides fault tolerance by restarting the execution from the beginning. Let us consider an experiment consisting in 88 tasks, each of them applies the structure prediction algorithm to a different sequence of the *Triosephosfate Isomerase* enzyme which is present in different organisms. The overall execution time for the bioinformatics application, when all the machines in the testbed are available, is 7.15 hours with an average throughput of 12 jobs per hour.

This experiment was reproduced in two new situations. In the first case, babieca is shut down for maintenance in the middle of the experiment during one hour. As a consequence, the framework stops scheduling jobs in this host and the average job turnaround is reduced to 10 jobs per hour. Once babieca is restarted, Grid*W*ay schedules jobs on it again and the throughput increases to nearly 12 jobs per hour. The second case starts with pegasus unavailable, and it is *plugged* in to the Grid 3.5 hours after the experiment started. As could be expected, the absence of pegasus decreases the average throughput (9 jobs per hour), and increases the overall execution time to 9.8 hours. Figure 3 shows the dynamic job turnaround time during the execution of the application in the above situations.

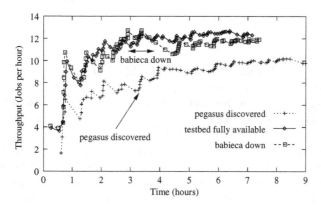

**Fig. 3.** Dynamic throughput in the execution of the application when the testbed is fully available, when pegasus is discovered and when babieca is down

# 5    Asynchronous Embarrassingly Distributed Paradigm

## 5.1    A Mars Impact Cratering Application

Our target application analyzes the threshold diameter for cratering the seafloor of an hypothetical martian sea during the first steps of an impact. Results of this analysis can be used to develop a search criteria for future investigations, including techniques that will be used in future Mars exploration missions to detect buried geological structures using ground penetrating radar surveys, as the ones included in the ESA Mars Express and planned for NASA 2005 missions.The discovery of marine-target impact craters on Mars would also help to address the ongoing debate of whether large water bodies occupied the northern plains of Mars and help to constrain future paleoclimatic reconstructions [15]. In any case, this kind of studies requires an huge amount of computing power, which is not usually available within a single organization.

Numerical simulations use the Eulerian mode of a 2D hydrocode based on SALES-2 [16]. The original hydrocode, Simplified Arbitrary Lagrangian-Eulerian (SALE), permits to study the fluid-dynamics of 2D viscous fluid flows at all speeds, from the incompressible limit to highly supersonic, with an implicit treatment of the pressure equation, and a mesh rezoning philosophy. The PDE solved are the Navier-Stokes equations.

We deal in this study with vertical impacts, as they reduce to 2D problems using the radial symmetry. All simulations were conduced with spherical projectiles. For a fixed water depth, we used 8 cases of projectile diameter in the range of 60 m to 1 Km, and 3 cases of impactor velocity: 10, 20 and 30 Km/s. Calculations were performed for 3 cases of water depth: 100, 200 and 400 m. Once fixed the projectile velocity and the water depth of the hypothetical ocean, we search to determine the range for the critical diameter of the projectile which can crater the seafloor [17]. Therefore, in this study we have to compute 72 cases. Its execution on a Grid environment allows to obtain the diameter range of interest within the research cycle time.

## 5.2    Results

Table 2 shows the characteristics of the machines in the research testbed, based on the Globus toolkit. The testbed joins resources from five sites, all of them connected by the Spanish Research and Education Network, RedIRIS. This organization results in a highly heterogeneous testbed, since it presents several architectures, processor speeds, DRMS and network links.

The execution time for each task is different and, what is more important, unknown beforehand, since the convergence of the iterative algorithm strongly depends on input parameters. Moreover, there is an additional difference generated by the changing resource load, availability and characteristics. Therefore, adaptive scheduling is crucial for this application. Figure 4 shows the dynamic turnaround time during the execution of this experiment. Total experiment time was 4.64 hours (4 hours, 38 minutes and 33 seconds), so the achieved throughput was 3.87 minutes (3 minutes and 52 seconds) per job, or likewise, 15.5 jobs per hour.

**Table 2.** Research testbed for the Mars impact cratering application

| Name | Site | Architecture | Speed | Mem. | OS | DRMS |
|------|------|--------------|-------|------|-----|------|
| hydrus | DACYA-UCM | 1×Intel P4 | 2.5GHz | 512MB | Linux 2.4 | fork |
| cygnus | DACYA-UCM | 1×Intel P4 | 2.5GHz | 512MB | Linux 2.4 | fork |
| cepheus | DACYA-UCM | 1×Intel PIII | 600MHz | 256MB | Linux 2.4 | fork |
| aquila | DACYA-UCM | 1×Intel PIII | 700MHz | 128MB | Linux 2.4 | fork |
| babieca | LCASAT-CAB | 5×Alpha EV67 | 450MHz | 256MB | Linux 2.2 | PBS |
| platon | REDIRIS | 2×Intel PIII | 1.4GHz | 512MB | Linux 2.4 | fork |
| heraclito | REDIRIS | 1×Intel Cel. | 700MHz | 256MB | Linux 2.4 | fork |
| ramses | DSIC-UPV | 5×Intel PIII | 900MHz | 512MB | Linux 2.4 | PBS |
| khafre | CEPBA-UPC | 4×Intel PIII | 700MHz | 512MB | Linux 2.4 | fork |

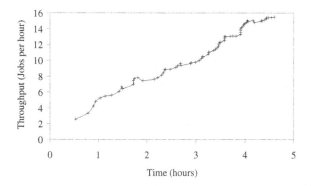

**Fig. 4.** Dynamic throughput in the execution of the application when the testbed is fully available

# 6    Master-Worker Paradigm

## 6.1    A Grid Oriented Genetic Algorithm

Genetics Algorithms (GA) are search algorithms inspired in natural selection and genetic mechanisms. GAs use historic information to find new search points and reach an optimal problem solution. In order to increase the speed and the efficiency of sequential GAs, several Parallel Genetic Algorithm (PGA) alternatives have been developed. PGAs have been successfully applied in previous works, (see for example [18]), and in most cases, they succeed to reduce the time required to find acceptable solutions.

In order to develop efficient Grid-oriented genetic algorithms [19], the dynamism and heterogeneity of a Grid environment must be considered. In this way, traditional load-balancing techniques could lead to a performance slowdown, since, in general the performance of each computing element can not be guaranteed during the execution. Moreover, some failure recovery mechanisms should be included in such a faulty environment. Taking into account the above considerations we will use a fully connected multi-deme genetic algorithm. In spite of this approach represents the most intense communication pattern (all demes exchange individuals every generation), it does not imply any overhead since the population of each deme is used as checkpoint files, and therefore transferred to the client in each iteration.

The initial population is uniformity distributed among the available number of nodes, and then a sequential GA is locally executed over each subpopulation. The resultant subpopulations are transferred back to the client, and worst individuals of each subpopulation are exchanged with the best ones of the rest. Finally, a new population is generated to perform the next iteration [20]. The scheme of this algorithm is depicted in figure 5.

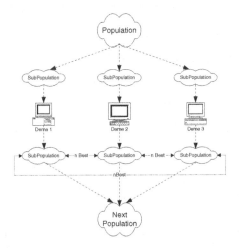

**Fig. 5.** Schema of fully-connected multi-deme genetic algorithm, with three computing nodes

The previous algorithm may incur in performance looses when the relative computing power of the nodes involved in the solution process greatly defers, since the iteration time is determined by the slowest machine. In order to prevent these situations we allow an *asynchronous* communication pattern between demes. In this way, information exchange only occurs between a fixed number of demes, instead of synchronizing the execution of all subpopulations. The minimum number of demes that should communicate in each iteration depends strongly on the numerical characteristics of the problem. We refer to this characteristic as *dynamic connectivity*, since the demes that exchange individuals differs each iteration.

## 6.2    Results

We evaluate the functionality and efficiency of the Grid-oriented Genetic Algorithm described above in the solution of the One-Max problem [21]. The One-

Max is a classical benchmark problem for genetic algorithm computations, and it tries to evolve an initial matrix of zeros in a matrix of ones. In our case we consider an initial population of 1000 individuals, each one a 20x100 zero matrix. The sequential GA executed on each node performs a fixed number of iterations (50), with a mutation and crossover probabilities of 0,1% and 60%, respectively. The exchange probability of best individuals between demes is 10%.

The following experiments were conducted on a research testbed made up of three different sites based on the Globus Toolkit. See table 3 for a brief description of the resources in the testbed.

**Table 3.** Research testbed for the Grid oriented genetic algorithm

| Name | Site | Architecture | Speed | Memory | OS | DRMS |
|------|------|-------------|-------|--------|-----|------|
| hydrus | DACYA-UCM | 1×Intel P4 | 2.5GHz | 512MB | Linux 2.4 | fork |
| cygnus | DACYA-UCM | 1×Intel P4 | 2.5GHz | 512MB | Linux 2.4 | fork |
| aquila | DACYA-UCM | 1×Intel PIII | 700MHz | 128MB | Linux 2.4 | fork |
| babieca | LCASAT-CAB | 5×Alpha EV67 | 450MHz | 256MB | Linux 2.2 | PBS |

Besides the need for both adaptive scheduling and execution we would like to remark the advantages of the DRMAA API to aid the rapid development and distribution across the rid of typical computational models. Figure 6 shows the execution profile of 4 generations of the GOGA, with a 5-way *dynamic connectivity*. Each subpopulation has been traced, and labelled with a different number ($P_{deme}$). As can be shown, individuals are exchanged between subpopulations $P1, P2, P3, P4, P5$ in the first generation; while in the third one the subpopulations used are $P1, P2, P4, P7, P8$. In this way the *dynamic connectivity*, introduces another degree of randomness since the demes that communicate differ each iteration and depend on the dynamism of the Grid.

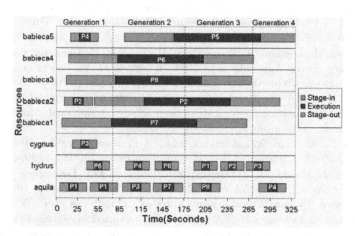

**Fig. 6.** Execution profile of four generations of the One-Max problem, each subpopulation has been labelled with $P_{deme}$

# 7   Conclusions and Acknowledgments

We have shown how an adaptive approach for job scheduling and execution is required due to both the changing conditions of the Grid resources and the asynchronous nature of some applications. The functionality, robustness and efficiency of a Grid environment consisting of GridWay and Globus have been analyzed through the execution of typical scientific applications. We have demonstrated that DRMAA is a suitable and portable framework to express the applications studied in this work: a protein structure prediction application, a Mars impact cratering application and a Grid oriented genetic algorithm.

We would like to thank all the research centers that generously contribute resources to the experimental testbed. They are the European Center for Parallelism of Barcelona (CEPBA) in the Technical University of Catalonia (UPC), the Department of Computer Architecture and Automatics (DACyA) in the Complutense University of Madrid (UCM), the Department of Information Systems and Computation (DSIC) in the Polytechnic University of Valencia (UPV), the Laboratory of Advanced Computing, Simulation and Telematic Applications (LCASAT) in the Center for Astrobiology (CAB), and the Spanish National Research and Education Network (RedIRIS). All of them are part of the Spanish Thematic Network on Grid Middleware.

# References

1. Foster, I., Kesselman, C.: The Grid: Blueprint for a New Computing Infrastructure. Morgan-Kaufman (1999)
2. Foster, I., Kesselman, C.: Globus: A Metacomputing Infrastructure Toolkit. Intl. J. Supercomputer Applications **11** (1997) 115–128
3. Schopf, J.M.: Ten Actions when Superscheduling. Technical Report WD8.5, The Global Grid Forum (2001) Scheduling Working Group.
4. Buyya, R., D.Abramson, Giddy, J.: A Computational Economy for Grid Computing and its Implementation in the Nimrod-G Resource Broker. Future Generation Computer Systems (2002) Elsevier Science.
5. Casanova, H., Legrand, A., Zagorodnov, D., Berman, F.: Heuristics for Scheduling Parameter Sweep Applications in Grid Environments. In: Proceedings of the 9th Heterogeneous Computing workshop (HCW2000). (2000) Cancun, Mexico.
6. Allen, G., et al.: The Cactus Worm: Experiments with Dynamic Resource Discovery and Allocation in a Grid Environment. International Journal of High-Performance Computing Applications **15** (2001)
7. Huedo, E., Montero, R.S., Llorente, I.M.: A Framework for Adaptive Execution on Grids. Intl. J. Software – Practice and Experience (SPE) **34** (2004) 631–651
8. Herrera, J., Huedo, E., Montero, R.S., Llorente, I.M.: Developing Grid-Aware Applications with DRMAA on Globus-based Grids. In: Proc. of 10th Euro-Par Conference. Volume 3149 of Lecture Notes on Computer Science. (2004)
9. Vadhiyar, S., Dongarra, J.: A Performance Oriented Migration Framework for the Grid. In: Proceedings of the 3rd IEEE/ACM Int'l Symposium on Cluster Computing and the Grid (CCGrid). (2003)

10. Giersch, A., Robert, Y., Vivien, F.: Scheduling Tasks Sharing Files on Heterogeneous Master-Slave Platforms. In: Proc. 12th Euromicro Conf. Parallel, Distributed and Network-based Processing (PDP 2004), IEEE CS (2004) 364–371

11. Huedo, E., Montero, R.S., Llorente, I.M.: Experiences on Adaptive Grid Scheduling of Parameter Sweep Applications. In: Proc. 12th Euromicro Conf. Parallel, Distributed and Network-based Processing (PDP 2004), IEEE CS (2004) 28–33

12. Medeiros, R., Cirne, W., Brasileiro, F., Sauvé, J.: Faults in Grids: Why Are They so Bad and What Can Be Done about It? In: Proc. of the 4th Intl. Workshop on Grid Computing (Grid 2003). (2003)

13. Huedo, E., Montero, R.S., Llorente, I.M.: Experiences on Grid Resource Selection Considering Resource Proximity. In: Proc. of 1st European Across Grids Conf. Volume 2970 of Lecture Notes on Computer Science. (2003)

14. van Ham, R., et al.: Reductive Genome Evolution in *buchnera aphidicola*. Proc. Natl. Acad. Sci. USA **100** (2003) 581–586

15. Ormö, J., Dohm, J.M., Ferris, J.C., Lepinette, A., Fairén, A.: Marine-Target Craters on Mars? An Assessment Study. Meteoritics & Planetary Science **39** (2004) 333–346

16. Gareth, S.C., Melosh, H.J.: SALES 2: A Multi-Material Extension to SALE Hydrocode with Improved Equation of State and Constitutive Model. Available at http://www.lpl.arizona.edu/~gareth/publications/sales_2 (2002)

17. Housen, K.R., Schmidt, R.M., Holsapple, K.A.: Crater Ejecta Scaling Laws: Fundamental Forms Based on Dimensional Analysis. Journal of Geophysical Research **88** (1983) 2485–2499

18. Kang, L., Chen, Y.: Parallel Evolutionary Algorithms and Applications. (1999)

19. Imade, H., Morishita, R., Ono, I., Ono, N., Okamoto, M.: A Grid-oriented Genetic Algorithm Framework for Bioinformatics. New Generation Computing **22** (2004) 177–186

20. Cantú-Paz, E.: A Survey of Parallel Genetic Algorthms (1999)

21. Schaffer, J., Eshelman, L.: On Crossover as an Evolutionary Viable Strategy. In Belew, R., Booker, L., eds.: Proceedings of the 4th International Conference on Genetic Algorithms, Morgan Kaufmann (1991) 61–68

# A Framework for the Design and Reuse of Grid Workflows

Ilkay Altintas[1], Adam Birnbaum[1], Kim K. Baldridge[1,2], Wibke Sudholt[2],
Mark Miller[1], Celine Amoreira[2], Yohann Potier[2], and Bertram Ludaescher[1,3]

[1] San Diego Supercomputer Center, University of California at San Diego,
9500 Gilman Drive, La Jolla, CA 92093, USA
{altintas, birnbaum, kimb, miller, ludaesch}@sdsc.edu
[2] Institute of Organic Chemistry, University of Zurich, Winterthurerstrasse 190,
CH-8057 Zurich, Switzerland
{kimb, wibke, ypotier, amoreira}@oci.unizh.ch
[3] Dept. of Computer Science & Genome Center, University of California at Davis,
One Shields Ave, Davis, CA 95616, USA
ludaesch@ucdavis.edu

**Abstract.** Grid workflows can be seen as special scientific workflows involving
high performance and/or high throughput computational tasks. Much work in
grid workflows has focused on improving application performance through
schedulers that optimize the use of computational resources and bandwidth. As
high-end computing resources are becoming more of a commodity that is
available to new scientific communities, there is an increasing need to also improve the design and reusability "performance" of scientific workflow systems.
To this end, we are developing a framework that supports the design and reuse
of grid workflows. Individual workflow components (e.g., for data movement,
database querying, job scheduling, remote execution etc.) are abstracted into a
set of generic, reusable tasks. Instantiations of these common tasks can be functionally equivalent atomic components (called *actors*) or composite components
(so-called *composite actors* or *subworkflows*). In this way, a grid workflow designer does not have to commit to a particular Grid technology when developing a scientific workflow; instead different technologies (e.g. GridFTP, SRB,
and *scp*) can be used interchangeably and in concert. We illustrate the application of our framework using two real-world Grid workflows from different scientific domains, i.e., cheminformatics and bioinformatics, respectively.

## 1   Introduction

With the increase in the volume of scientific data and knowledge, the demand to utilize the largest portion thereof in an efficient and simple way has become one of the
main challenges in today's science. Many scientific domains need computing methods
and resources for continued improvement of the quality of their research. Important
examples include computational problems in bio- and cheminformatics. Technical
challenges also arise through the introduction of different, heterogeneous distributed
network computing systems that make up the Grid [1,2]. While an increasing number
of computational tools for the Grid become available, they are generally difficult to

P. Herrero, M.S. Pérez, and V. Robles (Eds.): SAG 2004, LNCS 3458, pp. 120–133, 2005.
© Springer-Verlag Berlin Heidelberg 2005

use for the domain scientist. Scientific workflow user environments, e.g., Kepler [7], Taverna [8], and Triana [9], aim at improving this situation by "wrapping" Grid tools and making them available in a user-friendly visual programming environment.

*Grid Workflows* can be seen as special scientific workflows that exhibit features of high-performance computing (HPC) workflows and/or high-throughput computing (HTC) workflows. While the focus of the former is on maximal peak performance, e.g., in terms of floating point operations per second (FLOPs), the latter can deliver large amounts of processing capacity over long periods of time [3]. HTC systems are effective for problems that deal with the management and tracking of data movements and the efficient assignment of tasks to resources.

We first discuss the practice of and the challenges in assembling HTC Grid workflows, and describe a Grid workflow framework that can help scientists develop HTC workflows for their research problems (Section 2). This is followed by a discussion of two real-world use cases from the cheminformatics and bioinformatics domains, respectively (Section 3). We conclude in Section 4 with a brief outlook on future work.

## 2 Grid-Workflow Framework

With the existing Grid infrastructure, building scientific applications for large-scale collaborative Grid workflows is complicated. Many scientists do not have the technical expertise to use the existing Grid components, so they need to recruit additional Grid expertise to assist them with their applications. One of the main reasons for these difficulties is that the basic Grid services to authenticate, access, manage, and discover remote resources are not easily obtained, nor easy to utilize once they are obtained. The goal of our Grid framework is to design abstract components and templates that facilitate Grid-based workflow construction, and to integrate multiple such Grid components into a single system with an intuitive graphical user interface (GUI).

Such a Grid workflow framework can be useful at several levels, e.g. as a modeling environment to capture the scientists' high-level ideas as a model of a scientific process, to design application-specific data analysis pipelines, or even to control the actual computational experiments, track the provenance of derived data, etc. The workflows generated by the system can be saved and reused in other studies. Another function of such a framework is to interface multiple technologies in one composition infrastructure, and use them interchangeably (e.g., GridFTP get vs. SRB get vs. *scp* etc.) To the best of our knowledge, ours is the first such workflow framework and system with this capability.

### 2.1 Grid Workflows: The Ingredients

We summarize below some common Grid service functions and then describe the abstract components that correspond to these functions in our framework.

**Authentication.** The Grid community has generated tools for authentication and authorization via generated proxy certificates. As summarized in [4], certificate management tools are developed for generating credentials for users and services, for getting users "signed up" to use a Grid, and for getting users' Grid credentials to wherever they are needed in a system. The Globus Toolkit [5] provides software development kits for the core security software in Globus-based Grid systems and applications. These Software Development Kits (SDKs) include libraries and Java APIs for a certificate-based authentication system that conforms to the Grid Security Infrastructure (GSI) and that can be used to generate proxy components. The toolkit also provides a web services implementation of the same package.

As straightforward as it sounds, these tools still require programming in order to be used in an end-user application. An abstract component in a visual workflow programming environment simplifies such programming (see Section 3).

**Data Movement.** Access and management of remote data are basic functions in distributed Grid computing. There are several methods for moving data from one location to another, e.g., GridFTP, SRB put/get, *scp* and others. GridFTP is a secure data transfer protocol optimized for wide-area networks. The SDSC Storage Resource Broker (SRB) is a client-server middleware that provides a uniform interface for connecting to heterogeneous data resources over a network and for accessing replicated data sets, e.g., based on metadata attributes [6]. While the former two are designed and optimized for file sharing of very large data over the Grid, sometimes a simple *scp* (secure copy) Unix command may be sufficient and easier to use for the scientist. *scp* is a shell command that allows users to copy files between systems quickly and securely, without the need for expertise in Grid systems. Such a tool can be as helpful in some workflows as any of the other file transfer mechanisms, even for data that will be used by a Grid job. Most systems provide interfaces to one or more of these tools. Ideally these methods should be usable interchangeably, depending on the user's needs, preferences, and abilities.

**Remote Service Execution.** Most scientists today are familiar with the use of web-based resources, and can make their work available through such distributed systems. However, manual copy/pasting or programming is usually required when using multiple of these resources in a data analysis or transformation pipeline. Often software developers are needed to write custom workflows that automate large-scale scientific workflows and processes. The use of generic tools for service-based execution can simplify the problem somewhat. A service is a component within the Internet computing model that provides a particular function through a simple remote invocation mechanism. Through the introduction of Web and Grid services, many new resources for different scientific domains are becoming available. However, services do not necessarily "fit together" (in the sense that they can be composed into a chain or pipeline of services) unless they have been designed to do so. Hence service composition (e.g., via "shim services") is an active field of research and development in scientific workflow systems [7, 8, 9].

The *ssh* (secure shell) Unix-command provides a simple way of connecting to a remote resource and executing a program there. A special actor component for this command is available in Kepler [7] as an easy way of executing a function on a remote machine, and getting back the results of the execution.

**Grid Job Submission.** A Grid job is an executable or command that runs on a (typically remote) Grid resource. The remote resource, also referred to as a 'contact' or 'gatekeeper', must have a Grid environment such as the Globus toolkit [5] installed to recognize this submission. Once submitted, a job can run in *batch* mode or *non-batch* mode. The jobs submitted in batch mode are assigned a job-id, which is returned immediately and can be used for subsequent monitoring of the submitted job. The non-batch jobs return the result of the computation once they are finished. Batch mode submission is useful for jobs that take a long time, such as process-intensive computations [10]. The jobs to be submitted can be described using the Resource Specification Language (RSL), a common interchange language to describe resources.

**Job Scheduling and Resource Management.** In order for a high-throughput application to make use of distributed resources, a solution must exist for the scheduling problem, i.e. there must be a mapping between tasks and resources. Solving this problem in an ideal system has been shown to be NP-hard [39], and research has largely focused on the development of scheduling heuristics, which have been built into the commonly-used high-throughput systems such as Condor [3], Nimrod/G [11,14], and the AppLeS Parameter Sweep Template (APST) [12]. In building practical systems, it is difficult to isolate the issues of scheduling from those of managing the heterogeneity and instability of component subsystems. All three of the aforementioned high-throughput scheduling tools have the ability to constantly monitor and adjust to changing load and performance. In addition, they all provide some ability to monitor the state of the running application, as they all maintain job databases that may be polled and updated during experiment execution. It is one of our goals in this work to show how these systems can be leveraged in the construction of Grid workflows.

**Fault Tolerance.** Because Grid workflows depend on distributed computational resources under diverse controlling authorities, they are exposed to high risk of component failure, including failures in computational platforms, network, application services or the workflow system itself. Many of these issues fall into the domain of system and network administrators, who must design infrastructure to provide redundant components. In this work, we address only the parts that are under our control; in particular, the workflow system can retry to connect to failed resource or service after a certain amount of time. Redundant resources may be either found in a service registry, or may be hard-coded into workflows. The decision on which approach has to be taken depends on the fail-over policy/strategy of a particular workflow system.

**Logging and Provenance.** In scientific applications it is often necessary to keep track of data and processes that were used to produce the results of a computational experiment or scientific workflow, in particular to facilitate reproducibility. This *provenance* information can be associated with a result data set or workflow run, effectively providing an execution trace of certain crucial provenance information. Logging services, e.g., of the Globus Toolkit [13], can be customized and integrated into a scientific workflow system for this purpose. Such services provide interfaces to modify log filters and monitor and create views over previous logs.

**User Interaction and Reporting.** Scientific workflows may require user interaction at runtime, e.g., to determine which data subsets should be routed through which of several alternate paths of the workflow, or for computational steering. Workflow engines already maintain information of intermediate steps and execution details of processes. The challenge is to display that information in a way that it will satisfy the needs of different users, with different detail levels and provisions for a variety of different publishing methods.

## 2.2  Component Composition and Interaction

Kepler [16] is an active cross-project collaboration bringing together several large-scale NSF/ITR projects (including SEEK [18], GEON [17], and ROADNet [19]), the DOE/SciDAC SDM project [20], and several other projects including Research Surge Enabled by Cyberinfrastructure (Resurgence) [21] and Encylopedia of Life (EOL) [22], to develop an open source scientific workflow system. The emerging Kepler system allows scientists from different domains (bioinformatics, cheminformatics, ecoinformatics, geoinformatics, astrophysics etc.) to design and execute scientific workflows. Scientific workflows can be used to combine data integration, analysis, and visualization steps into larger, automated "knowledge discovery pipelines" and "grid workflows" [23, 33].

Kepler is build on top of the mature Ptolemy II system developed at UC Berkley [24]. Ptolemy II is a system along with a set of APIs for heterogeneous hierarchical modeling. Not unlike the electrical circuit design, the focus of the Ptolemy II system is to build models of systems based on the assembly of predesigned components. These components are called *actors* [25]:

> *"An actor is an encapsulation of parameterized actions performed on input data to produce output data. An actor may be state-less or state-full, depending on whether it has internal state. Input and output data are communicated through well-defined ports. Ports and parameters are the interfaces of an actor. A port, unlike methods in Object-Oriented designs, does not have to have a call-return semantics. The behaviors of a set of actors are not well-defined without a coordination model. A framework is an environment that actors reside in, and defines the interaction among actors."*

The interaction styles of actors are captured by *models of computation* (MoC). A MoC defines the communication semantics among ports and the flow of control and data among actors.

A framework implements a model of computation. Frameworks and actors together define a system [25]. In our Grid Workflow framework, we define a set of grid actors in Kepler that work in dataflow-based computation models such as Process Network (PN) and Synchronous Data Flow (SDF). *Directors* are responsible for implementing particular MoCs, and thus they define the "orchestration semantics" workflows. Simply by changing the director of a workflow, one can change the scheduling and overall execution semantics of a workflow, without changing any of the components or the network topology of the workflow graph.

The theoretical basis for the PN director are *Kahn Process Networks*. A process network is a directed graph, comprising a set of nodes (processes) connected by a set of directed arcs (representing FIFO queues). Each process executes a sequential program and is wrapped as a Ptolemy II actor. The one-way FIFO channels are used for the communication of processes and, in Kahn's process networks, have unbounded capacity, i.e., each channel can carry a possibly infinite sequence (a *stream*) of atomic data objects (*tokens*). Since channels have in principle unbounded capacity, writes to channels are non-blocking, while reads are blocking [26]. The PN domain in Ptolemy and the director implementing it in Ptolemy (and thus in Kepler) employ an extended model due to Lee and Parks [27, 28]. The SDF domain is a special variant of PN in which a sequential execution order of actors can be statically determined prior to execution. This results in execution with minimal overhead, as well as bounded memory usage and a guarantee that deadlock will never occur.

## 2.3   Abstract Grid Workflow Actors

Grid workflows often exhibit similar flow patterns [29, 30], including the basic workflow patterns [31]. A very common scenario is the following: a user needs to copy (or *stage*) a set of files from one resource (e.g., the local environment) to a remote resource, run a computational experiment on that remote resource, and then fetch the results back to the local environment or copy them to another resource/database. We call these types of workflows *stage-execute-fetch* workflows. A script can implement a workflow that conforms to this pattern. However, a script does not specify the details of the scheduling of tasks and communication between the resources while the workflow is running. Also, scripts are often platform dependent and specific to a scenario, despite the fact that the pattern can be parameterized and used in many workflows. Users could more easily specify their own workflows via GUIs or a well-defined set of reusable components (actors) that can be connected to each other through some interfaces. The Kepler scientific workflow system, through its modeling foundation inherited from Ptolemy, provides an environment with such reuseable building blocks for Grid workflows. Motivated by the need to develop a simple, extensible, platform independent, and client-controllable grid workflow framework, we propose the following set of abstract actors that can be used as building blocks for the construction of Grid workflows.

**Authenticate Actor.** This component acts as a certificate source for other actors. All actors that use the same certificate can use the output of this actor. For the Globus Grid authentication, the actor initializes a proxy that creates a Globus proxy certificate from an X.509 key and certificate pair, when provided a pass-phrase. For SRB and remote database actors, this actor is generating the connection and can forward a connection token to the following steps in the workflow.

**Copy Actor.** This fundamental actor copies sets of files from one resource to another resource during workflow execution. The abstract copy actor can be instantiated to a simple FTP actor, a secure copy (*scp*) actor, a GridFTP actor, or an SRB-based put/get actor. For example, a GridFTP actor involves a Globus-grid proxy certificate, source and destination resources including directories, and a set of file names to be transferred. Similarly, SRBPut and SRBGet can be used to instantiate the abstract copy actor. Special variants include:

- **Stage Actor.** This variant copies files from the local host to a remote host.
- **Fetch Actor.** This variant retrieves files from the remote host to the local host.

**Job Execution Actor.** The purpose of this actor is to submit and run a remote job. Submission methods and clients can include special wrappers for *ssh*-based execution, web service-clients, Grid job runner proxies, and actors for Nimrod- and APST-based submission. Kepler provides a variety of these instantiations, which have proven to be useful for remote job execution in different scientific application domains [32, 33].

**Monitoring Actor.** Monitoring actors and tools of our framework are designed to be scalable depending on user needs. We propose three different levels of monitoring, namely, *light*, *standard*, and *heavy*. In the standard monitoring level, the user is notified only if an actor fails to execute. Polling the job database of Nimrod/G or APST is an example mechanism for checking the state of execution of an actor. The overall workflow execution monitoring is done via a monitoring subsystem that interacts with the director. The light monitoring system is one that watches the execution but does not notify the user about failures until the workflow has finished or stalled. The heavy monitoring verbosely reports every communication between the workflow entities and also notifies the user about failures immediately.

**Reporting Actor.** The reporting actors work in coordination with the other actors to report regular intermediate results or exceptional conditions such as actor failures. This actor can also be implemented as a separate utility rather than as a Kepler actor. It talks to the monitoring unit and director, and allows users to report information wherever they would like, e.g., at a remote Grid resource, in a provenance database, or directly on a website.

**Filter Actor.** Filtering and subsetting data is a very common function. For example on a tuple stream, or a stream of XML elements, filtering corresponds to a selection operation $\sigma$. In contrast, cutting a certain region of interest from a map image can be seen as a data subsetting operation. A common requirement in Grid applications is to filter or subset data at the (usually remote) site of origin before passing it on to subsequent processing steps of the workflow.

**Storage Actor.** Once results are produced, they need to be stored on different resources, file systems, or databases. Sometime this step is preceded by a filtering step so that only interesting data will be saved. Stored information can include the primary data flowing through a workflow as well as process and provenance related metadata. Different incarnations of this actor can be used to save data on a number of storage devices, e.g. directly to a file system or databases, or indirectly to SRB.

**Data Discovery Actor.** Previously stored results should be searchable in various ways, e.g., through simple keyword based search, or more advanced ontology-based search mechanisms that "understand" how to expand a given search term (or a metadata annotation of a dataset). Since discovery of relevant datasets is very common tasks, the data discovery component is being integrated into the Kepler graphical user interface (i.e., Vergil, which is Ptolemy's GUI).

**Service Discovery Actor.** Kepler provides a web service harvester component for importing web services (or, more precisely, their interfaces) from a service repository or website. For the latter, the harvester can search text/html pages or repositories for appropriate links to WSDL web service descriptions. After parsing and analyzing these descriptions, the harvested web services appear in Kepler as any other actors; in particular, their input and output parameters and types are inferred from the WSDL descriptions. Different operations from a single web service "package" are grouped together via the web service name and stored in the Kepler actor library. Once imported, web service actors are given a local LSID and can be annotated using a Kepler actor classification ontology. In this way, different dynamic view can be created on the actor library, depending on the chosen "view ontology" and the given search terms (concept names). Annotations can refer to a (web service) actor as a whole, or to the specific inputs and outputs of the actor. After the web service import is completed, actors representing the different operations can be searched, dragged and dropped onto Kepler's Vergil design interface, etc. like any other predefined actor.

**Transformation and Querying Actors.** When chaining together actor components to form larger workflows, consecutive actors or services do not necessarily "fit together". Data transformation actors and query actors can be used as "shims" to bridge structural and/or format mismatches between the output of a data producing actor and the input of a subsequent data consuming actor. Kepler provides various data transformation and querying actors, e.g., XSLT and Perl actors for data transformations, and XQuery and SQL actors for querying.

### 2.4  A Grid Workflow Pattern: *Stage-Execute-Fetch*

The abovementioned set of abstract Grid-related actors and their concrete instantiations allow a Kepler user to design and execute Grid workflows using a number of different tools, e.g., SRB for data handling including replica management, and Globus, Condor, and Nimrod, for remote execution and scheduling, respectively. In this way, the most suitable of a number of Grid tools become available to the scientist in a uniform manner. In addition to employing existing concrete Grid actors or their abstract counterparts[1], our framework for Grid workflows also includes *patterns* of Grid workflows. Such patterns correspond to *abstract workflows*, i.e. which might not be immediately executable and which involve abstract actors like the ones discussed above. An *abstract actor* can be seen as a "stub" or placeholder for a yet to be specified function, but whose input and output ports have already been pre-configured to capture the essential arguments of the operation. For example, the abstract copy actor will contain as inputs at least descriptions of the files/objects to be copied and their source and target locations. Concrete instantiations might require additional information, e.g., one or more authentication or connection tokens to access the various involved resources.

Using Ptolemy's hierarchical modeling capabilities, combined with the notion of abstract actors, larger templates of workflow patterns can be represented as abstract workflows. A very common pattern involves only three core abstract actors, i.e., *stage, execute,* and *fetch*, and is described as a linear chain of these actors. This Grid workflow pattern or template can be retrieved from the workflow repository (which is identical to the service/actor repository, modulo the fact that workflows are composite actors) and instantiated using suitable concrete actors to make the abstract workflow executable. The next section discusses in more detail two instantiations of this pattern, i.e., two real-world scientific workflows from very different domains.

---

[1] At design-time; they have to be substituted/instantiated with concrete ones at runtime.

# 3  Instantiating the Framework Using the Kepler Workflow System

The proposed Grid framework and its incarnation in Kepler have proven useful in different application domains, including those from computational chemistry and biology described below. Thanks to its generality, the approach and framework are applicable in other scientific domains as well.

## 3.1  Use Case 1: GAMESS Workflow for Quantum Chemistry

RESearch sURGe ENabled by CyberinfrastructurE (RESURGENCE) [21] is a project to develop a general workflow infrastructure for computational chemistry that allows high-throughput calculations distributed on computational grids. The project was initiated by the need to make the evolving technologies, such as computational grids and web services, available to scientists. In addition, such infrastructure provides a mechanism for researchers to couple different scientific codes within one overall calculation pipeline, spanning across domain sub-fields, input and output formats, and computational resources. The goal is thus to build a tool that provides a common user interface so that users do not have to be concerned with the particulars of grid computing, web services nor their associated underlying code, computational platforms, or with data file formats. However, the focus is not to generate complete predefined workflows, but large enough workflow chunks so that scientists can string them together according to their individual interests. With this purpose in mind, the Resurgence project became a part of the Kepler collaboration for developing common scientific workflow systems for a variety of disciplines [30, 34, 35].

The first target of the project is to build a pipeline from the base of Kepler composite actors, which automatically prepares and executes quantum chemical calculations for a number of molecules, with the individual input files generated on the fly (see Figure 1). For this, the *General Atomic and Molecular Electronic Structure System* (GAMESS) [36, 37] is employed, a program for ab initio molecular quantum chemistry. The program is an important internationally used software tool for the study of molecular and biomolecular research problems. Using this software, one can make reliable predictions of the structure, molecular properties and reactivity of molecules, which are useful for understanding complex problems in the real world. There are many standardized methods that can be invoked within the software package, and a very large variety of options and capabilities exist. Results of these computations can be compared to experimentally determined properties of the same type, used for predictions of properties before an experiment is performed, or, in some cases provide information that can not be obtained experimentally. As such, results of these computations can fill important gaps in our scientific knowledge. The software can be run on a variety of computer platform types, and many enhancements have been made to GAMESS both scientifically, as well as in terms of the latest middleware technology developments. Therefore, the software serves as an excellent testbed and driving application for further development of the Kepler system.

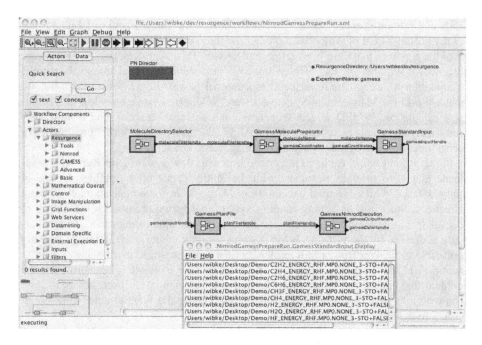

**Fig. 1.** Development version of the Resurgence GAMESS pipeline during execution

One principle of workflows in the Resurgence project is that the complex file preparation, transformation and analysis pipeline components should be mainly executed on the same machine where Kepler is running, while the highly compute-intensive molecular calculation pipeline components should be executed on dedicated, typically remote, compute servers, if possible. This allows access to helper tools that are often only installed on the central machine, to safeguard intermediate files after each workflow step and collect all outcomes in one place, but also means that input and output files have to be transferred back and forth between local and grid machines. This is of course an instantiation of the general stage-execute-fetch pattern, refined by other steps, including data transformations. For the preparation of GAMESS input files, the Open Babel program [38] is used to convert between different molecular file formats. For the execution of GAMESS jobs, the Nimrod/G toolkit [11, 14] is applied. For the future, there are plans to extend the Resurgence interface to additional molecular modeling software, particularly for the treatment of large biomolecules by classical mechanics. In addition, input and output data are planned to be directly read from and stored into molecular databases using concrete instances of the abstract storage actor.

### 3.2 Use Case 2: The Encyclopedia of Life/iGAP Workflow for Protein Sequence Annotation

It is hard to think of a better example of the explosion of data than computational molecular biology. Biologists are currently hard at work in digesting an over-abundance of

DNA and protein sequence data. One such effort is the Encyclopedia of Life Project (EOL) [22], the goal of which is to predict the three-dimensional protein structures for all of the genomes that have been sequenced to date. This is a calculation of such a huge scale that it requires the use of bleeding-edge grid technology and massively-parallel computation to access the requisite computational power. In previous work [40], we built a Workflow Management System daemon (WMSD) to manage the logistics of this large calculation. WMSD selects sequences from an input database, and continuously feeds many thousands of tasks to APST. APST manages the low-level complexities of job submission, heterogeneous resource management, and scheduling.

In the present work, we have integrated this workflow system with Kepler. Our ultimate aim is to provide biologists with the ability to set up a flexible pipeline of analysis tasks, which are then executed on a large scale for a huge number of input sequences. Since this is a long-running system, a key requirement is the ability to recover from major system failure – an instance of the monitoring actor. This is partially addressed by the fact that WMSD stores its state in an Oracle database, making it possible to recover from a failure of APST. In such a case, Kepler enables the automation of higher-level error recovery mechanisms. For example, after correcting the problem that caused the jobs to fail, it is easy for a scientist to insert actors to reset jobs with a "failed" state to "new", which would cause the WMSD actor to resubmit these jobs to APST at the next update.

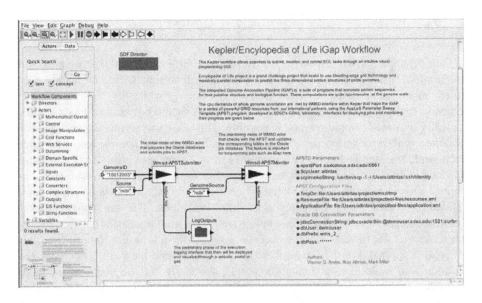

**Fig. 2.** The Encyclopedia of Life iGAP workflow

In the first implementation of this system, the workflow of tasks to be executed for each genome sequence is hard-coded into logic in the WMSD. The benefit of Kepler to date has been primarily in the areas of error recovery and resource management. In the future, we would like to allow the scientist to specify these workflows using the full power of the Kepler system. In essence, this would allow users to assemble workflows consisting of "pseudo-actors", whose sole behavior would be to emit WMSD configuration files specifying the workflow to be executed in high-throughput mode.

## 4 Discussion and Outlook

We have described a framework for Grid workflows based on abstractions of common Grid workflow components such as authentication, data movement, and remote execution, and monitoring. Abstract workflows, consisting of abstract and possibly concrete actors provide the workflow designer with common components and workflow patterns that can be reused and instantiated to create executable Grid workflows. A main advantage of this approach is that (a) it frees the designer from making technology decisions early on in the design process, and (b) at instantiation time, it allows the user to chose and even combine different concrete technologies such as Globus, SRB, and Nimrod. In future work we plan to automate the instantiation process of our framework using a reasoning approach that aims at automating the "wiring" of different actor instances, based on their semantic port types [41].

## References

1. Berman, F., Wolski, R., Casanova, H., Cirne, W.,Dail, H., Faerman, M., Figueira, S., Hayes, J., Obertelli, G., Schopf, J., Shao, G., Smallen, S., Spring, N., Su, A., Zagorodnov, D. : Adaptive computing on the Grid using AppLeS. Parallel and Distributed Systems, IEEE Transactions on, Vol. 14, Issue 4, 369-382, April 2003.
2. F. Berman, G. Fox, and A. Hey, editors. Grid Computing: Making the Global Infrastructure a Reality. John Wiley & Sons, 2003.
3. The Condor Project Homepage: http://www.cs.wisc.edu/condor/
4. GRIDS: Grid Research Integration Deployment and Support Center, The Grid Ecosystem: Software Components for Grid Systems And Applications: http://www-unix.grids-center.org/r6/ecosystem
5. The Globus Toolkit: http://www-unix.globus.org/toolkit/
6. Storage Resource Broker: http://www.npaci.edu/DICE/SRB/
7. Kepler Project: http://kepler-project.org
8. Taverna Project: http://taverna.sourceforge.net
9. Triana Project: http://www.trianacode.org/
10. Vladimir, S.: Grid Job submission using the Java CoG Kit, IBM Developer Works
11. Nimrod/G Project: http://www.csse.monash.edu.au/~nimrod/nimrodg/
12. AppLeS Parameter Sweep Template (APST) Project: http://grail.sdsc.edu/projects/apst/
13. Configuring Globus Toolkit Logging Services: http://www-unix.globus.org/toolkit/docs/3.2/core/admin/configuringlogging.html
14. Abramson, D., Giddy, J., Kotler, L.: High Performance Parametric Modeling with Nimrod/G: Killer Application for the Global Grid?, IPDPS'2000, Mexico, IEEE CS Press, 520-528, USA, 2000.
15. Schwiegelshohn, U., Yahyapour, R..: Attributes for Communication Between Scheduling Instances, in Global Grid Forum (GGF), December 2001.
16. Altintas, I., Berkley, C., Jaeger, E., Jones, M., Ludäscher, B., Mock, S.: Kepler: An Extensible System for Design and Execution of Scientific Workflows, In the 16th Intl. Conference on Scientific and Statistical Database Management(SSDBM), Santorini Island, Greece, June 2004.

17. NSF/ITR: GEON: A Research Project to Create Cyberinfrastructure for the Geosciences, http://www.geongrid.org
18. NSF/ITR: Enabling the Science Environment for Ecological Knowledge (SEEK), http://seek.ecoinformatics.org
19. ROADNet: Real-time Observatories, Applications and Data Management Network, http://roadnet.ucsd.edu
20. Scientific Data Management (SDM) Center, http://sdm.lbl.gov/sdmcenter
21. Resurgence Project Home Page: http://www.resurgence.unizh.ch/~resurgence/
22. EOL Project: http://eol.sdsc.edu
23. Altintas, I., Berkley, C., Jaeger, E., Jones, M., Ludäscher, B., Mock, S.: Kepler: Towards a Grid-Enabled System for Scientific Workflows, In the Workflow in Grid Systems Workshop in GGF10 - The Tenth Global Grid Forum, Berlin, Germany, March 2004.
24. 24.E.A. Lee et al., Ptolemy II project and system, Department of EECS, UC Berkeley, http://ptolemy.eecs.berkeley.edu/ptolemyII
25. Liu, X., Liu, J., Eker, J., and Lee, E. A.: Heterogeneous Modeling and Design of Control Systems, in Software-Enabled Control: Information Technology for Dynamical Systems, Tariq Samad and Gary Balas (eds.), Wiley-IEEE Press, April 2003.
26. G. Kahn, "The Semantics of a Simple Language for Parallel Programming", Proceedings of International Federation for Information Processing Congress 74, pp. 471-475, North Holland Publishing Co., Aug 1974.
27. E.A. Lee and T.M. Parks, "Dataflow Process Networks", Proceedings of the IEEE, Vol. 83 No. 5, pp. 773-801, May 1995.
28. Hylands, C., Lee, E. A., Liu, J., Liu, X., Neuendorffer, S., Xiong, Y., Zheng, H. (eds.): Heterogeneous Concurrent Modeling and Design in Java (Volume 3: Ptolemy II Domains), Technical Memorandum UCB/ERL M03/29, University of California, Berkeley, CA USA 94720, July 16, 2003.
29. van Laszewski, G., Amin, K., Hategan, M., Zaluzec, N., J., Hampton, S., Rossi, A.,: GridAnt: A Client-Controllable Grid Workflow System, 37th Hawaii International Conference on System Sciences (HICSS-37), Hilton Waikoloa Village, Island of Hawaii, January 2004.
30. K. K. Baldridge, W. Sudholt, J. P. Greenberg, C. Amoreira, Y. Potier, I. Altintas, A. Birnbaum, D. Abramson, C. Enticott, S. Garic, "Cluster and Grid Infrastructure for Computational Chemistry and Biochemistry", in "Parallel Computing for Bioinformatics", A. Y. Zomaya (Ed.), John Wiley & Sons, submitted for publication
31. van der Aalst, W., M., P. , Barros, A., P., ter Hofstede, A., H., M., and Kiepuszewski, B.: Advanced Workflow Patterns, in Conference on Cooperative Information Systems, pp. 18–29, 2000.
32. I. Altintas, E. Jaeger, K. Lin, B. Ludaescher, A. Memon, A Web Service Composition and Deployment Framework for Scientific Workflows, In the 2nd Intl. Conference on Web Services (ICWS), San Diego, California, July 2004.
33. B. Ludaescher, I. Altintas, C. Berkely, D. Higgins, E. Jaeger, M. Jones, E.A. Lee., J. Tao, Y. Zhao, Scientific Workflow Management and the KEPLER System, special issue of Distributed and Parallel Systems, to appear, 2005.
34. K. K. Baldridge, J. P. Greenberg, W. Sudholt, S. Mock, I. Altintas, C. Amoreira, Y. Potier, A. Birnbaum, K. Bhatia, M. Taufer, "The Computational Chemistry Prototyping Environment", Proceedings of the IEEE Special Issue on Grid Computing, in print
35. W. Sudholt, K. K. Baldridge, D. Abramson, C. Enticott, S. Garic, C. Kondric, D. Nguyen, "Application of grid computing to parameter sweeps and optimizations in molecular modeling", Future Generation Computer Systems 21 (2005) 27-35

36. Schmidt, M. W., Baldridge, K. K., Boatz, J. A., Elbert, S. T., Gordon, M. S., Jensen, J. H., Koseki, S., Matsunaga, N., Nguyen, K. A., Su, S. J., Windus, T. L., Dupuis, M., Montgomery, J. A., J. Comput. Chem. 1993, 14, 1347-1363
37. GAMESS Home Page: http://www.msg.ameslab.gov/GAMESS/
38. Open Babel: A Package to Decypher Computational Chemistry: http://openbabel.sourceforge.net/
39. O. H. Ibarra and C. E. Kim, "Heuristic algorithms for scheduling independent tasks on nonindentical processors," *Journal of the ACM*, 24(2): 280-289, Apr. 1977.
40. A. Birnbaum, J. Hayes, W. W. Li, M. A. Miller, P. W. Arzberger, P. E. Bourne, H. Casanova. To appear in *Proceedings of LNCS, Springer Lecture Notes in Computer Science, 2005*.
41. S. Bowers and B. Ludäscher, An Ontology-Driven Framework for Data Transformation in Scientific Workflows, Intl. Workshop on Data Integration in the Life Sciences (DILS'04), March 25-26, 2004 Leipzig, Germany, LNCS 2994.

# Towards Peer-to-Peer Access Grid

Milena Radenkovic[1] and Igor Miladinovic[2]

[1] School of Computer Science & IT,
University of Nottingham,
Nottingham, NG8 1BB, UK
Tel. +44-115-8467670
mvr@cs.nott.ac.uk

[2] Telecommunication Research Center Vienna (ftw.),
Tech Gate Vienna,
Donau-City-Strasse 1, 1220 Vienna, Austria
Tel. +43-1-5052830-54
miladinovic@ftw.at

**Abstract.** The paper is concerned with supporting natural patterns of scientific collaboration in Access Grid environments. We reveal that no current approach to Access Grid allows dynamic session invocation within on-going Access Grid sessions nor workflow driven session triggering among users involved in that workflow. A model for a lightweight signaling architecture integrated within Access Grid is proposed that allows transparent demand-driven session management. The architecture is configurable both in terms of dynamically changing user preferences and resource requirements. The core of the architecture is the advanced SIP stack embedded both within Access Grid nodes and heterogenous end nodes. This is important in order to allow maximum flexibility of audio,video and workflow presentation to the end users.

**Keywords:** Access Grid, P2P, SIP, Video Conferencing.

## 1 Introduction

Access Grid (AG) [5] is already becoming widely accepted standard for collaborative environments predominantly used within GRID and e-Science community. Despite that, it is still a long way from providing truly satisfactory collaborative experience for the end users. Substantial research effort has been invested in extending and improving various aspects of AG. These efforts are mainly focused around richer collaborative visualization facilities in AG [7], richer user semantic descriptions [9] and record and replay facilities that keep provenance of the past meetings for subsequent use [10]. In this paper we focus on the limited interaction space within active AG sessions and propose mechanisms for tailoring them to better suit patterns of scientific collaboration. Our original motivation came from multiple HCI and user requirements analysis [11] that found that during structured meetings and workshops, people tend to be more productive in an

P. Herrero, M.S. Pérez, and V. Robles (Eds.): SAG 2004, LNCS 3458, pp. 134–145, 2005.

unstructured manner with lots of brainstorming, problem solving, casual conversation and spontaneous idea generation. Flat single AG session structure that follows traditional strict turn-taking teleconferencing scenario does not allow for any of that and often results in very long meetings with several tens of participants being silent during the entire meeting and only few active speakers. This paper argues that in order to provide more natural and effective meetings, AG needs to support multiple modes of interaction, from very structured to more informal and casual. For example, this refers to enabling the users to have richer discussions about spontaneous ideas among a subset of participants without disturbing the main discussion topic of the meeting. We propose a lightweight signaling architecture based on advanced SIP that is integrated within the current AG architecture and serves as the main enabling mechanism for moving towards more natural and productive AG. Furthermore we argue that peer-to-peer paradigm is much better suited for future streaming Grid applications such as audio, video and scientific instrumentation applications. We believe that current Web services have a limited time span in terms of being the only building block for AG and other streaming collaborative applications in e-Science. Scientific collaborative scenarios should at least include support for scenarios such as: spotting trends in streaming scientific data or spotting cross references in newly added annotations, alerting involved users by triggering/initiating sessions among them; or enabling users to transparently start/end sessions among each other. Even though fundamental and important, these scenarios are not yet supported in either AG1.0 [5] or emerging proposals for AG2.0 [2].

The reminder of this paper is organized as follows. Section 2 discusses current AG and SIP architectures, and identifies their limitations in a systematic manner. Section 3 introduces architectural overview of the proposed infrastructure that aims to provide support for a configurable, more ubiquitous and dynamic AG. This infrastructure is based on a collection of standardized messages that allow inspection and update of resource properties and transparent triggering of sessions among participants. Section 4 describes SIP protocol stack needed for basic AG conferences. Section 5 discusses more advanced SIP features for more advanced AG conferences. Session 6 concludes the paper and outlines future work.

## 2    Background Information

### 2.1    Access Grid

Access Grid (AG) aims to develop a large scale collaborative environment based on the idea of video walls that are dramatically scaled up in terms of the number of simultaneous participants, flexibility and functionality. AG combines data resources, computational services and people in order to provide support for the scientific method. The two key features of the scientific method include workflows and provenance. When we talk about 'workflow' in this paper we mean the specification and execution of ad-hoc in-silico experiments using scientific resources.

A workflow-based approach allows the e-Scientist to describe and enact their experimental processes in a sharable, structured, repeatable and verifiable way. Provenance data can be broken down into two categories: derivation data and annotations. Derivation data provides the answer to questions about what initial data was used for a result, and how was the transformation from initial data to result achieved. In the case of an in silico experiment that consists of coordinating a set of services, the derivation data is about which services were used and how did they transform the initial inputs into the overall result. Annotation data provides more contextual information that might be of interest: who performed an experiment, when, did they supply any comments on the specific methods and materials used. AG utilizes this idea to allow users to collaboratively monitor and discuss their Grid resources and services, use their computer-based repositories and computational analysis adopted for testing hypothesis or to demonstrate known fact. The underlying infrastructure also aims to allow dynamic formation of virtual groups/sub-groups to solve problems, describe them, search for resources and support provenance.

In order to make these high-level AG goals more specific, we give a brief architectural overview of AG. AG consists of a number of AG nodes distributed across multiple sites that provide support for group to group communication without imposing constraints on bandwidth or encoding algorithms i.e. multiple cameras can to be used simultaneously and at higher quality. AG is heavily multicast based with only one statically pre-allocated multicast group per virtual venue. The virtual venue software underlines web pages providing abstract meeting rooms that implicitly provide scoping, presence and persistence of the AG sessions. AG sessions are initiated statically, prior to start of the session by the AG managers. Protocol standards used for audio, video, text-based and network communication are still very basic and they include RAT, VIC, MUD and H.323 respectively. Protocol standards used for audio, video, text-based and network communication are still very basic and they include RAT, VIC, MUD and H.323 respectively. AG 2.0 Reference Release [2] has proposed a more flexible layered AG architecture and a set of new services including identity, network and virtual venues services. In order to provide a more usable and configurable sessions, AG2.0 design has introduced venues server client interface, venues description standard, per venue scheduling and authorization and venues server configuration.

This design methodology of AG has been adopted for its simplicity and robustness. However, it also has a number of adverse implications that are concerned with its scalability and ubiquity:

- Current AG sessions allow no ad-hoc and on-demand user driven session management because they are statically configured.
- AG nodes are still not wide spread and their user interfaces are less then user friendly.
- Even though there are multiple projects underway (including initiatives of more dynamic and flexible Access Grid 2.0) to link more novel devices, there is still no standardized architecture to support this transparently within AG.

Despite the additional services in AG2 and being heavily based on multicast, both generations of AG lack real control and flexibility that individual end users have because of the key role AG nodes have. Some combination of P2P synchronization, signaling and notification is necessary within the AG in order to be better suited for large communities working and discussing wide annotations of data collections and workflows. We aim to enable AG to be gracefully extended both in terms of heterogeneous clients (i.e. not only AG nodes) and new forms of user communication and data integration.

## 2.2    Session Initiation Protocol

The Session Initiation Protocol (SIP) [15][17] is an application layer peer-to-peer signaling protocol for Internet Protocol (IP) networks. It is able to establish, modify and terminate any kind of multimedia sessions. SIP was originally developed by the Multiparty Multimedia Session Control (MMUSIC) working group of the Internet Engineering Task Force (IETF). Meanwhile, a SIP working group has been formed that continues the development of this protocol.

Like many other protocols in the Internet today, SIP is a text-based protocol. Messages are divided into requests and responses. There are six types of requests defined in the SIP specification [15]: INVITE, ACK, BYE, CANCEL, OPTIONS and REGISTER. Some SIP extensions define new requests that provide additional functionality. For example, the SIP extension for Instant Messaging [3] introduces the MESSAGE request used for exchange of instant messages. Each SIP requests, with the exception of the ACK request, is confirmed by a response. Responses are divided into provisional and final responses. Provisional responses are optional and they provide additional information about processing of a request. Final responses, in contrast, represent a definitive answer to a request.

A SIP message comprises a message header and optionally a body. The header is composed of several header fields that carry information about the message, or additional information for message routing. The body of a SIP message usually contains information about the session. For audio and video sessions, this information is mainly described by the Session Description Protocol (SDP) [6]. However, the body of a SIP message can contain any MIME [4] type and hence, it can be used to carry content of an instant message, for example. The media data in a real-time session are usually carried by the Real Time Transport Protocol (RTP) [16].

Basically, there are two types of entities in SIP – User Agents (UAs) and network servers. A UA represents an end point for a SIP network. A user terminal is a typical example of a UA. Network servers are divided into proxy servers, redirect servers, and registrar servers. A proxy server is an application layer router that forwards SIP requests to the next hop server that can be either a UA or another network server. A redirect server, in contrast, replies an incoming request with a response that contains the address of the next hop server. This means that it simply redirects incoming requests instead of forwarding them.

In order to uniquely identify its resources, SIP has its own addressing mechanism. Each SIP resource is identified by a special type of Uniform Resource

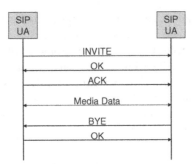

**Fig. 1.** Basic SIP Call

Identifier (URI), called SIP URI. On the other side, each SIP user is provided with a unique SIP URI that is referred to as *address-of-record (AOR)*. In order to be reachable, a user has to register at a SIP registrar server with this user's AOR and the SIP URI of the device that this user is currently using. This URI is called *contact address*. The registrar server stores these bindings of AOR to zero or more contact addresses for each user. This information is used for routing of messages, so that a registered user can be reached independently of the device that this user is currently using. A registrar server is often combined with a proxy or with a redirect server, so that the separation between them is only logical.

Figure 1 shows the message flow in the most simplest scenario of the initialization of a SIP session. There are no network servers between SIP UAs, and all messages are exchanged directly between them. The initiation of a session comprises three messages: INVITE, OK, and ACK. This is referred to as three way handshake. After the initialization, media data between UAs can be exchanged using RTP (marked with dotted line). A session is terminated when one of the UAs sends the BYE request that is confirmed with an OK response.

## 2.3   Advanced SIP Services

The basic SIP specification defines methods needed for session initialization, modification, and termination. Additionally, there is a possibility to query the capabilities of a server using the OPTIONS request. These features do not fulfill all the needs expected from a modern signaling protocol today. On the other side, SIP is designed to be an extensible protocol, and it allows introduction of new methods and header fields. There is a number of SIP extensions that have been defined in the last few years. They provide SIP with additional features, including messaging and event notification.

In this section we briefly describe some SIP extensions that are directly relevant for video conference, and can be applied on AG. SIP-Specific Event Notification [12], for example, enables asynchronous notification of users whenever an event occurs. First, a user has to subscribe for a resource and gets the current state of it. For the duration of the subscription, this user will be notified after any change of the state of this resource. This extension does not define any type of event, but only a general framework. Additional, so-called event packages must be defined for each particular event. One example is the Presence event package [13], used for Presence Service in SIP. The presence information can be used to start a conference when all the potential participant are available. We will discuss this scenario in Section 5.2.

Another SIP extensions useful in a conference is the extension for Instant Messaging [3]. It provides SIP with the capability of exchanging instant messages between users. These users can be involved in a conference, but need not to be.

The identity of participants can be distributed along participants in a conference. The identity is represented trough the SIP URI of participants. This feature is useful, for example, for initialization of sub-conferences within an existing conference. We will discuss sub-conferences in Section 5.1.

In a conference, it is usually desired that participant can dynamically join in the conference. This means that existing participants need a mechanism to invite other users to participate. The SIP REFER method [18] can be used for this purpose. It simply refers a user to contact a certain resource, for example a conference server.

The IETF working group for Centralized Conferences (XCON) [1] is standardizing a suite of protocols for centralized multimedia conferences. Privacy, security, and authorization mechanisms play an important role in the proposed solution. A basic floor control will also be provided. XCON uses SIP as the reference signaling protocol in their examples.

# 3   Proposed Architecture

As mentioned in Section 2.1, in the current AG architecture there no signaling protocol. Media data are distributed over certain multicast addresses and any user that obtains these multicast addresses and port numbers is able to receive data. Participants in a conference are not aware about identities of other participants. There is no possibility to easily start an add-hoc sub-conference, which is useful when a user wants to discuss a particular topic within a sub-group of conference participants.

To solve these problems, we propose the introduction of a signaling protocol in the AG architecture. More concrete, as the signaling protocol we propose SIP (Section 2.2). Figure 2 shows the architecture of a SIP enabled AG Node and its connection to the network. Because of clarity, the Echo Canceller and Mixer, as well as the Control Computer for audio streams are not shown in the figure. Dotted lines indicate SIP traffic and the solid ones media data. The figure also shows some single UAs that participate in the conference. They can be running on a Personal Computer (PC) or even on a Personal Digital Assistant (PDA) [19].

The new component in the AG node architecture is the SIP Stack. It is responsible for the SIP communication with other SIP components. On the other side, it has an interface with existing AG node components, including display

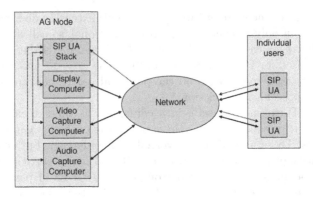

**Fig. 2.** AG Node architecture with SIP

```
v=0
o=AGNode1 9847392 3948273 IN IP4 129.131.88.99
s=AG session
m=audio 32000 RTP/AVP 0
c=IN IP4 234.5.66.7/127
m=video 34000 RTP/AVP 34
c=IN IP4 234.5.66.32/127
m=video 34000 RTP/AVP 34
c=IN IP4 234.5.66.33/127
m=video 34000 RTP/AVP 34
c=IN IP4 234.5.66.34/127
m=video 34000 RTP/AVP 34
c=IN IP4 234.5.66.35/127
```

**Fig. 3.** SDP description with multiple media streams

computer, video capture computer, and audio capture computer. These interfaces need not necessarily to be standardized. However, this would bring more flexibility and allow to combine components of different vendors.

An SIP enabled AG Node obtains session parameters, such as multicast addresses, port numbers, and codecs for audio and video streams, over SIP. These session parameters are described in SDP format [6]. SDP is capable of specifying multiple media streams, each of which can have an own codec, IP-address (that can also be a multicast address), and port number. Given that each AG Node sends out four video streams, and receives multiple streams, this feature of SDP is very important for AG conferences.

Figure 3 shows an example of a SDP description with multiple media streams. This description includes one audio stream in PCMU codec, and four video streams in H.263 codec. This is indicated by the numbers at the end of the media (m) line. Each of these streams is distributed over a separate multicast address that is specified in the contact (c) line. More information about SDP can be found in [6].

# 4    Basic Operations

This section describes basic SIP operation in an AG conference, including initialization of a conference, participation in a conference, and leaving a conference. Although SIP can support centralized and decentralized conferences [14], we focus on centralized conferences only, because they offer better control of the conference participants. Basically there are two types of centralized conferences: dial-in and dial-out. They have in common that they use a central component for conference management that is called Conference Server (CS). Therefore, we can differentiate between a dial-in and a dial-out CS.

## 4.1    Initialization of a Conference

Dial-in conferences are created by an AG node. This node generates a unique Conference Identifier (CID) and creates a conference SIP URI. Using this SIP URI, the AG node initialize a point-to-point SIP session with the conference server using the same set of messages as shown in the upper part of Figure 1. At this point, the only participant in this conference is the AG node that has initiated the conference. Other nodes can participate only if they obtain the conference SIP URI.

Dial-out conferences are initiated by CS. They are usually pre-arranged with a specified start time and a list of initial participants. Additionally, an end time can also be specified. At the start time, CS generated a unique conference SIP URI, and initiate a SIP session with each participant from the list. These sessions are logically associated in a single conference session by CS.

## 4.2    Participation in a Conference

Basically, there are two possibilities to participate in a conference for both, dial-in and dial-out conferences. The first possibility is when an AG node, sends an INVITE message to the conference server. A precondition for this is that this AG node obtains the corresponding conference SIP URI. It can be distributed by several means, including Web, E-mail, Short Message Service (SMS), or SIP. The SIP REFER message, defined in [18], can be used for this purpose. This message demands from a SIP UA, which has received it, to initiate a session with the SIP URI given in that message.

Let us suppose that there is a conference with there AG nodes, and a further AG node is to be invited in this conference. Figure 4 shows this scenario. AG nodes 1, 2, and 3 are involved in a conference and at some time AG node 3 decides to invite AG node 4 to participate in the conference. In order to do this, AG node 3 sends a REFER request with the conference SIP URI to AG node 4 (marked with 1 in Figure 4). AG node 4 replies this message with a 200 OK response (2), and sends an INVITE request with the conference SIP URI to CS (3). If CS allows AG node 4 to participate in the conference, it replies with a 200 OK (4), and finally, AG node 4 confirms this response with an ACK request (5). As mentioned before, the conference SIP URI can also be distributed by

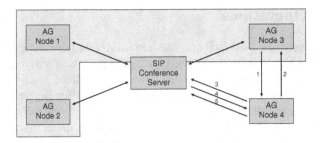

**Fig. 4.** Participation in a Conference

other means, like web, e-mail, or sms. In that case, steps 1 and 2 in Figure 4 are omitted.

The second possibility for an AG node to participate in a conference is that this node is invited by CS. CS is usually instructed by an AG node, which actively participates in the conference, to do this. In our example, AG node 3 would sent a REFER request with the SIP URI of AG node 4 to CS. This would instruct CS to send invite AG node 4 to participate in the conference.

### 4.3    Leaving a Conference

When an AG node wants to leave a conference, it simply sends a BYE message to CS and stops receiving and sending video and audio streams. CS replies this message with a 200 OK response as shown in the lower part of Figure 1. Other participants can transparently continue communication.

## 5    Advanced Operations

Until now, we have seen how SIP can be used in AG for providing basic conferencing functions. These functions are also present in the today's AG architecture, although they are realized on a different way (see Section 2.1). In this section we will go into some advanced functionalities that are not provided by the today's AG architecture, but that can be provided with our architecture.

### 5.1    Sub-conferences

An AG conference usually involves several AG nodes. There is also growing need that individual users attend such a conference [19], giving the AG architecture a p2p character. These users participate in the conference with their PCs or PDAs. Because of limited resources, these users should have the possibility to choose a subset of the conference streams that they want to receive [19]. This functionality is provided by SIP as stated in Section 3. In this section we will use term *participant* meaning either an AG node or an individual user.

In an AG conference there is often a need that certain issues, which are not of general interest, are discussed under a subset of conference participants. For example, it is useful that geographically distributed participants are able

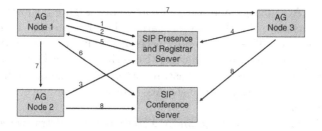

**Fig. 5.** Conference initialization with Presence service

to exchange their opinions about the current presentation or to clarify some ambiguities in a small group. A special case is when this group consists of only two participants. Given that this kind of communication is common in everyday life, the AG architecture should be able to support such sub-conferences.

From the point of view of SIP, such a sub-conference is a new conference that has to be initiated. A precondition is that the participants are aware of other participants' identities (SIP URIs). This information can be provided using SIP extension for multiparty conferencing [8], or using SIP event notification framework described in Subsection 2.3 with an appropriated event package. Depending on the number of participants, there are several possibilities to realize a sub-conference. In the special case when only two participants are involved in a sub-conference, it is necessary to initiative a new two-party session between these two participants as shown in Figure 1. In any other case, a new SIP conference has to be initiated on the same way as described in Subsection 4.1. We propose a hierarchical structure of CIDs in order to indicate which sub-conferences belong to the same conference. Therefore, sub-conferences CID should contain the conference CID and an extension which must be unique for this sub-conference. In this way, CS knows the organization of the conferences and it is able to better manage them. For example, it can be allowed that only participants in a conference can participate in its sub-conference.

Media data in a sub-conference can be exchanged in two ways. First, if there are just a few streams, they can be exchanged over unicast using an RTP mixer. Second, they can be exchanged over multicast, similarly to streams in a AG conference.

## 5.2   Access Grid Conference with Presence Service

The presence service can be excellently combined with the conferencing since it provides information about availability of potential conference participants. For example, it is possible to automatically start a conference as soon as all the potential participants become available. In this section we want to show how the presence service can be used in our architecture.

Let us consider a scenario where AG node 1 wants to start a conference with AG nodes 2 and 3. However, in order to be sure that other nodes are available, AG node 1 will request presence information of AG nodes 2 and 3, and it will get notified when AG nodes 2 and 3 become available. Figure 5 shows the message flow in this scenario. For the sake of clarity, the presence and registrar server are placed together. This is not really necessary, but these two servers need to be able to communicate with each other. Note that presence information can be obtained by several sources, the registrar server is just one of them. A common used source are SIP UAs (in our case AG nodes), enabling users to state their presence information.

First, AG node 1 goes online and registers at the registrar server (1). Note that Figure 5 shows only the requests – in fact each of them is followed by a response. Thereafter, AG node 1 subscribes for the presence information of AG nodes 2 and 3 (2). At some time, AG nodes 2 and 3 also go online and register at the register server (3,4). AG node 1 gets notified about this event (5), creates an empty conference at the conference server (6), and invites AG nodes 2 and 3 to participate by sending corresponding REFER requests (7). In the last step, AG nodes 2 and 3 join in the conference (8).

In this scenario, presence server and conference server are not able to communicate with each other. This is the reason why AG node 1 has to start the conference. However, if presence and conference server are able to communicate, conference server can be implemented to start the conference by itself in a dial-out manner when all the participants become available. For example, conference server can subscribe for presence information of participants by itself and it will be notified when they become available.

### 5.3    Other Operations

There is a number of other advanced operations required or desired in a multimedia conference. Privacy, security, floor control, and authorization are some of them. All these operation are hardly possible without a signaling protocol. Introducing SIP to the AG architecture could be the right step towards the implementation of these features in the AG architecture. There is a large community of IETF engineers that improve SIP conferencing capabilities permanently. An important role here plays the XCON working group. Although they are developing a solution that is independent of any signaling protocol, their examples uses SIP as the reference signaling protocol.

## 6    Conclusion

The paper addressed design of Access Grid environment that actively supports collaboration among large numbers of heterogenous simultaneous users. With the rapid increase in deployment of AG applications and large AG sessions, there might be severe consequences to the end user experiences if problems of static, pre-configured sessions and dominant role of AG nodes are ignored. The paper introduced lightweight SIP-enabled AG architecture that allows peer-to-peer sub-session (sessions within sessions) and session management. This is based on a collection of standardized messages that allow inspection and update of resource properties and transparent triggering of sessions among participants. A number of real-world experiments should be conducted to examine the behaviour of such AG in real networks. Our immediate future plans are to integrate and evaluate our prototype proposal with the real semantic Grid middleware (myGrid) for use in bioinformatics community.

# References

1. http://www.ietf.org/html.charters/xcon-charter.html.
2. www-unix.mcs.anl.gov/fl/events/agtech/materials/access
3. B. Campbell, J. Rosenberg, H. Schulzrinne, C. Huitema, and D. Gurle. Session Initiation Protocol Extension for Instant Messaging. RFC 3428, Internet Engineering Task Force, December 2002.
4. N. Freed and N. S. Borenstein. Multipurpose Internet Mail Extensions (MIME) Part One: Format of Internet Message Bodies. RFC 2045, Internet Engineering Task Force, November 1996.
5. T. A. Grid. http://www.accessgrid.org/.
6. M. Handley and V. Jacobson. SDP: Session Description Protocol. RFC 2327, Internet Engineering Task Force, April 1998.
7. G. Kong, J. Stanton, S. Newhouse, and J. Darlington. Collaborative Visualisation over the Access Grid using the ICENI Grid Middleware. In *UK e-Science All Hands 2003, Nottingham, UK*, September 2003.
8. I. Miladinovic and J. Stadler. Closed Conference Signalling using the Session Initiation Protocol. *Internet Research: Electronic Networking Applications and Policy*, 13(2):126–133, April 2003.
9. T. A. R. Ontology. http://www.aktors.org/ontology/.
10. T. C. project. http://www.aktors.org/coakting/.
11. M. Radenkovic, R. Stevens, and A. Wipat. Requirements for Performing e-Science Experiments. In *Requirements Capture for Collaboration in eScience, Edinburgh*, January 2004.
12. A. Roach. Session Initiation Protocol (SIP)-Specific Event Notification. RFC 3265, Internet Engineering Task Force, June 2002.
13. J. Rosenberg. A Presence Event Package for the Session Initiation Protocol (SIP). Internet draft, work in progress, Internet Engineering Task Force, January 2003.
14. J. Rosenberg and H. Schulzrinne. Models for Multi Party Conferencing in SIP. Internet draft, work in progress, Internet Engineering Task Force, July 2002.
15. J. Rosenberg, H. Schulzrinne, G. Camarillo, A. Johnston, J. Peterson, R. Sparks, M. Handley, and E. Schooler. SIP: Session Initiation Protocol. RFC 3261, Internet Engineering Task Force, June 2002.
16. H. Schulzrinne, S. L. Casner, R. Frederick, and V. Jacobson. RTP: A Transport Protocol for Real-Time Applications. RFC 1889, Internet Engineering Task Force, January 1996.
17. H. Schulzrinne and J. Rosenberg. The Session Initiation Protocol: Internet-Centric Signaling. *IEEE Communications Magazine*, 38(10):134–141, 2000.
18. R. J. Sparks. The Session Initiation Protocol (SIP) Refer Method. RFC 3515, Internet Engineering Task Force, April 2003.
19. M. Thorson, J. L. adn Gabriel Maajid, K. Park, A. Nayak, P. Salva, and S. Berry. AccessGrid-to-Go: Providing AccessGrid Access on Personal Digital Assistants. White paper, Electronic Visualization Laboratory, 2002.

# A Service Oriented Architecture for Integration of Fault Diagnostics

Xiaoxu Ren[2], Max Ong[2], Geoffrey Allan[2], Visakan Kadirkamanathan[2], Haydn Thompson[1,2], and Peter Fleming[1,2]

[1] Rolls-Royce University Technology Centre in Control and Systems Engineering
[2] Department of Automatic Control and Systems Engineering,
University of Sheffield,
Sheffield S1 3JD, UK
{X.Ren, M.Ong, Jeff.Allan, Visakan, H.Thompson, P.Fleming}@shef.ac.uk

**Abstract.** Many model-based fault diagnosis approaches have been proposed so far and some of them have been put into industrial practices. But for modern complex processes, due to the variable nature of faults and model uncertainty, no single approach can diagnose all faults and meet different contradictory criteria. In this paper, the importance of integration of different fault diagnostic schemes in a common framework is emphasised. A service-oriented architecture for the integration is proposed based on Grid technologies. As an implementation, a decision support system for the gas turbine engine fault diagnosis is presented and some deployed services are discussed.

## 1   Introduction

In the aviation industry, a great number of efforts have been put for reducing the number of in-flight engine shutdowns, aborted take-offs and flight delays through the use of the engine fault diagnostic and health monitoring technologies. Among these technologies, model-based approaches are promising modern approaches for aero engine fault detection and isolation (FDI). Model-based FDI is based upon the idea that measurements from dissimilar sensors are functionally related because they are all derived from the same state of the system. Any violation of these relationships indicates the occurrence of faults. Although the model-based approach is commonly accepted as a promising approach for fault diagnosis, due to model uncertainties, intense computational requirements and unknown complicated nature of fault diversity, there is no single widely accepted generic solution of fault diagnosis. Researchers working in this area have proposed different approaches of using different algorithms under the name 'model-based' [8,14,5]. Each approach, however, has its own focus and none of them is a universal approach, neither suitable nor available for all fault types. To overcome these shortfalls and exploit advantages of different approaches, an integration of different methods or hybrid schemes are highly recommended [15,9].

The modern aero engines are being instrumented with engine monitoring units possessing significantly greater capability to record and analyse data. Each

P. Herrero, M.S. Pérez, and V. Robles (Eds.): SAG 2004, LNCS 3458, pp. 146–157, 2005.

engine on a civil airliner is capable of generating at least 1Gbyte of data per flight. As a result in future one can envisage terabyte of engine monitoring data being transmitted every day for analysis of a whole fleet. Thus the challenge is not only provide a set of fault diagnostic tools for FDI and high-level maintenance decision support, but also provide the suitable infrastructure to manage the large amounts of data and perform the high performance, high throughput computing to support these fault diagnostic algorithms and decision-making.

With the latest development in Internet and Intranet technologies, especially with the development of the Grid computing, it is now possible to provide different algorithms as individual Grid services and combine these services dynamically to generate a 'virtual organisation' for fault diagnostic purposes. In this paper, a service-oriented architecture on the Grid for integration of different fault diagnostic schemes is proposed. Different fault diagnosis algorithms and analysis tools are provided as Grid services in this framework. Through configuration and workflow management, these services can be dynamically invoked to form a flexible distributed decision support environment for aero engine fault diagnosis and maintenance.

This paper is organised as follows: Section 2 presents an overview of model-based fault diagnosis. Different approaches developed for model-based fault diagnosis are summarised and compared. In Section 3, the concept of Grid computing is introduced. The service-oriented architecture on the Grid for fault diagnosis is proposed and the advantages are highlighted. In Section 4, the DAME project is introduced and some experimental work on the FDI integration are presented. The developed gas turbine engine simulation services for fault detection and case-based reasoning services for high-level decision support are detailed. Finally, some concluding remarks are made.

## 2  Model-Based Fault Diagnosis

Model-based approaches are widely accepted modern approach for solving fault diagnosis problems. Model-based fault detection and isolation focuses on dynamic consistency (parity) relations and parameter estimation. The basic procedure of using model-based FDI is firstly to generate the analytic symptoms by using analytical knowledge about the process based on process observation. Then the generated analytic symptoms as well as heuristic symptoms are analysed at the fault diagnosis stage for finding the type, size and location of a fault as well as its time of detection.

In general, model-based FDI is a two-step procedure: residual generation and residual evaluation. Residual generation is a process in which the input and output of a system are monitored and manipulated to generate a signal or vector, the so-called *residual*. The residual should be normally zero or close to zero when no fault is present, but is distinguishably different from zero when a fault occurs. Residual generation is thus a procedure for extracting fault symptoms from the system, with the fault symptom represented by the residual signal. The residual should ideally carry only fault information. To ensure reliable

FDI, the loss of fault information in residual generation should be as small as possible.

Residual evaluation is the analysis of the residual to examine the likelihood of faults. A decision is made based on the knowledge about the process and the symptoms. If a fault has occurred, more analysis should be made to isolate or even identify the fault. A decision process may consist of a simple threshold test on the instantaneous values or moving averages of the residuals, or it may consist of methods of more sophisticated decision theories.

From the various approaches used for the residual generation and evaluation, there are roughly four different approaches used by model-based FDI:

- Observer approach or parity relations approach. The underlying idea of observer approach is to estimate the system outputs from the available inputs and output of that system. The residual will then be a weighted difference between the estimated and actual outputs. In a similar way, the parity relations approach is based either on a technique of direct redundancy, making use of static algebraic relations between sensor and actuator signals or alternatively, upon temporal redundancy, when dynamic relations between inputs and outputs are used.
- Parameter estimation approach. This approach makes use of the fact that component faults of a dynamic system can be thought of as reflected in the physical parameters of the system, e.g. friction or mass velocity resistance. A fault is then can be detected through the parameter estimation or model identification.
- Statistical approaches. Mainly used to improve the fault detection capability, statistical approaches such as the generalised likelihood ratio (GLR) test can be used to find changes of the residual signal more quickly and accurately. Principle component analysis (PCA) and Fisher discriminant analysis (FDA) are the most widely used techniques for dimensionality reduction and pattern classification on FDI.
- Qualitative approach. The qualitative approach is based upon the concept of a qualitative model which unlike its quantitative counterpart only requires declarative (heuristic) information. An expert system, for example, is one of the quantitative approaches that use if-then rules to represent the human knowledge of the relation between the normal/abnormal system behaviour and the causes of faults. The fault tree approach traces the evolution of the fault through the dynamic system described by a fault tree, event trees or causal networks. There are also qualitative model-based approaches which use a qualitative model derived directly from the physical laws of the system under consideration. Bond Graphs and Petri Nets, for example, can be used to assist this modelling purpose.

In general, a fault diagnosis technique should be able to complete the following two main tasks:

- detect and isolate different faults occurring in a process, which include sensor faults, actuator faults and component faults.
- detect and isolate incipient faults as well as abrupt faults.

**Table 1.** A comparison of different model-based approaches for FDI

| FDI Scheme | Suitability | Promptness and Sensitivity | Design and Implementation | Modelling and Robustness |
|---|---|---|---|---|
| Observer and Parity relation approaches | Suitable for fault detection and isolation in actuators and sensors. | Reaction to both abrupt and incipient fault is fast. Sensitive to sensor fault. | Design procedure is systematic and simple. Easy to implement. | Nonlinear observer is difficult to design. Mature techniques are available for robust observer. |
| Parameter estimation approach | Suitable for fault detection and isolation in system components. | Reaction to abrupt faults is slow. More suitable for incipient faults. | Design procedure is systematic but not simple. Difficult to implement. | Nonlinear system parameter estimation is possible to handle. Robustness depends on methods used. |
| Statistical approach | Suitable for both fault detection and isolation. | Depend on methods used, reaction to abrupt faults could be slow. | Design procedure is systematic. Easy to implement. | Kernel density estimation is possible to handle. Very Robust. |
| Qualitative approach | Suitable for fault isolation. | Reaction to incipient faults is usually slow. | Design is difficult. Easy to implement. | Suitable symbolic model is not easy to obtain. Very robust. |

While at the same time, a fault diagnosis scheme should also consider following criteria for better fault diagnosis performance:

- Promptness of fault detection
- Sensitivity to incipient faults
- False alarm rate and missed fault detection
- Incorrect fault identification

Although different model-based approaches are designed to solve fault diagnosis problems, each approach has its own focus and none of the above mentioned methods is a generic solution for complex modern system fault diagnosis. This is due to the complicated nature of the monitored system and faults, the applicability of different modelling approaches or the insufficient knowledge about the monitored process. Table 1 is a summarised comparison of different selected model-based approaches for fault diagnosis. From this comparison, it is clear that none of these approaches can fully satisfy the requirements of modern fault diagnosis such as promptness, accuracy and sensitivity to faults. It is commonly agreed that hybrid schemes would provide better solutions for future complex system fault diagnostics [1, 11]. Thus an evaluation of different FDI approaches and the integration of assorted FDI approaches in an open computational environment are crucial. Additionally, it is important to consider how these approaches should be used in conjunction to provide the most accurate diagnosis in the decision-making process.

Another restriction of using some model-based FDI techniques often lies with the inherent demands for intensive computing power for modelling and simulation. These computation requirements also limit its application on large scale complex systems. The Grid technology provides the necessary high-performance, high-throughput computing power to overcome these restrictions. The distributed computing structure and the organised resource sharing features provide excellent opportunities to integrate different FDI schemes to obtain better fault diagnostic performance.

## 3    Service-Oriented Architecture on the Grid for FDI Integration

Service-oriented architecture (SOA) is not a new concept. The early service-oriented architecture uses the Distributed Component Object Model (DCOM) [12] or Object Request Brokers (ORBs) based on the CORBA specification [13]. Over the last few decades, software has slowly been decoupled. The introduction of the Client/Server structure removed the database from the fat client. The thin-client decoupled the user interface from the business logic. Service-oriented architectures were proposed to decouple the integration logic from the business logic. Basically, services and service-oriented architectures are about designing and building systems using heterogeneous network addressable software components. A service-oriented architecture is thus an architecture made up of components and interconnections that stresses interoperability and location transparency. With the introduction of Web services and Grid services, there has been a renewed interest in building service-oriented architectures for 'virtual organisations' [4].

The technology of Web services is the most likely connection technology of service-oriented architectures. Web services essentially use XML to create a robust connection. At the core of the Web services model is the notion of a service, which is defined as a collection of operations that carry out some types of tasks. Within the context of Web services, there are three components, namely *service providers, service requestors* and *service brokers*. A service is deployed on the Web by the service provider. The functions provided by a given Web service are described using the Web Services Description Language (WSDL) [18] and published on the Web. A service broker helps the service provider and service requester find each other through a UDDI (Universal Description, Discovery, and Integration) [17] based registry. A service requester uses the standard API to ask the service broker about the services it needs and then uses SOAP (Simple Object Access Protocol) [16] to invoke the remote service provider side applications.

The Grid is a name that was first coined in the mid-'90s to describe a vision for a distributed computing infrastructure for advanced science projects. First properly explained by Ian Foster and Carl Kesselman [3], the Grid should enable 'resource sharing and coordinated problem solving in dynamic, multi-institutional virtual organisations'. With the first generation Grid involving 'Metacomputers' and second generation Grid focused on middle ware and communication protocols, now it is claimed that the third generation Grid is combining service-oriented architecture concepts and Web services technologies to create Open Grid Services Architecture (OGSA) [6], whereby a set of common interface specifications support the interoperability of discrete, independently developed services. The Open Grid Services Infrastructure (OGSI) service specification is the keystone in implementing this architecture, followed by the recent Web Service Resource Framework (WSRF) [19], which is a set of six Web services specifications that try to meld Web service with Grid Computing by defining how to model and manage state in a Web services context.

Defined by OGSA, a Grid service is basically a Web service, which is a set of Internet-based distributed processes. Based on standards such as XML, SOAP, WSDL and UDDI, the promise of Grid services is to enable a distributed environment in which any number of applications, or application components, can interoperate seamlessly among organisations in a platform-neutral, language-neutral fashion on the Grid.

To support the complex system fault diagnostics, a methodology have been proposed to integrate suites of modelling, estimation and analysis tools for fault diagnosis on the Grid. The service-oriented architecture is adopted here to support this integration and the latest development on the Grid has been implemented to meet the specifications of OGSA and WSRF.

By adopting this open SOA for the integrated fault diagnostics, the most commonly used techniques for FDI, which include parameter estimation, state

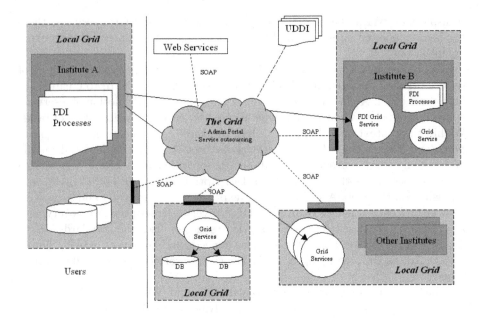

**Fig. 1.** Integrated fault diagnostics on the Grid

observer, parity relations, statistic approaches and symbolic approaches, can all be developed individually as fault diagnostic services. As illustrated in Figure 1, these services can be created and maintained by different institutions for different fault diagnostic purposes and are all defined through a commonly accepted description format, namely the Web Service Description Language (WSDL). Registered with the Universal Description, Discovery, and Integration (UDDI) registry, these fault diagnostic services can be discovered and organised in a flexible way. The result is a versatile virtual FDI toolbox on the Grid. Users can access this toolbox by using an Internet browser via a Grid portal, and they can select different FDI schemes to fit their own unique requirements. When an individual service is invoked, it can use the global or local Grid resources to fulfil its commitment. This service can also invoke other Grid services if possible. At the low level, the physical Grid infrastructure provides the potential high-performance computing power and large-scale data handling capabilities. By adopting the OGSI specification, the proposed architecture is a Grid solution to integrated fault diagnostics, which allows different FDI applications to share algorithms, data and computing resources as well as to access them across multiple organisation in an efficient and secure way.

## 4    Implementation

The UK e-Science pilot project Distributed Aircraft Maintenance Environment (DAME) is developing a distributed diagnostics and prognostics system for maintenance of civil aerospace engines. The techniques will generalise to other diagnostic domains such as medicine, transport and manufacturing. The DAME system uses Grid technology to demonstrate how remote and diverse applications and services can be linked into a virtual diagnostic environment. Various techniques are employed in the project, which include advanced pattern matching to search very large data sets (Terabytes), modelling for fault diagnosis and simulation for decision making, case based advice, workflow management and collaboration environments [2].

As one effort carried out on the DAME project, the proposed service-oriented architecture for integrated fault diagnostics has been implemented. A gas turbine engine performance model was firstly provided as a Grid service to facilitate the exploitation of further development and analysis of different model-based FDI approaches. Figure 2 illustrates a running scenario of this Grid service through a Web portal.

Figure 3 shows one basic usage of the engine simulation Grid service for fault diagnosis. When an accurate system performance simulation is available on the Grid, the experienced maintenance engineers can invoke this simulation against the real monitored process data. The system that is being analysed is compared against the simulation results. The differences between the current state of the engine and the ideal model generate residuals. These residuals then need to be intelligently analysed to form a decision about the current state of the engine.

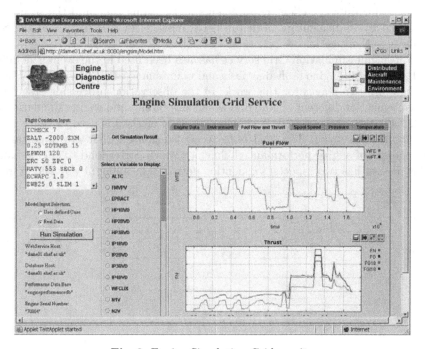

**Fig. 2.** Engine Simulation Grid service

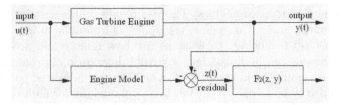

**Fig. 3.** Simulation-based fault diagnosis

This can be used to track changes in engine parameters which may indicate impending faults.

The advantages of providing an engine performance simulation as a Grid service is that the engine simulation service is identified by a URI, whose public interfaces and bindings are defined and described using XML. Authorised users can perform the engine performance simulation through a Web browser remotely without knowing details of the execution of the simulation. The simulation service itself is distributed among a set of high-performance computers on the Grid. Based on the Globus Toolkit 3 (GT3) [7], this engine simulation Grid service can be invoked simultaneously in different 'Virtual Organisations' for different applications. The usage and management of the Grid resources are made through the Globus middleware and are transparent to users. Through its public interface, authorised developers can also invoke this service to develop their own applications. The factory service can generate a bunch of engine simulation instances for different client requirements at the same time and the security is enhanced by implementing both the GT3 message level security and the SSL two-way authentication.

The engine simulation Grid service has also been used in the event generation and analysis for engine fault diagnosis and maintenance. As illustrated in Figure 4, there are two stages for this work. In the observation processing stage, raw measurement of different engine performance variables and engine simulation results as inputs are analysed. A change detection method is used to characterise the input time series. The goal is to recognise changes that are important in the context of engine performance behaviour which correspond to engine faults. This process has two aspects: segmenting data in a meaningful way and extract-

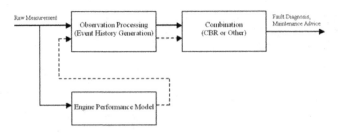

**Fig. 4.** Event generation and analysis

ing features that are useful about whether the engine is exhibiting normal or abnormal behaviour. In the combination stage, two event sequences from both the raw measurement and the engine simulation are compared, any discrepancy will indicate possible fault.

The advantage of introducing a separate event history based on the engine simulation is that a reference of health engine history is provided to assist the fault diagnostic decision-making. The comparison of two discrete event histories instead of the original binary time series data can help to overcome the model uncertainty and unmodeled noise. As the result, the robustness of the fault diagnosis is improved.

Another effort of the DAME project on the integration of fault diagnostics on the Grid is the use of Case-Based Reasoning (CBR) [10] services to correlate and integrate fault indicators from different aero engine input monitoring systems, BITE reports, maintenance data and dialog with maintenance personnel to allow troubleshooting of faults. As a qualitative fault diagnosis approach, case-based reasoning is a problem-solving paradigm that resolves new problems by adapting the solutions used to solve problems of a similar nature experienced in the past. A further advantage of this approach is that it allows consolidation of rule knowledge and provides a reasoning engine that is capable of probabilistic-based matching. With CBR technology, development can take place in an incremental fashion facilitating rapid prototyping of an initial system. The development of robust strategies for integration of multiple health information sources can be achieved with reasoning algorithms of progressively increasing complexity.

Also deployed as Grid services on the Grid environment, the CBR services can be invoked by other authorised Grid services or maintenance analyses to perform the high-level fault diagnostics and decision-making, as illustrated in Figure 5. The advantage of deploying CBR as the Grid service is that maintenance personnel can access a secured connection to the service via a web browser on

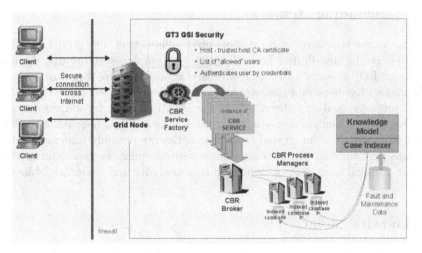

**Fig. 5.** Case-based reasoning Grid services

any computer connected to the Internet. The maintenance personnel will then have access to stores of accumulated diagnostic knowledge and maintenance data as well as large computing resources to support the fault analysis and the decision-making process. Other fault diagnostic services can be used to perform the preliminary fault diagnosis and the results can be used to facilitate the CBR analysis. As standard Grid services, the CBR services can be invoked to produce useful outcomes that are profitable to other decision-making services as well. In the future, the CBR services can be upgraded to accommodate a dynamic learning process. Anomalous data (data containing unknown faults) may be analysed in DAME to produce new fault cases that are dynamically appended to the casebase, further increasing the knowledge of the system.

A typical use case which encompasses both the engine simulation and CBR services in the fault analysis and maintenance process is described as follows. Data downloaded from an aircraft is first analysed for novelties (known fault occurrences). The existence of fault and the possible fault type can be checked against the engine simulation. If a novelty exists, then further information is extracted from the data and other available fault diagnostic services to form a query within the CBR services. The result returned to the maintenance personnel consists of previous similar fault cases, known solutions to the problem, as well as a confidence ranking for each case. The maintenance analyses and domain experts can further take advantages of the integrated fault diagnostic tools to confirm the fault diagnosis findings. For example, the domain experts can substantiate a proposed fault analysis by injecting the similar fault into an engine model and perform a simulation to check the uniformity.

By using the Grid technologies and the proposed serviced-oriented architecture, more modelling, simulation, and decision-making services from different providers or institutes can be shared, coordinated and integrated for fault diagnostics, prognostics and engine maintenance.

## 5    Concluding Remarks

In this paper the using of service-oriented architecture and Grid technologies to support the distributed fault diagnosis of complex systems was discussed. Different FDI schemes have been summarised and the importance of integrated diagnostics has been emphasised. An open framework based on the OGSA has been proposed and demonstrated on the DAME project to address the after-market requirements of aero engine industry. The business benefits of this open, flexible approach to integrated fault diagnostics are not only improved fault diagnosis performance, but also reusable service assembly, better maintainability, better parallelism in development, higher availability and better scalability.

## Acknowledgment

This work and the DAME project are supported by the UK EPSRC under contract 2382.

# References

1. J. Chen and R. J. Patton. *Robust Model-based Fault Diagnosis for Dynamic Systems.* Kluwer Academic Publishers, USA, 1999.
2. DAME. Distributed Aircraft Maintenance Environment project. URL: http://www.cs.york.ac.uk/dame/, 2003.
3. I. Foster and C. Kesselman. *The Grid: Blueprint for a New Computing Infrastructure.* Morgan Kaufmann, 1999.
4. I. Foster, C. Kesselman, J. M. Nick, and S. Tuecke. The physiology of the Grid: An open services architecture for distributed systems integration. 2002.
5. J. Gertler. *Fault Detection and Diagnosis in Engineering Systems.* Marcel Dekker, 1998.
6. GGF. Global Grid Forum. URL: http://www.ggf.org, 2003.
7. Globus. Globus alliance. URL: http://www.globus.org, 2003.
8. R. Isermann. Supervison, fault-detection and fault diagnosis methods - an introduction. *Control Engineering Practice*, 5(4):639–652, 1997.
9. R. Isermann and P. Balle. Trends in the application of model-based fault detection and diagnosis of technical processes. *Control Engineering Practice*, 5(5):709–719, 1997.
10. J. Kolodner. *Case-based Reasoning.* Morgan Kaufmann, 1993.
11. Y. G. Li. Performance-analysis-based gas turbine diagnostics: A review. *Proc. Instn. Mech. Engrs, Part A*, 216:363–377, 2002.
12. Microsoft. Distributed Component Object Model. URL: http://www.microsoft.com/com/tech/DCOM.asp, 2003.
13. OMG. Object Management Group. URL: http://www.omg.org, 2003.
14. R. J. Patton. Robust model-based fault diagnosis: the state of the art. In *IFAC Symposium on Fault Detection, Supervision and Safety for Technical Processes*, pages 1–24, Espoo, Finland, 1994.
15. R. J. Patton, F. J. Uppal, and C. J. Lopez-Toribio. Soft computing approaches to fault diagnosis for dynamic systems: A survey. In *4th IFAC Symposium on Fault Detection supervision and Safety for Technical Processes*, pages 198–211, Budapest, Hungary, June 2000.
16. SOAP. The Simple Object Access Protocol. URL: http://www.w3.org/TR/2000/NOTE-SOAP-20000508/, 2003.
17. UDDI. The Universal Description, Discovery and Integration protocol. URL: http://www.uddi.org/, 2003.
18. WSDL. The Web Services Description Language. URL: http://www.w3.org/TR/wsdl, 2003.
19. WSRF. The Web Services Resource Framework. URL:http://www.globus.org/wsrf/, 2004.

# GAM: A Grid Awareness Model for Grid Environments

Pilar Herrero, María S. Pérez, and Víctor Robles

Facultad de Informática, Universidad Politécnica de Madrid,
Campus de Montegancedo S/N,
28.660 Boadilla del Monte, Madrid, Spain
{pherrero, mperez, vrobles}@fi.upm.es

**Abstract.** In this paper, we present a new extension and reinterpretation of one of the most successful models of awareness in Computer Supported Cooperative Work (CSCW), called the Spatial Model of Interaction (SMI), which manages awareness in Collaborative Virtual Environments (CVEs) through a set of key concepts. This work, carried out at the Universidad Politécnica de Madrid, proposes a couple of special features: the management of the data information from the user point of view and the co-ordinated sharing of computational resources in a virtual organisation. The final awareness model allows users to be aware of the data grid information in a grid computing infrastructure.

## 1 Introduction

There has been a surge of interest in grid computing, a way to enlist large numbers of machines to work on multipart computational problems. There are excellent reasons for this attention among scientists and engineers. Grid computing enables the use and pooling of computer and data resources to solve complex data-intensive problems. The technique is the latest development in an evolution that earlier brought forth such advances as distributed computing, the Worldwide Web, and collaborative computing.

Grid computing harnesses a diverse array of machines and other resources to rapidly process and solve data-intensive problems. Academic and government researchers have used it for several years to solve large-scale problems, and the private sector is increasingly adopting the technology to create innovative products and services, reduce time to market, and enhance business processes.

Grids are networks that may include personal or desktop computers, computer clusters, clusters of clusters, or special data sources. This definition reflects a desire to take advantage of vastly powerful but relatively inexpensive networked resources. In our work, we focus on the use of grids to manage large amounts of data in geographically distributed environments, getting what is usually known as Data Grid.

Grid computing is becoming a critical component of science, business, and industry. Making grids easy to use could lead to advances in fields ranging from industrial design to financial management. Grids could allow the analysis of large investment portfolios in minutes instead of hours, significantly accelerate drug development, and reduce design times and defects. With computing cycles plentiful and inexpensive,

P. Herrero, M.S. Pérez, and V. Robles (Eds.): SAG 2004, LNCS 3458, pp. 158–167, 2005.

practical grid computing would open the door to new models for compute utilities, a service similar to an electric utility in which a user buys computing time on-demand from a provider.

In this paper we present the research work carried out at the Universidad Politecnica de Madrid with the aim of formalising a Grid Computing Model (GCM) to manage the scalability and the interaction on a Grid Computing infrastructure.

This formalisation is based on the extension and reinterpretation of an awareness model – called the Spatial Model of Interaction (SMI) [1] - and the concepts that this SMI defines as its key concepts.

In this paper we give an overview to the theoretical principles of the SMI and its key concepts before introducing our own interpretation of them. The paper continues with brief description of our preliminary implementations, and finalise with a brief summary of our ongoing and future work.

## 2 The Spatial Model of Interaction (SMI)

The Spatial Model of Interaction (SMI), defined for application to any Computer Supported Cooperative Work (CSCW) system where a spatial metric can be identified, has been driven by a number of objectives [1]:

- Scalability: It is based on the concept of aura. Each object has an aura for each medium in which it can interact, because the aura defines the volume of space within which this interaction is possible. The use of aura facilitates scaling to many users by limiting the number of object interactions that must be considered. This number will be governed by the extent of the object auras and by the population density of the space.
- Interactions: The SMI assumes a space populated by potentially communicating objects. These objects may represent anything: human users or data in a database, for example. The space itself may have any form, for example, a three-dimensional Cartesian space, an abstract higher-dimensional space or a graph. The SMI provides a framework for these objects to manage their interaction, and communication between every pair of objects. A key component of this management of interaction is the use of the space itself. Thus by controlling their geometrical information the objects are able to modify their interaction and communication [7,8,9].

The model itself defines five linked concepts: medium, focus, nimbus, aura and awareness (see Fig. 1 and Fig. 2). These are extended by the additional concepts of adapters and boundaries.

- Medium: A prerequisite for useful communication is that two objects have a compatible medium in which both objects can communicate. This medium might include audio, video, graphics and text.
- Aura: In 1992, Fahlén and Bowers defined aura as the sub-space which effectively bounds the presence of an object within a given medium and which acts as an enabler of potential interaction [4]. Once aura has been used to determine the potential for object interactions (see Fig. 1), the objects themselves

are subsequently responsible for controlling these interactions. "When two auras collide, interaction between the objects in the medium becomes a possibility".

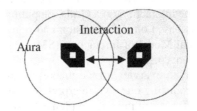

**Fig. 1.** Collision of two objects' auras

- Focus: In each particular medium, it is possible to delimit the observing object's interest. This idea was introduced by S. Benford in 1993 as "The more an object is within your focus the more aware you are of it", and it was called Focus.
- Nimbus: In the same way, it is possible to represent the observed object's projection in a particular medium. This area is called Nimbus: "The more an object is within your nimbus the more aware it is of you".

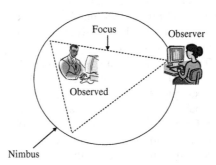

**Fig. 2.** Key concepts in The Spatial Model of Interaction

- Awareness: It is the main concept involved in controlling interaction between objects. It quantifies the degree, nature or quality of interaction between two objects. One object's awareness of another object quantifies the subjective importance or relevance of that object. The awareness relationship between every pair of objects is achieved on the basis of quantifiable levels of awareness between them and it is unidirectional and specific to each medium.

Therefore, awareness between objects in a given medium is manipulated via Focus and Nimbus, requiring a negotiation process. Considering, for example, A's awareness of B, the negotiation process combines the observer's (A's) focus and the observed's

(B's) nimbus. In the words of Benford and Fahlén: "The level of awareness that object A has of object B in medium M is some function of A's focus on B in M and B's nimbus on A in M".

For a simple discrete model of focus and nimbus, there are tree possible classifications of awareness values when two objects are negotiating unidirectional awareness [10]:

- Full awareness: The awareness that object A has of object B in a medium M is "full" when object B is inside A's focus and object A is inside B's nimbus.
- Peripheral awareness: The awareness that object A has of object B in a medium M is "peripheral" when object B is outside A's focus but object A is inside B's nimbus, or object B is inside A's focus but object A is outside B's nimbus.
- No awareness: An object A has no awareness of object B in a medium M when object B is outside A's focus and object A is outside B's nimbus.

In the Spatial Model of Interaction, an object can control its awareness in different ways [1] by modifying its own auras, foci and nimbi:

- Implicitly: By moving and changing direction within the space and hence its auras, foci and nimbi.
- Explicitly: By directly modifying the parameters which define auras, foci and nimbi.

Some extensions of the Spatial Model of Interaction are Adapters, from Benford and Fahlén [4], and Boundaries, from Bowers [3]. However, in this paper we are not going to take into account adapters, leaving this concept and its effects for future work.

Boundaries also are a way of structuring space and influencing awareness [3]. In this way, boundaries "divide space into different areas and regions and provide mechanisms for marking territory, controlling movement, and influencing the interactional properties of space" [10]. It is possible to identify several kinds of boundaries:

- Obstructive: The boundary blocks the property in question (aura, focus, nimbus)
- Conditionally obstructive: The obstruction can be removed when some condition is obeyed
- Transforming: The boundary alters the property in some way
- Non-obstructive: The boundary has no effect on the property

In this section we have provided readers with an overview of the SMI and its key concepts as they were introduced in the original model. In the next section we will describe in detail how we have reinterpreted and extended this awareness model in the context of a grid computing infrastructure.

The extension and reinterpretation of this awareness model has been made in two different phases. The first one, became a prototype, called MADEW, which was in charge of establishing the operability of the key awareness concepts as they were extended and reinterpreted for our purposes. The second one has to involve the design, implementation and operation of the grid infrastructure and constitute the main objective of this paper.

## 3  The SMI's Key Concepts in a Grid Environment

One of the major goals of grid computing is to provide efficient access to data. Nowadays, there is a huge number of data-intensive applications, e.g. data mining systems extracting knowledge from large volumes of data. Data-intensive applications have been used in several domains, such as physics, climate modelling, biology or visualisation.

Grids provide access to distributed computing and data resources, allowing data-intensive applications to improve significantly data access, management and analysis. Grid systems responsible for tackling and managing large amounts of data in geographically distributed environments are usually named Data Grid.

This research line presented in this paper started by a simple, abstract and preliminary interpretation of the SMI key concepts in the context of an asynchronous collaboration [11,12,13] and nowadays proposes an awareness infrastructure for grid computing.

This awareness infrastructure is based on reinterpreting some of the SMI key concepts into grid environments as follows:

Focus: It represents an observing data's interest. It can be interpreted as the subset of the space on which the user has focused his attention with the aim of looking for specific information. It can relate both to content and to other users. Regarding content, it can be computed by the type of information you are looking for in a geographically distributed environment. Regarding other users, it can be computed by collecting information about those users that, having areas of common interest and/or having had effective past interactions, you maybe interested in.

Nimbus: It represents an observed data's projection. It can be interpreted as the subset of the space in which information is geographically accesible. It also can relate both to content and to other users. Regarding content, it can be computed by the set of owned resources that the user is interested in sharing with others. Regarding other users, it can be computed by collecting information about those users could or should be informed about the shared information.

Awareness: This concept will quantify the degree, nature or quality of asynchronous interaction between a user and the distributed data resources. The interaction will manage how systems extract knowledge from large volumen of data, managing the efficiency to access to data. The more the interaction is managed the better the information is distributed.

Aura: This concept will be used to determine the potential for user interactions. The use of aura to makes easy scale to many users by limiting the interactions that must be considered. This concept will allow data-intensive applications to improve significantly data access and management.

Boundaries: They are used to divide the space into different areas and regions and provide mechanisms for marking territory, controlling movement and for influencing the interaction properties of the space.

We also propose an extension of the SMI to introduce some new concepts in our awareness infrastructure as a way of improving the data access and analysis. In this way, in this paper we propose to introduce the following concepts:

Sensorial Limitation: This concept will introduce new restrictions on the information to be shared in the distributed environment. Users in a grid environment could be aware of visual information, auditory information or both of them.

Data Limitation: Once the sensorial limitation has been established, user can be authorized to get all kind of visual (or auditory) information –such as images and videos- from the environment or just a part of it –such as text and images or just text.

Internal Filters: Focus and nimbus could be restricted by the user's internal state and desires. For instance, focus could be restricted through potential collaborator's profiles and through content filters. We will only be aware of those data that are within our focus and fall into our defined profiles. Social trends, users directions and the history of previous interactions - and their effects on our mood or internal state - can also restrict our focus or nimbus and therefore the data awareness. Thus, a successful interaction will increase our level of attention to users or contents that fall into a similar profile.

In this section we have introduced our proposal for reinterpreting and extending awareness into the context of grid environments. In the next section we will describe the first implementation we have made of this approach.

## 4  Implementing GAM

The first implementation of our interpretation was envisioned for educational purposes in an international company with a very strong alliance programme and a long list of partners along the world. The major goal of this application was to gather to communicate and collaborate with colleagues from other institutions world-wide on the subject, applying high-speed computational science and allowing:

Co-ordination and collaboration in or between physically dispersed and/or virtual organisations.

The exploitation of computational resources, data, software, storage and other resources available in the whole of the company.

Controlled access by resource providers, which defines who can share, what is shared, and which conditions allow sharing in a distributed heterogeneous computing and data storage.

The resulting application would facilitate resource and data sharing, transfer and dynamic replication of data, and synchronisation of databases; and the interoperability of this inter-networked environment transforms the grid of servers into a single, large virtual computer for the end user.

Nowadays, the Grid Computing community is changing its directions towards services model. The new Open Grid Services Architecture (OGSA) [5], defined by the Global Grid Forum (GGF) [6], shows an abstract view of the new trend of Grid environments. OGSA provides support by the creation, maintenance and lifecycle of services offered by the different Virtual Organizations (VOs) - a set of persons, users, individuals or institutions that share the same access.

The new trend is trying to fuse Web Services and Grid Services defined by the OGSA in a single development line. The GGF and the organization in charge of Web Services, World Wide Web Consortium (W3C), are making great efforts to become true this union.

Having in mind these two stages of this new tendency, our plan consisted of implementing the application in two phases:

Phase I establishes the operability of the key awareness concepts extended and reinterpreted in the previous section, having been implemented in a prototype system, called MADEW (Awareness Models developed in Web Environments) [11,12,13]

Phase II involves design, implementation and operation of the awareness infrastructure on a grid infrastructure.

Besides the typical set of operations associated to a training course and to the management of users and data in a software application –such as introduce, remove or modify data and user's details -, MADEW controls employee access to some specific areas, the circumstances in which employees could access this information (visual or auditory) and the kind of information they could pick up from the course.

The hierarchy of permissions was established by the enterprise depending on the status of the employee. To make it possible, each and every resource in the course (not just visual but also audial) must be registered (Fig. 3) and the person in charge of the course has to associate some privileges to each and very employee in the enterprise given the application's data limitations (Fig. 4, Fig. 5). For example, those

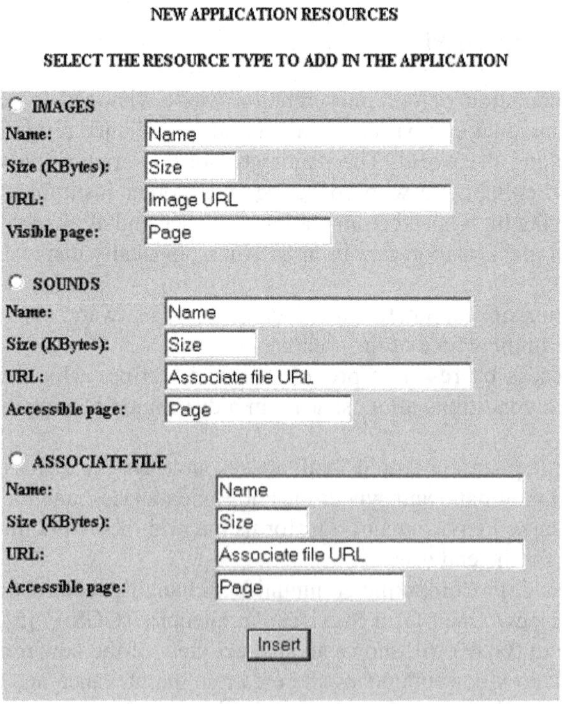

**Fig. 3.** Registering new resources in MADEW

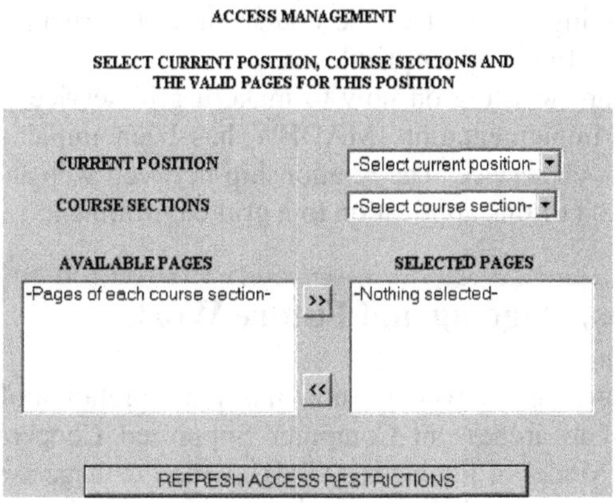

ACCESS MANAGEMENT

SELECT CURRENT POSITION, COURSE SECTIONS AND
THE VALID PAGES FOR THIS POSITION

CURRENT POSITION               -Select current position- ▼

COURSE SECTIONS                -Select course section- ▼

AVAILABLE PAGES                          SELECTED PAGES

-Pages of each course section-    >>    -Nothing selected-

                                  <<

REFRESH ACCESS RESTRICTIONS

**Fig. 4.** Access Management in MADEW

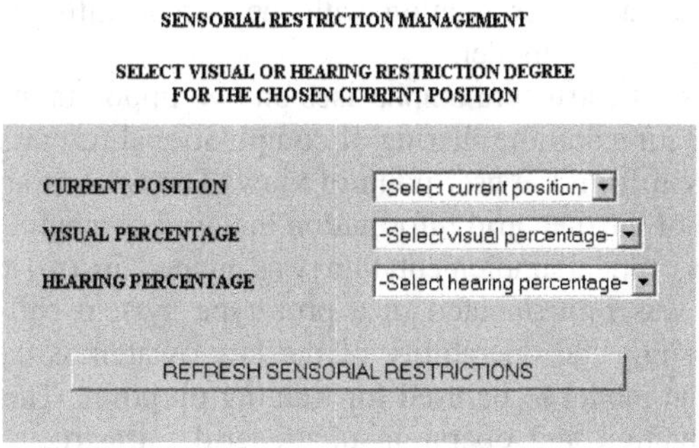

SENSORIAL RESTRICTION MANAGEMENT

SELECT VISUAL OR HEARING RESTRICTION DEGREE
FOR THE CHOSEN CURRENT POSITION

CURRENT POSITION               -Select current position- ▼

VISUAL PERCENTAGE              -Select visual percentage- ▼

HEARING PERCENTAGE            -Select hearing percentage- ▼

REFRESH SENSORIAL RESTRICTIONS

**Fig. 5.** Data Limitations

employees with a high position in the company would have access to all the course information (including text, images, videos and sound files), beginners could only access to textual information, and images but perhaps not to audio files.

If the information is available a user and he is interested in it, there will be a full awareness of interaction. However, if the user tries to access a specific part of the course where there is a boundary, the application will threw an error message (Fig. 6) advertising to the user that he (or she) is trying to access a restrictive part of the course material for which he (or she) has not permission. If the user could justify the

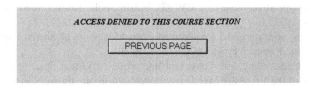

RESTRICTION MESSAGE

ACCESS DENIED TO THIS COURSE SECTION

PREVIOUS PAGE

**Fig. 6.** Denied message in MADEW

necessity of accessing that part of the course or that particular resource, the course manager could modify his or her privileges.

Currently we are working on how to make a grid service with the starting point from MADEW's implementation. MADEW has been implemented as both a web application and a web service. The relationship between web and grid services makes easier the adaptation of this application to a grid environment.

## 5 Conclusions, Ongoing and Future Work

In this paper, we present a new extension and reinterpretation of one of the most successful models of awareness in Computer Supported Cooperative Work (CSCW), called the Spatial Model of Interaction (SMI), which manage awareness in Collaborative Virtual Environments (CVEs) through a set of key concepts [1,2].

This awareness infrastructure extends the key concepts of the SMI introducing some new factors– such as Sensorial Limitation, Data Limitation or Internal Filters - as well as it makes a reinterpretation with the aim of introducing them as the key concepts of this awareness model.

Our awareness infrastructure emphasises on two important items: the management of the data information and the sharing of computational resources in a virtual organisation, both of them from the user point of view. The final awareness model to allow users to be aware of the data grid information in a grid computing infrastructure.

The awareness model implementation was planed in two different phases. The first one, which was implemented in a prototype system called MADEW, was in charge of establishing the operability of the key awareness concepts extended and reinterpreted in the model to be used for training purposes. The second one involves design, implementation and operation of the grid infrastructure and constitute our ongoing work.

## Acknowledgements

The work presented in this paper has been supported by the Communication Research Group (CRG), led by Steve Benford and Chris Greenhalgh at the School of Computer Science and Information Technology in the University of Nottingham, in UK.

## References

[1] Benford S.D., and Fahlén L.E. A Spatial Model of Interaction in Large Virtual Environments. Published in Proceedings of the Third European Conference on Computer Supported Cooperative Work (ECSCW'93). Milano. Italy. Kluwer Academic Publishers, pp. 109-124, 1993.

[2] Benford S. and Mariani J Requirements and Metaphors of Shared Interaction. COMIC Esprit Basic Research Project 6225. D4.1, 1993.

[3] Bowers J. Modelling Awareness and Interaction in Virtual Spaces. Supplement to Proceedings of the 5th MultiG Workshop. Stockholm-Kista, pp. S9-S24, 1993.

[4]  Fahlén, L. E. and Brown, C.G., *The Use of a 3D Aura Metaphor for Compter Based Conferencing and Teleworking*, Published in Proceedings of the 4th Multi-G Workshop, Stockholm-Kista, pp. 69-74, 1992.

[5]  Foster I., Kesselman C., Nick J., Tuecke S. The Physiology of the Grid: An Open Grid Services Architecture for Distributed Systems Integration; Open Grid Service Infrastructure WG, Global Grid Forum, June 22, 2002.

[6]  Global Grid Forum http://www.ggf.org

[7]  Greenhalgh C. An experimental implementation of the spatial model. In Pehrson B. and Skarback E. (Eds.) Published in Proceedings of the 6th ERCIM workshops. Stockholm, pp.53-71, June 1994.

[8]  Greenhalgh, C. M., and Benford, S. D. MASSIVE: A Virtual Reality System for Teleconferencing, ACM Transactions on Computer Human Interfaces (TOCHI), 2 (3), pp. 239-261, ISSN 1073-0516, ACM Press, September 1995

[9]  Greenhalgh, C. *Dynamic, embodied multicast groups in MASSIVE-2*, Technical Report NOTTCS-TR-96-8, Department of Computer Science, University of Nottingham, UK, 1996.

[10]  Greenhalgh, C., *Large Scale Collaborative Virtual Environments*, Doctoral Thesis. University of Nottingham. October 1997.

[11]  Herrero P., De Antonio A., *A Formal Awareness Model for 3D Web-Based Collaborative Environments*. Published in Proceedings of the Workshop on Awareness and the www. ACM 2000 Conference on Computer Supported Cooperative Work (CSCW 2000). Philadelphia, Pennsylvania, USA , 2000.

[12]  Herrero P. *A Human-Like Perceptual Model for Intelligent Virtual Agents* PhD Thesis. Universidad Politécnica de Madrid, June 2003.

[13]  Herrero P., De Antonio A., MADEW: Modelling a Constraint Awareness Model to Web-Based Learning Environments. Published in Proceedings of the International Conference on Computational Science (ICCS 2004). Krakow, Poland, June 2004.

# Grid Accounting Service Infrastructure for Service-Oriented Grid Computing Systems

Jemal H. Abawajy

Deakin University,
School of Information Technology,
Geelong, Victoria 3217, Australia
jemal@deakin.edu.au

**Abstract.** In this paper, we propose an architecture of accounting and payment services for service-oriented grid computing systems. The proposed accounting and payment services provide the mechanisms for service providers to be paid for authorized use of their resources. It supports the recording of usage data, secure storage of that data, analysis of that data for purposes of billing and so forth. It allows a variety of payment methods, it is scalable, secure, convenient, and reduce the overall cost of payment processing while taking into account requirements of Grid computing systems.

## 1 Introduction

Grid computing [4] is a distributed computing platform that integrates resources across multiple organizations and administrative domains. In a Grid environment, resources belonging to different organizations work in a shared, coordinated and collaborative manner to solve large scale scientific and engineering problems. Recently, Grid computing is evolving towards a service-oriented architecture [4]. As a result, service-oriented grid computing is attracting increasing attention from the grid computing research community.

Service-oriented grid computing nicely deals with the challenges in a dynamic, heterogeneous, and geographical Grid environment and provides a universal resolution for Grid computing system architecture [1, 4, 8]. Also, it provides efficient mechanism whereby incentives are offered for resource owners to contribute resources to the grid system while at the same time encourage users to optimally utilize grid resources. Moreover, users will be able to buy exactly the amount of service they need, without concerns about buying, housing and maintaining computers, and without the expense of idle equipment. The Grid audit allows clients to evaluate application performance and adapt to changes in resource availability and cost dynamically [2]. Resource providers can analyze the demand for their resources and adjust prices accordingly. In order to conduct the audit there is a need for a global Grid accounting infrastructure. Most resource management systems such as cluster systems and operating systems log accounting information against local system accounts. The resources they account for, such as CPU time, main memory, secondary storage and

P. Herrero, M.S. Pérez, and V. Robles (Eds.): SAG 2004, LNCS 3458, pp. 168–175, 2005.

network consumption, vary from one system to another. Also the internal format of the accounting data is different between the systems.

An example of a service-oriented grid computing is the Open Grid Services Architecture (OGSA) [4], which is basically the fusion of the Globus Toolkit and the Web Services technologies that meets the demands of an increasingly complex and distributed computing infrastructure: by providing a set of interfaces from which all Grid services are implemented, the OGSA allows for consistent resource access across multiple heterogeneous platforms with local or remote location transparency; it also allows the composition of services to form more sophisticated services regardless of how the services are implemented, and supports integration with various underlying native computing platforms facilities.

Unfortunately, there are several obstacles, most notably security and accounting, to the widespread adoption of the service-oriented Grid computing. Accounting is the process of keeping track of a user's activity while accessing the network resources, including the amount of time spent in the network, the services accessed while there and the amount of data transferred during the session. Accounting data is used for trend analysis, capacity planning, billing, auditing and cost allocation. The accounting process provides valuable security information for incidence response and other security processes. Although the significance of computational accounting has been widely recognized recently and Global Grid Forum Accounting Working Group has been established to address a component of the Grid accounting problem [9], accounting services has until recently been a sparsely-addressed problem, particularly in practice.

Our goal in this paper is to close this gab by building secure grid accounting service infrastructure. our principal subject of study, is how users can pay for computing services received; we decided to address this problem through the use of economic transactions between producers (the resources) and consumers (the users), within the context of an economic model. In this model, users pay in order to execute their job on the resources and the owner of the resources earns credits by executing the user jobs.

The rest of the paper is organized as follows: Section 2 presents related work and discusses various technical challenges that have to be addressed in order to realize service-oriented grid systems. In Section 3, we describe the proposed system architecture along its main components. The conclusion and future directions are presented in Section 4.

## 2 Related Work

Service-oriented grid computing is the computing paradigm that utilizes services as fundamental elements for developing applications/solutions. A service, in the context of service-oriented grid computing, is defined as a resource (e.g., compute, communication and storage) that is provided by resource owners for use by any interested parties for a fee. In the service-oriented Grid system of interest, we have a set of sites, $S = \{S_1, \cdots, S_s\}$, each site is owned and managed by a single grid service provider. In general, there are three key entities involved in service-oriented Grid systems: (1) Grid service users (GSC); (2) Grid service provider (GSP); and (3) Grid bank service (GBS).

The GBS provide tools for its clients to withdraw and deposit funds in their account. Resource owners (GSP) are allowed to solicit an open market price in a way that achieves maximum profit and resource consumers (GSC) are allowed to select resources that meet their special need and quality of service. Grid service users can be individuals, groups or organizations with the need to access large resources in order to solve the most challenging computational problems and willing to pay for resource utilization using an *electronic payment* system.

Some of the challenges to be addressed when designing and deploying service-oriented systems include: (1) provide GSC with a secure way of paying for the service over network; (2) a GSP must be protected from dishonest GSC; (3) a GSC should be able to rightfully repudiate bogus transactions; (4) grid sites must be able to exchange basic accounting and usage data in a common format; and (5) a grid bank service (GBS) should generally be representative of real-world banking system in that it should be scalable, secure, convenient; and provide all the operations supported by traditional banking systems. Hence, in order to realize the full potential of service-oriented grid systems, new services such as service pricing, accounting, charging and payment mechanisms are required in addition to the issues (e.g., information directory, resource allocation, execution management, and scheduling) that have already been addressed by existing grid systems [8]. These new middleware services form the backbone of any service-oriented grid system.

There are several obstacles, most notably security and accounting, to the widespread adoption of the service-oriented Grid computing. As noted in [8], the problem of grid accounting will be of increasing importance to high-performance service providers. Moreover, the significance of grid accounting service has been widely recognized recently and Global Grid Forum Accounting Working Group has been established to research issues such as a Resource Usage Service [9] for global Grid accounting. However, satisfactory solutions to this problem in the context of grid computing do not yet exit [8]. Existing Grid accounting systems present a solution only in the context of local resource management systems. Although several initiatives are engaged in the development of Grid technologies, Grid accounting and payment issues are yet to be addressed [8]. To overcome this limitation, we propose an infrastructure that provides services for authorization, payment, accounting, and audit. It is a secure authorization, payment, accounting and audit system leveraging the Globus Toolkit technologies.

The idea of applying economics to resource management in distributed systems has been explored in a number of systems and architectures [2]. Unfortunately, many of them have mentioned but do not address the problem of accounting for resource consumption and conducting an audit to determine which allocations have been utilized. Grid Economic Services Architecture (GESA) [1] concentrates on providing the enabling infrastructure by defining additional service data and ports (interfaces) compliant with the Open Grid Services Architecture. An implementation of GASA, called the GridBank is discussed in [1]. The GRid Architecture for Computational Economy [] concentrates on pricing mechanisms independent of middleware implementation. A third-party trusted Grid banking service and a resource usage service are considered as separate outside services and are not defined. Service Data Elements, which describe potential chargeable resource items, provided by the ChargableGridService abstraction are categorised but are not defined syntactically. The work is in progress and promises to improve future releases of the Globus Toolkit by providing integrated accounting services.

The area of computational accounting has not been formally researched in traditional computing environments. Such environments usually span only one organization or administrative domain and resource usage is recorded against local system accounts. Such accounts are local to the site (administrative domain) and all accounting information recorded against the accounts is in proprietary format and cannot be shared with other sites. The GGF Accounting Working Group has been formed as part of the Global Grid Forum to overcome billing and authorization limitations present in distributed Grid systems. The goal of the group is to collaborate research and development in the accounting field of Grid computing such as research a Resource Usage Service [9] for global Grid accounting.

# 3   Service-Oriented Grid Computing Architecture

The service-oriented Grid system architecture being proposed in this paper is designed to offer low-level service that co-exits with existing Grid infrastructures [3, 4, 6, 7]. Access to the service-oriented Grid resources are controlled by service providers and software libraries that allow service buyers to negotiate as shown in Figure 1. Note that for the sake of brevity, we deliberately left out some middleware technologies (e.g., information directory, resource allocation, execution management, and scheduling) from Figure 1 as these technologies are already provided by a number of Grid systems [2, 4] and remain the same in our service-oriented Grid structure as well. As in [1], the proposed system uses SOAP (e.g., over Globus toolkit's sockets), which are optimized for security. A user proxy is a certificate signed by the user, which is later used to repeatedly authenticate the user to resources [9]. This avoids the problem of making the user enter password for each resource to be used.

## 3.1   Grid Service Providers

Grid Service Provider (GSP) contributes its resources to the Grid and charge for their usage. The components of the GSP can be divided into three main groups: Negotiators, Verifiers and Billers that are responsibilities for direct accounting system for recording resource consumption and billing the user according to the agreed pricing policy.

The *Verify subsystem* provides three essential services necessary for GSP: (1) *authorization verification*; (2) *conflict resolution*; and (3) *contract verification*. The authorization verification service establishes securely and accurately the identity and credentials of each user for which GSP accepted to perform some services. The contract verification is responsible for making sure that there are enough funds before actually undertaking the request for a user. In case there is a disagreement on given transactions, the GSPs should be able to prove that the service took place. The verify subsystem is called upon in this situation which uses the resource utilization information in a database about each completed services.

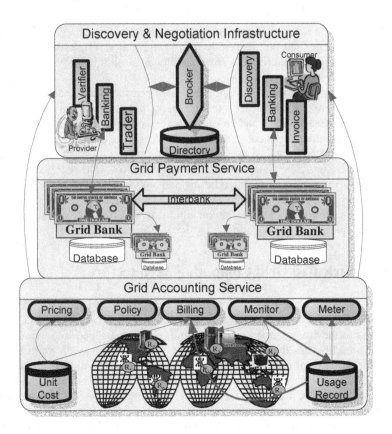

**Fig. 1.** An overview of the generic service-oriented Grid architecture

The *Grid Resource Monitor (GRM)* and the *Grid Service Billing (GSB)* subsystems are responsible for collecting the raw usage information, aggregate them into a record usage format proposed in [13] and enable assigning of the charges and value to these usage records. The *GRM* collects statistics on the utilization of various resources types (e.g., CPU time, storage, connection set-up cost, etc.) for each user and store them in a file with read and append permissions only. This will address security of usage collection as it is related to fraud of falsifying usage records, which we believe that it is one of the most important aspects of the service-oriented Grid system. The GRM is user configurable with respect to how often as well as what resources to monitor. In addition, data collection is performed, as much as possible, in a non-invasive manner.

A cumulative usage of each resource type along the identity of the user is stored in a database where the *GSB* will generate invoices from. The GSP will keep the information for a specific period after which time it is archived or deleted. Invoices can be produced on-demand as well as in a batch at specific period (e.g., monthly). The GSB supports different types of usage calculations (e.g., ALL-RESOURCES, CPU-ONLY, STORAGE-ONLY, and MEM+CPU). This is accomplished by making the usage calculation user configurable such that the GSP can tune resources to meet specific needs.

The *trader*, *e-pay* and *price subsystems* are collectively responsible for negotiation with users or their agents with the objectives of maximizing GSP profit. The trader advertises the available services in *business directory*, provide rates and quotes for potential users and also responsible for the negotiation of how to handle services that run over the purchased time. Note that queries with respect to service rate quotes are not binding and have time-to-live. The system can be configured to send acknowledgement/rejection message to requesting entity if need be. Three possible scenarios supported by the trader to handle overrun cases are: *suspend and notify*, *kill* or allow the service to *complete*.

The *pricing subsystem* allows GSPs to competitively set the price using pricing strategies that have been proposed in the literature [see 4 and reference thereafter]. GSP may keep track of payment history for each user to minimize loses of revenue due to unpaid service. GSP can accept one or some or all payment methods described in previous section. GSPs can also tailor the payment methods accepted through the *e-Pay subsystem* to the GSCs trust-level or credit rating. For instance, new clients will start with prepaid method while established clients can have any methods of payments. This flexibility will be attractive to both GSP and GSC in that the GSP can minimize revenue losses while GSCs can build their ratings slowly with the GSP.

## 3.2  Grid Service Customer

Grid service users (GSC) interact with the system by defining their requirements through the grid service broker. An example of user requirement is "Solve this problem within 30 minutes (i.e., deadline), to be paid in rubies (i.e., currency to be used) after the service is rendered (i.e., payment methods)". If a suitable GSP is available, the broker (described in the next section) will send the particulars of the chosen GSPs.

Costs of resource usage and service level agreements are negotiated between the service providers and service users before access to the resource is granted. Specifically, ff GSC decides to use the service provider suggested by the broker, it will provide permission to GSP to verify the availability of enough funds and any other necessary information needed before beginning the required service.

## 3.3  Grid Service Broker

The *grid service broker (GSB)* provides the means to negotiate and acquire resources that meet the GSCs requirements. In general, GSB has two main components: *negotiator* and *service-level agreement enforcer*. Every GSC supplies sufficient resource requirement information to allow the *negotiator* to determine the cost of the resource that will be needed by GSC. It then attempts to maximize user utility by simply choosing the GSPs through the cost-benefit analysis.

The negotiator communicates with the GSPs *trader* or *grid market directory* (GMD) and then selects the appropriate GSP that meets the GSC requirements. Note that in service-oriented Grid environment, how each GSC will pay for the service must also be considered at the time of resource selection. For instance, if a given GSP do not offer services in the user-preferred currencies (e.g., rubies) and intended user payment methods (e.g., pay-after-usage), then the recruitment of this particular GSP despite of its attractive price cannot be considered. Therefore, we extended the basic negotiator by including information needed to select an appropriate GSP for the GSCs.

The negotiation between the GSB and GSP will result in a binding agreement between the two parties in that the GSP will deliver end-to-end quality of services depending on user requirements whereas the GSB agrees to pay the agreed upon price promptly. It is the responsibility of the *service-level agreement enforcer* to ensure that GSC get their moneys worth. In this paper, we assume that both parties don't renege on their contractual obligations and the case where this is not true will be addressed in the future.

### 3.4   Grid Bank Service

A grid bank service (GBS) is a multi-party protocol between a number of grid service users, $U = \{u_1, \cdots, u_n\}$, and a number of banks, $B = \{b_1, \cdots, b_n\}$, in the system. It is a virtual financial institution that establishes an account for all participants (i.e., GSP, GSC and GBS) and guarantees payment for authorized transactions in accordance with electronic payment (*e-payment*) method regulations and local legislation.

*Digital Note (DN)* is used as a piece of data that represents monetary value within the system. Each bank generates its own DN with *value, serial number, bank id, from, to*, and due dates (i.e., *valid* and *expiry dates)* fields. Every client of a bank will be assigned a set of DN at the time of opening account or on-demand from the client. Each DN is digitally signed by the bank using public key cryptography to make them valid currency. Also, a unique serial number is assigned to each DN by the bank.

In addition to providing exchange rate functionality to its clients, the GBS provides a number of different types of accounts including: (1) project-level account (PLA); (2) individual-level account (ILA); and (2) group-level account (GLA). The PLA accounts are appropriate for many users working on the same or related projects. In PLA, resource usage is charged against the project. Group-level accounts are appropriate for organizations such as institutions that have many projects going simultaneously and the cost of these projects is charged on the group-level account. Individual accounts are appropriate for grant-level projects or small organizations.

Moreover, each bank provides tools for its clients to *withdraw* and *deposit* funds, *account enquiry* and *inter-bank clearing*. Only a client with appropriate credentials can use the account enquiry, withdraw and deposit tools. Clients use the same user proxy/component to access their bank as they use to access other resources on the s-Grid. Inter-bank clearing (IBC) handles issues involving fund transfers and request for information between different banks. So, IBC operation is restricted to by different banks.

## 4   Conclusions and Future Directions

In this paper, we proposed a scalable, secure and easy to use and implement service-oriented grid computing architecture. We described an important component of such system which is the electronic payment system along many other components necessary for realizing the service-oriented Grid systems. All components in the proposed architecture are user configurable as such can be integrated into the existing systems.

In addition, the proposed system protects both users and service providers against theft and forgery. Moreover, it provides the grid service providers with tools that help them maximize the profit (e.g., tools for expressing their pricing policies and minimize bogus transactions) and recording service use and accounting. We are currently exploring a potentially common usage collection framework with web services.

**Acknowledgements.** The help Maliha Omar is very much appreciated. Without her help, this paper would not have been completed on time.

# References

1. Barmouta A., Buyya R.: GridBank: A Grid Accounting Services Architecture (GASA) for Distributed Systems Sharing and Integration. IPDPS (2003) 245
2. Elmroth E., Gardfjäll P.: An OGSA-based Bank Service for Grid Accounting Systems, PARA'04 Workshop in State-of-the-Art in Scientific Computing, 2004.
3. Buyya R., Abramson D., Giddy J.: A Case for Economy Grid Architecture for Service Oriented Grid Computing. HCW'98, (1998) 4-18.
4. Foster I., C. Kesselman, Nick J., Tuecke S.: The Physiology of the Grid: An Open Grid Services Architecture for Distributed Systems Integration, 2002.
5. Foster I., C. Kesselman, Nick J., Tsudik G., Tuecke S.: Security Architecture for Computational Grids. In Proc. 5th ACM Conference on Computer and Communications Security Conference (1998). 83-92.
6. Medvinsky G., Neuman B.: NetCash: A Design for Practical Electronic Currency on the Internet. ACM Conference on Computer and Communications Security (1993) 102-106.
7. Novotny J., Tuecke S., Welch V.: An Online Credential Repository for the Grid: MyProxy. In Proceedings of the Tenth International Symposium on High Performance Distributed Computing (HPDC-10), IEEE Press, 2001.
8. Abawajy J.: Grid Accounting and Payment Architecture, Proceedings of IASTED International Conference on Parallel and Distributed Computing and Networks, (2004) 82 - 88.
9. Resource Usage Service Working Group, Globus Grid Forum. http://www.doc.ic.ac.uk/~sjn5/GGF/rus-wg.html
10. Grid Economic Services Architecture, Working Group, http://www.doc.ic.ac.uk/~sjn5/GGF/gesa-wg.html.
11. Foster I., Kesselman C., Nick J., Tuecke S.: Grid Services for Distributed System Integration. *Computer*, 35(6), 2002.
12. Basney J., Chetan S., Qin F., Song S., Tu X., Humphrey M.: An OGSI CredentialManager Service. UK Workshop on Grid Security Practice, Oxford, July 2004.

# Mercatus: A Toolkit for the Simulation of Market-Based Resource Allocation Protocols in Grids

Daniel Grosu and Umesh Kant

Department of Computer Science,
Wayne State University, 5143 Cass Avenue,
Detroit, MI 48202, USA
dgrosu@cs.wayne.edu
ap5651@wayne.edu

**Abstract.** Grid technologies enable the sharing and coordinated use of diverse resources distributed all over the world. These resources are owned by different organizations having different policies and objectives which need to be considered in making the resource allocation decisions. In such complex environments market-based resource allocation protocols are a better alternative to the classical ones because they take into consideration the policies and preferences of both users and resource owners. The only suitable solution for investigating the effectiveness of these resource allocation protocols over a wide range of scenarios with reproducible results is to consider simulations. Thus in this paper we present Mercatus, a simulation toolkit that facilitates the simulation of market-based resource allocation protocols. We describe the model and the structure of Mercatus and present experimental results obtained by simulating three types of auction-based resource allocation protocols.

## 1   Introduction

Grid technologies enable the sharing and coordinated use of diverse resources distributed all over the world [1]. Resources may provide computing services, data storage services, or may be sensors providing data capture services. The resources in a grid environment are typically heterogeneous and are operated by their owners under different policies. Moreover users and resource owners have different objectives, sometimes contradictory. The resource management mechanisms used in traditional computing systems cannot be simply applied to these complex environments because they assume complete control over resources. Thus we need new resource allocation protocols that take into account the objectives of both users and resource owners. The solution is to consider market-based resource allocation protocols [2, 3] which are based on trading and resource brokering policies between resource owners and users. These protocols are suitable for grid environments because of their decentralized structure and the use of incentives for resource owners to contribute resources.

P. Herrero, M.S. Pérez, and V. Robles (Eds.): SAG 2004, LNCS 3458, pp. 176–187, 2005.

There exist two broad categories of market-based models for resource allocation in grids: commodities markets and auctions [2]. In the *commodities markets model* various services provided by the resource owners are treated as interchangeable commodities. The resource owners determine the price for their services and charge users depending on the amount of resource they consume. In the *auction model* resource owners auction resources using different types of auction mechanisms for establishing the price. Auctions are easier to implement than commodities markets models because they require very little knowledge about the global price. Auctions can be classified into two classes depending on the type of interactions between sellers and buyers. In *one-sided auctions* bids are submitted by the grid users to a central auctioneer. The auctioneer decides the winner based on different auction mechanisms. Examples of one-sided auctions are: First-price auction (the highest bidder wins and pays the amount he bid) and Vickrey auction (the highest bidder wins and pays an amount equal to the second highest bid) [4]. In *two-sided auctions*, also called double auctions, both users and resource owners submit bids. To distinguish the bids we call 'asks' the bids submitted by the resource owners. The selling price and the users and the resource owners that trade are decided by the central auctioneer according to different types of double auction mechanisms.

The only suitable solution for investigating the effectiveness of these resource allocation protocols over a wide range of scenarios with reproducible results is to consider simulations. Thus in this paper we present Mercatus, a simulation toolkit which provides a set of core abstractions and functionalities which allow researchers to easily build simulators for the study of market-based resource allocation protocols in grids.

**Related Work.** There exist a large body of work on economic-based resource management models in distributed systems [3, 5, 6]. For a comprehensive survey of economic models for resource management see [2]. A number of research projects addressed the simulation of scheduling and resource allocation protocols in grids [7, 8, 9]. We discuss here three projects, SimGrid [9], GridSim [8] and OptorSim [7] which are closely related to our work.

SimGrid [9], developed at UCSD, is a simulation toolkit which targets the simulation of specific application domains and computing environments topologies. SimGrid's C API provides functions for generation of resources and tasks, and functions to schedule and unschedule tasks on resources. The main difficulty when simulating market-based resource allocation protocols using SimGrid comes form the fact that there is no support for implementing market-based allocation protocols and the time accounting during the execution of these protocols is not implicit. In Mercatus time accounting is implicit from the design of the toolkit and it does not require special actions from the user.

GridSim [8], developed at the University of Melbourne, is a Java-based simulation toolkit which supports the simulation of application scheduling on heterogeneous Grid resources. GridSim API provides methods for task creation, resource management and scheduling. The main difficulty when simulating auction-based resource allocation protocols comes from the fact that the resource broker which acts on behalf of the user and performs scheduling of user's work on suitable resources, does not support mechanisms for continuous bidding as required in the case of auction-based protocols. Also, the base class in GridSim does not have support for implementing auctions. Thus in our simulation toolkit we provide a grid market auctioneer class which supports registration of resources and conducts auctions supporting various bidding policies.

OptorSim [7], developed within the EU Data Grid project, is a Java based simulator which allows the simulation of data replication algorithms in data grids. It provides support for simulating peer to peer auctions for optimal replica selection. The main focus is on data transfer and replication and not on job execution.

**Our Contributions.** In this paper we introduce a new simulation toolkit, Mercatus, which provides basic constructs necessary to building simulators for the study of market-based resource allocation protocols in grids. Currently, Mercatus supports the simulation of several types of resource allocation protocols based on one-sided and two-sided auctions. It allows the study of economic efficiency in terms of costs, profits and payments and the study of system efficiency in terms of execution time and resource utilization.

**Organization.** In Section 2 we present the simulation model and the resource allocation protocols. In Section 3 we describe the design and structure of Mercatus and show how the resource allocation protocols are implemented. In Section 4 we show how to build simulations using Mercatus. In Section 5 we present several simulation experiments showing the capabilities of our simulation system. In Section 6 we draw conclusions and present future work.

## 2    Mercatus Simulation Model

Mercatus assumes a grid system model in which there exist several heterogeneous resources each offering services and several users that consume these services. The resources are characterized by the following parameters:

($i$) *Processing rate*: It is given in million instructions per seconds (MIPS).
($ii$) *Reservation price*: It is defined as the minimum price accepted by a resource for one second of task execution.
($iii$) *Cost*: Represents the cost incurred by a resource for one second of task execution.

Users are characterized by the following parameters:

($i$) *Work*: It is defined as the total amount of work in millions of instructions for all the tasks of a user.
($ii$) *Number of tasks*: Represents the number of tasks of one user.
($iii$) *Budget*: It is the maximum amount of 'grid dollars' (G$) a user can pay to resources for executing his tasks.

The goal of the users is to finish their work at the earliest time and to pay as little as possible out of their budget, whereas the resources are concerned with maximizing their utilization and hence their profit. The price at which the trade takes place is decided by the auction-based protocols. In Mercatus these auctions are conducted by a Grid Market Auctioneer (GMA). Depending on the type of auction, users or/and resources send bids to GMA. GMA decides the winner depending on the auction mechanism used and declares the auction results to users so that a winning user can send his task to be processed at an appropriate resource. Auction results are also sent to resources so that they can identify the winning user. The GMA keeps on conducting auctions until there is no user with any task left. A user continuously participates in consecutive auctions until he has no tasks left or he exhausted his budget. A resource continuously participates in the auction until there is no user left with any tasks not executed. GMA, users and resources are continuously interacting with each other. Mercatus does not support the simulation of data transfers and data replications.

Mercatus allows the programmer to specify the bidding policy of each grid user. The bidding policy can be constant or variable (depending on the budget remaining, deadline, resource processing rate and a percentage increase specified by the programmer). Also in two-sided auctions the asks of resources can be constant or variable (a resource can decrease its asks if it didn't win in the last auction). Currently, Mercatus supports three types of resource allocation protocols based on First-price, Vickrey [4] and Double auctions [10]. All these protocols are implemented as part of the GMA. All the bids submitted by the users are for a second of task execution at a given resource. In the following we briefly describe these protocols.

**First Price Auction Protocol (FPA):** This protocol is run by GMA in behalf of one resource. Users participating in this protocol bid without knowing what the bid values of the other users are. The user who bids the highest wins the auction and pays the amount he bid. The winning user sends the task to the resource involved in the auction.

**Vickrey Auction Protocol (VA):** This protocol is run by GMA in behalf of one resource. This protocol is based on Vickrey auction which is also called the second-price auction. Users participating in this protocol bid without knowing what the bid values of the other users are. The user who bids the highest wins the auction and pays an amount equal to the second highest bid. The winning user sends the task to the resource involved in the auction.

**Double Auction Protocol (DA):** Users send bids for a group of resources where each resource has the same characteristics. We assume that $m$ users decided to participate in a double auction for a group of $n$ resources. After GMA collects all the bids $\{b_1, b_2, \ldots, b_m\}$ and all the asks $\{a_1, a_2, \ldots, a_n\}$, it does the following:

(i) Sorts bids in decreasing order and asks in increasing order:

$b_{\pi(1)} \geq b_{\pi(2)} \geq \ldots \geq b_{\pi(m)}$

$a_{\sigma(1)} \leq a_{\sigma(2)} \leq \ldots \leq a_{\sigma(n)}$

where $\pi$ and $\sigma$ are the permutations defining the orders statistics above.

(ii) Finds $k$ such that $b_{\pi(k)} \geq a_{\sigma(k)}$ and $b_{\pi(k+1)} < a_{\sigma(k+1)}$.

(iii)  Determines the trading price, $t = \frac{1}{2}(b_{\pi(k+1)} + a_{\sigma(k+1)})$

(iv)  If $a_{\sigma(k)} \leq t \leq b_{\pi(k)}$ notifies resource $\sigma(i)$ and user $\pi(i)$, $i = 1, 2, \ldots, k$, that they can trade at price $t$.

(v)  If $t \geq b_{\pi(k)}$ or $t < a_{\sigma(k)}$ notifies resource $\sigma(i)$ and user $\pi(i)$, $i = 1, 2, \ldots, k-1$, that they can trade. Each resource gets $a_{\sigma(k)}$, and each user pays $b_{\pi(k)}$.

(vi)  GMA sends reject messages to resources and users that do not trade.

Users that trade send tasks to the corresponding resources and they execute them. After receiving the results of the execution, users send payments to the corresponding resources. If the condition in (v) holds, resource $\sigma(i)$ receives $a_{\sigma(k)}$ and user $\pi(i)$ pays $b_{\pi(k)}$, for $i = 1, 2, \ldots, k-1$. As a result of this trade there is a surplus of $(k-1)(b_{\pi(k)} + a_{\sigma(k)})$. We assume here that this surplus is kept by GMA which plays the role of a budget balancer. We also assume that $b_{\pi(m+1)}$ is the lowest possible valuation of the users, $a_{\sigma(n+1)}$ is the highest possible valuation of the resources and that $b_{\pi(m+1)} < a_{\sigma(n+1)}$ holds.

## 3    Architecture and Implementation of Mercatus

Mercatus is a toolkit for the simulation of market-based resource allocation protocols in grid environments. It is a discrete event simulation toolkit written in Java, based on the SimJava discrete event model [11]. We will first briefly describe the SimJava package and then present the architecture and implementation of Mercatus.

**SimJava Simulation Package.** SimJava simulation package [11], implements a discrete event model suitable for implementing general simulations. Events are used at implementation level to model the behavior of respective entities in terms of interactions. The entities interact with each other by passing events. These events may be just simple notifications or may carry additional information related to the notification. Each entity runs in a separate Java thread and has a body() method which encodes its behavior. These threads run concurrently and entities communicate to each other through ports. The Sim_system object is responsible for initializing the simulation environment and linking the various entities through their ports. It also takes care of the events ordering by guaranteeing that the events dispatched by various entities are received by other entities in the same order. Sim_system also takes care of time accounting. More details about SimJava discrete event model can be found in [11].

**Mercatus Architecture.** There are three major players in our grid simulation model: users, resources and GMA. We model each of these three grid players as SimJava entities, where User entity represents users, Resource represents resources, and grid market auctioneer, GMA is the trusted party which resolves the trading between users and resources. Each entity has two ports, 'in' and 'out'. An entity uses the 'in' port to receive events from other entities and the 'out' port to send events to other entities.

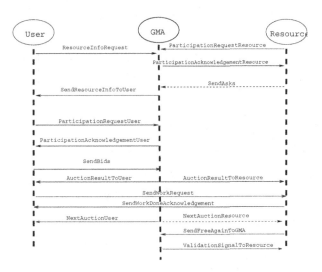

**Fig. 1.** Events passed between entities

We describe the sequence of interactions among User, Resource and GMA entities and the events passed during these interactions. The events being passed can contain data corresponding to that particular event. The sequence of interactions for *one-sided auctions* is as follows:

*Phase I: Information collection and participation decisions*

1. Resources notify GMA of their willingness to participate in an auction by sending the ParticipationRequestResource event. The resource information is sent to GMA together with this event. GMA acknowledges the receipt of resource information by sending ParticipationAcknowledgementResource.

2. Users request information about resources willing to participate in auctions by sending ResourceInfoRequest. GMA provides resource information to users by sending SendResourceInfoToUser. Users receive the information and after analyzing it they decide to participate in some of the auctions. A user notifies GMA about his decision to participate by sending Participation RequestUser to GMA. After the event ParticipationAcknowledgementUser is received by the user, he is ready to participate in the auction.

*Phase II: Conducting the Auction*

1. Participating users send bids by using the event SendBids.

2. GMA runs the auction and notifies User (by sending AuctionResultsToUser) and Resource (by sending AuctionResultToResource) about the result of the auction.

3. The winning user sends the task to the corresponding resource using Send WorkRequest. The resource acknowledges the receipt of the work by sending SendWorkDoneAcknowledgment.

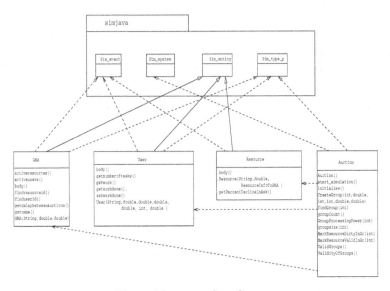

**Fig. 2.** Mercatus class diagram

4. A new auction starts which involves the resources that are idle and willing to participate. GMA informs users and resources that it is ready to start the next auction by sending `NextAuctionUser`. `SendFreeAgainToGMA` is used by a resource to inform GMA that it is idle again and will participate in the next auction. `ValidationSignalToResource` acknowledges that the resource is validated and it can participate in the next auction.

The sequence of event passing is shown in Figure 1. In case of the two-sided auctions two other events are needed, `SendAsks` and `NextAuctionResource`. They are represented in Figure 1 using dotted lines.

The main SimJava classes used to build the Mercatus toolkit are: `Sim_system`, `Sim_entity`, `Sim_event`, and `Sim_type_p`. Based on these classes provided by SimJava our toolkit implements nine classes. We can categorize these nine classes into three groups: (i) `Auction` class (main class), (ii) entity classes, and (iii) wrapper classes. In Figure 2 we present the class diagram of the Mercatus toolkit.

(i) `Class Auction`: This class is responsible for running the simulation. The `initialise()` method initializes the simulation and defines various parameters such as the number of users and the number of resources. It also declares objects of these entities each with different bidding policy parameters. The Auction class provides a method for starting the simulation (`start_simulation()`) and methods for managing groups of resources: `CreateGroup()`, creates a group of resources all having the same characteristics; `findGroup()`, finds and returns the group number of a resource with a given id; `groupcount()`, returns the total number of groups of resources; `GroupProcessing Power()`, returns the processing power of a resource belonging to a group; `groupsize()`, returns the number of resources belonging to a particular group; `MarkResourceDirtyInGr()`, marks resource availability as false; `MarkResourceValidInGr()`, marks resource availabilit y as true; `ValidGroups()`, returns the number of valid group of resources; and `ValidityOfGroup()`, returns true or false depending on whether the group has at least one resource available or not.

(ii) *Entity classes:* These classes model the users, resources and GMA.

**Class User:** The `body()` method is used to model the behavior of `User`. This method is inherited from `Sim_entity` class of SimJava. This class provide methods for: getting the number of tasks of a user, `getnumberoftasks()`; getting and updating the work completed, `getworkdone()` and `setworkdone()`; and getting the total work of a user, `getwork()`.

**Class GMA:** The `body()` method is used to model the behavior of GMA. This method is inherited from `Sim_entity` class of SimJava. GMA provides methods for: getting the number of resources currently available, `activeresources()`; getting the number of users currently willing to participate, `activeusers()`; finding a resource in the list of all resources, `findresourceid()`; finding a user in the list of all users, `finduserid()`; returning the delay between two successive auctions (the delay is set in the constructor of GMA), `getdelaybetweenauctions()`; and getting the name of GMA, `getname()`.

**Class Resource:** The `body()` method is used to model the behavior of the resource. This method is inherited from `Sim_entity` class of SimJava. It provides a method for getting the percent decline parameter in asks of a resource, `getPercentDecline InAsk()`.

(iii) *Wrapper classes:* We implemented several wrapper classes which are used to pass information between entities along with an event. Due to space limitation we are not able to describe these classes here.

## 4     Building Simulations with Mercatus

In Figure 3 we present a simple example of Mercatus code fragment in which we simulate ten resources and five users. This example shows that Mercatus is a very efficient tool and it is very simple to use.

The first step of any simulation is to initialize the simulation environment by calling `initialise()` method with the following parameters: auction type, number of resources, number of users, number of rounds, bidding policy and network latency. Next we add as many users as we specified in the above step by calling `addUser()`. The parameters of `addUser()` method are: user name, total work, deadline, budget, number of tasks, and percentage increase of bids. Resources are added by calling `CreateGroup()` method once for each group of resources with identical characterstics. The parameters of this method are: number of members, processing rate, cost and percentage decrease in asks. The total number of resources over all groups should be equal to the total number of resources specified in the `initialise()` method. Finally, we call `start_simulation()` which links the ports of all entities and starts the simulation.

```
public static void main(String[] args) {

        Auction.initialise(0, 5, 10, 25, 0, 0.1 );

        Auction.addUser("User0", 4.2, 5, 100, 4, 56);
        Auction.addUser("User1", 6.5, 6, 150, 4, 80);
        Auction.addUser("User2", 3.0, 4, 180, 5, 70);
        Auction.addUser("User3", 4.0, 10, 100, 3, 61);
        Auction.addUser("User4", 4.25, 5, 100, 5, 76);

        Auction.CreateGroup(6, 50, 400, 30);
        Auction.CreateGroup(4, 100, 800, 80);

        Auction.start_simulation();

    }
}
```

**Fig. 3.** Sample code fragment for creating simulations

## 5    Simulation Experiments

In order to show the capabilities of Mercatus we present a case study in which we simulated a grid environment consisting of 15 resources shared by 10 users. The resources are divided into two groups. The parameters of users and resources are given in the Table 1 and Table 2. The work of each user is in millions of instructions. Members indicate the number of resources belonging to the group. In these experiments we assume that the reservation price is equal to the resource cost. All the simulation experiments are run for 25 auction rounds and considering a network latency of $10^{-5}$ seconds.

Mercatus facilitates the evaluation of market-based resource allocation protocols in terms of their economic efficiency by reporting user spending, resource cost and resource profit. It also also allows the study of system efficiency in terms of execution time and resource utilization. In the following simulation study we present a number of plots showing some of these metrics.

**Resource Profit.** In Figure 4 we present the profit of each resource as percentage of the cost. For most of the resources the profit obtained in VA is less than that in FPA. This is because in VA the winning user pays an amount equal to the second highest bid, while in FPA the winning user pays an amount equal to the highest bid. The exceptions are resources 4, 10, 11 and 12 which gain a higher profit than in FPA. This is because resources register in random order and the order of resources in FPA and VA is not the same.

In DA we observe that resource 9 gains a very low profit. This is because resource 9 won three times during the 25 rounds, but every time it won according to the second case of DA protocol where the seller gets $a_k$. Resources 5 and 7

**Table 1.** Users' parameters

| User | 0 | 1 | 2 | 3 | 4 | 5 | 6 | 7 | 8 | 9 |
|---|---|---|---|---|---|---|---|---|---|---|
| Work | 4.2 | 6.5 | 3.0 | 4.0 | 4.25 | 5.9 | 4.0 | 5.0 | 4.6 | 3.1 |
| Budget | 100 | 150 | 180 | 100 | 100 | 140 | 100 | 160 | 200 | 140 |
| Number of tasks | 4 | 4 | 5 | 3 | 5 | 5 | 6 | 7 | 4 | 5 |

**Table 2.** Resources' parameters

| Group | Members | Processing rate (MIPS) | Cost ($G) |
|-------|---------|------------------------|-----------|
| 0     | 6       | 50                     | 400       |
| 1     | 9       | 100                    | 800       |

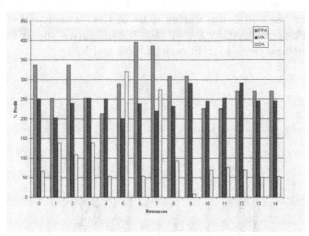

**Fig. 4.** Resource profit

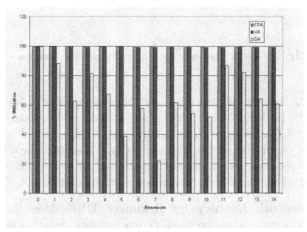

**Fig. 5.** Resource utilization

gain high profit in DA because both resources won only one task each during the 25 rounds of DA. Furthermore they won according to the first case of DA protocol where winner gets $t$. Since the budget of the users is high the value of the trading price $t$ is also high.

**Resource Utilization.** The resource utilization for each resource in the system is presented in Figure 5. We observe that for FPA and VA the utilization is very high because during most of the auction rounds of these protocols all available resources get a user task. In the first auction one of the users has seven tasks, so seven out of fifteen resources will get a task. In the next auction these seven resources will be busy servicing user tasks, but remaining eight resources will be available and will get and execute other user tasks. In this way during most of the auction rounds the number of available resources is less than the total number of tasks a user has and hence during most of the auctions either a resource is winning a task or is servicing a user task it won during the last auction. Thus the resource utilization is high in case of FPA and VA.

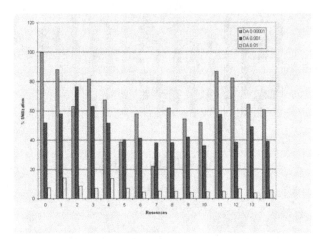

**Fig. 6.** Effect of network latency on resource utilization

For DA the resource utilization is not always high and is less than that of FPA and VA. This is because in case of DA at least two resources should be in a group for the DA protocol to be applied. Also DA protocol is based on the equilibrium of buyers bid and sellers ask and any resource which is beyond this equilibrium point does not win the auction. So in case of DA it is not guaranteed that a resource will win a task even if there are sufficient users.

**Effect of Network Latency on Resource Utilization.** In Figure 6 we present the resource utilization for different network delay values and considering the DA protocol. In most of the cases the resource utilization decreases as network latency increases. This is because more time is spent in communication as compared to the time spent executing tasks. There are two exceptions at resources 2 and 7 where the utilization is high even though the network latency is increased from $10^{-5}$ to $10^{-2}$ seconds. This is because DA requires that at least two resources should be available and as latency is high it is highly probable that during the next auction more resources will be available. Hence it is more probable that for each auction there are enough resources to apply DA and thus utilization is increased.

# 6    Conclusion

In this paper we introduced Mercatus, a simulation toolkit that facilitates the simulation of market-based resource allocation protocols. We described the model and the structure of Mercatus and presented experimental results obtained by simulating three types of auction-based resource allocation protocols. In the future versions of Mercatus we will provide support for implementing other market-based resource allocation protocols (e.g. combinatorial auctions, commodities markets) and also more features that will make it more flexible. Mercatus v1.0 has been released and it is available at `http://mercatus.cs.wayne.edu`.

# References

1. Foster, I., Kesselman, C.: The Grid: A Blueprint for a New Computing Infrastructure. 2nd edn. Morgan Kaufmann, San Francisco, CA (2003)
2. Buyya, R., Abramson, D., Giddy, J., Stockinger, H.: Economic Models for Resource Allocation and Scheduling in Grid Computing. Concurrency and Computation: Practice and Experience. **14** (2002) 1507-1542
3. Wolski, R., Plank, J. S., Brevik, J., Bryan, T.: Analyzing Market-based Resource Allocation Strategies for the Computational Grid. Int. J. of High Performance Computing Applications. **15** (2001) 258-281
4. Vickrey, W.: Counterspeculation, Auctions, and Competitive Sealed Tenders. J. of Finance. **16** (1961) 8-37
5. Abramson, D., Buyya, R., Giddy, J.: A Computational Economy for Grid Computing and its Implementation in the Nimrod-G Resource Broker. Future Generation Computing Systems. **18** (2002) 1061-1074
6. Gomoluch, J., Schroeder, M.: Market-based Resource Allocation for Grid Computing: A Model and Simulation. Proc. of the 1st Int. Workshop on Middleware for Grid Computing. June (2003) 211-218
7. Bell, W. H., Cameron, D. G., Capozza, L., Millar, A. P., Stockinger, K., Zini, F.: OptorSim - A Grid Simulator for Studying Dynamic Data Replication Strategies. Int. J. of High Performance Computing Applications. **17** (2003) 403-416
8. Buyya, R., Stockinger, M.: GridSim: A Toolkit for the Modeling and Simulation of Distributed Resource Management and Scheduling for Grid Computing. Concurrency and Computation: Practice and Experience. **14** (2002) 1175-1220
9. Casanova, H.: SimGrid: A Toolkit for the Simulation of Application Scheduling. Proc. of the IEEE/ACM Int. Symp. on Cluster Computing and the Grid. May (2001) 430-437
10. McAfee, R. P.: A Dominant Strategy Double Auction. J. of Economic Theory. **56** (1992) 434-450
11. Howell, F., McNab, R.: SimJava: A Discrete Event Simulation Package for Java with Applications in Computer Systems Modeling. Proc. of the 1st Int. Conf. on Web-based Modeling and Simulation. January (1998) 252-259

# A Resource Monitoring and Management Middleware Infrastructure for Semantic Resource Grid

Fawad Nazir[1], Hafiz Farooq Ahmad[2], Hamid Abbas Burki[1],
Tallat Hussain Tarar[1], Arshad Ali[1], and Hiroki Suguri[2]

[1] National University of Science & Technology,
Rawalpindi, Pakistan
{arshad.ali, fawad.nazir, hamid.abbas,
tallat.tarar}@niit.edu.pk
[2] Communication Technologies,
Sendai, Japan
{farooq, suguri}@comtec.co.jp

**Abstract.** The Semantic Grid is an extension of the current Grid in which information will be given well-defined meaning, better enabling computers and resources to work in cooperation and coordination. The architecture of Semantic Grid adopts a service-oriented perspective in which distinct entities are represented as software agents, provide services to one another. Traditionally Grid management frameworks are based upon fixed management functionality and fixed interaction interfaces that cannot satisfy the flexibility and complexity that the dynamic Semantic Resource Grid demands. Agent technology is promising in this domain since it facilitates automatic negotiation of services contracts a dynamic configuration of those services, thus enhancing the provisioning for semantic grid services. In this paper we propose an infrastructure for resource monitoring and management in Semantic resource Grid. Our architecture unifies sharing and managing of heterogeneous resources across the Grid. The resources will be able to actively find and advertise services. The resources will be arranged into groups which will enable the resource to have common understanding. We used agents in our architecture which enable the resources to have effective negotiation, support dynamic services and services utilization and advertisement. In this way we can achieve self-controllability and self-coordinability among Grid resource. We argue that semantics is a key to autonomy of the operation and management in emerging complex dynamic systems, such as Semantic Grid. Our architecture could be a part of resource monitoring and management middleware in the Semantic Resource Grid.

## 1 Introduction

Resources are an integral part of the Grid which is an emerging technology for enabling resource sharing and coordinated problem solving in dynamic multi-institutional virtual organizations [1, 2]. Grids resources are identified by their attributes. Resource attributes have various degrees of dynamism, from mostly static attributes, like operating system version, to highly dynamic ones, like network bandwidth or CPU load [1]. Most of the computational resources in the world are underutilized. The Grid can

P. Herrero, M.S. Pérez, and V. Robles (Eds.): SAG 2004, LNCS 3458, pp. 188–196, 2005.

unify these resources to be used as a single resource. Sharing computing resources naturally increases the computing capacity available to all participants, since one research project may use many computing resources while other projects are not using computational power. Computational Grids [2] utilize internet connected resources as a source of cheap computational power. The resources in computational grids can be computers, storage space, sensors etc. The grid is made up of a variety of remote resources that are owned by many different people and organizations. Wide varieties of geographically distributed resources such as computers, supercomputers, storage systems, data sources are unified forming a Grid. In distributed systems such as the Grid, resources are reserved and released dynamically, network links fail independently and unpredictably, machines and servers connect and disconnect in an arbitrary way. The Grid being built in this third generation is heading towards what is termed as the Semantic Grid. The Semantic Grid is characterized as an open system in which computational resources (owned by different organizations), software components, users come and go on a continual basis [4].The realization of the Semantic Grid requires an infrastructure where all resources, including services, are adequately described in a form that is machine-process able. The Semantic Grid is addressing the way that *information* is represented, stored, accessed, shared and maintained - information is understood as data equipped with semantics. The 'semantics' permeates the full vertical extent of the Grid and is not just a semantic (or knowledge) layer on top: it is semantics in, on and for the Grid. The Semantic Grid involves all three conceptual layers of the Grid: knowledge, information and computation/data. The complementary layers will ultimately provide rich, seamless and pervasive access to globally distributed heterogeneous resources [5]. The Grid requires a high degree of automation in order to support flexible collaborations and resource utilization. Moreover, this environment should be personalized to the individual participants and should offer seamless interactions with both software components and other relevant users. The Semantic Grid is comprised of easily deployed components whose utility transcends their immediate application, providing a high degree of easy-to-use and seamless automation and in which there are flexible collaborations and computations utilizing the available resources in an intelligent and efficient way. In our approach we will be providing the capability of monitoring distributed computational resources effectively is a crucial factor for high-performance distributed computation. Monitoring the behavior of the resources of a distributed computation system is necessary, both for determining the cause of performance problems, and for tuning the system, in order to optimize its use and therefore its performances. As long as the distributed systems on which we operate become bigger and are more widely distributed (as it happens for Grid environments), the automating the operations of monitoring becomes important. Our architecture for monitoring and management of Semantic Resources Grid is based on autonomous entities like agents and they are used for activating all monitoring tools for the different resources involved with an application, collecting such data and filtering them for obtaining useful information. We have used the mobility property of the agent that enables the dynamic monitoring components to be loaded on the machine automatically. The monitoring of those resources is based upon publish subscribe model. Negotiation framework for agents is used to discuss the monitoring parameters and decide the mechanism and policy to monitor and utilize resources. If during negotiation some new parameter are identified to be monitored and not currently present in the resource. The particular module which will be used to monitor the new parameters is loaded dynamically on the resource and is published using the framework for utilization. Now in the later sections we will briefly discussing about the motivation of this research work and current related work.

## 2  Motivation

In the existing Grid implementations the monitoring of resources means getting the values of predetermined attributes from the resource which is to be monitored. The resources entertain monitoring requests for only a limited number of attributes and are unable to provide values of other attributes if requested. This is because of static monitoring mechanisms which only return the values of predetermined attributes. What is lacking is way of updating the internal monitoring mechanism of the resources so they can adapt to the monitoring requests for other parameters. Mobile agents are agents that can physically travel across a network, and perform tasks on machines that provide agent hosting capability therefore they can act as a means of updating the internal monitoring mechanisms of the resources by bringing new code implementation which is required to gather information about the requested attribute.

## 3  Related Work

Not much work has been done in this area of research. Even the concept of Grid resource monitoring is in the stage of refinement. The monitoring architectures need to be designed so that they can cope with the heterogeneity and dynamic nature of the Grid resources and changing requirements. The Grid Performance Working Group of GridForum [6] is currently dealing with the Grid monitoring. They have proposed a possible architecture, in one of the papers ([7]), for maintaining and accessing performance information. In another paper [8] a system for managing monitoring sensors is proposed in which software agents are used in a producer/consumer model. In another paper [9] the use of mobile agents is proposed for active monitoring in Grid environments. An approach for the dynamic measurement of the performances of an application in Grid environments is presented in the Pablo scalable information toolkit [10]. The Monitoring and Discovery Service (MDS), the information services component of the Globus Toolkit, is also dealing with resource monitoring [11]. The MDS provides Grid information such as the available resources and the state of the computational Grid. This information may include properties of the machines, computers, and networks in your Grid, such as the number of processors available, bandwidth, storage devices, network interfaces, CPU load, file system information, and memory. It uses the Lightweight Directory Access Protocol (LDAP) to provide middleware information in a common interface. MDS includes two components: the Grid Resource Information Service (GRIS) and the Grid Index Information Service (GIIS). With the MDS, you can publish information about almost anything in your Grid [12].

# 4 Architecture

In this section we will discuss architecture of the framework, which will be used for resource monitoring and management in Semantic Resource Grid. In our approach we provide an agents based infrastructure over which multiple resources (services provided be computational and data resources) can register there services for other users to subscribe and utilize based on negotiated parameters. The framework also provides a provision to dynamically load and publish the modules which are not present in some remote resource for monitoring and management. The monitoring and management services are constructed, maintained and derived using specialized co-operating and negotiating agents. Now we will present four major agents which will be coordinating to provide this infrastructure.

## 4.1 Autonomous Grid Resource Management Agent

When ever a resource becomes part of Semantic Resource Grid it publishes its self. The autonomous grid resource management agent which is a software system is than dynamically downloaded, executed and published on that resource using mobile agent concept. This agent architecture is based on GMA so it provides functionalities such as publish subscribe model, filtering of the monitored data and support push model for monitoring parameters thus reducing unwanted network traffic. We argue that our proposed architecture is autonomous as it provides functionality of equality, locality and self-containment in all MoGiNMA implementations (sub-systems). Equality, locality and self-containment are main components of autonomic controllability in any sub system as part of Autonomous Distributed System (ADS).

## 4.2 Service Registrar Agent

A Service Registrar Agent provide the same functionality as the DF in a traditional network, i.e., it must be a yellow pages service in which agents may register their services, and search for services offered by other agents. As Services Registrar agent also keep the same functions specified for the DF in FIPA00023. So, agents do not need to modify the way they interact with the DF. Therefore, it will have the following functions: register, deregister, modify and search. A Service Registrar Agent must provide flexible service search mechanisms that include both local services (in the same platform) and remote services. In the semantic Grid environment the remote services will be dynamic as the resources will join and leave the group continually.

## 4.3 Information Services Agent

Resource discovery and utilization are challenging issue in the semantic grid. In Semantic Grid dynamic and Distributed Resource Sharing is done. In the current implementation Grid users, administrators, and the Grid services themselves need directories to keep track of these entities and to maintain relationships between them. Grid information services are a significant part of the "Resource" and "Collective" layers. Keeping in view the concept of VO as a set of institutions, users, and resources, grouped together for sharing resources in the grid we can think of semactic grid as dynamic pool of resource in which resource become part of Grid for limited time and resource and giving limited services. So now in our proposed architecture we can not call information services we will call it dynamic pool of resources which will be monitored and managed by remotely downloaded monitoring and management components.

### 4.4  Resource Broker Agent

The Resource Broker (RB) is a middleware that supplies distributed clients with job execution at the more likely Computing Element (CE) in a heterogeneous computing environment. Client applications are provided with a set of API for sending requests and receiving response to/from RB servers. The RB server is responsible for carrying out tasks to satisfy the client requests. In our case we will be providing load services of dynamic resources pools on which the job will be scheduled. In this way user job can be predicted and user will be will given a time and resource estimations based on the prediction of the monitoring parameter.

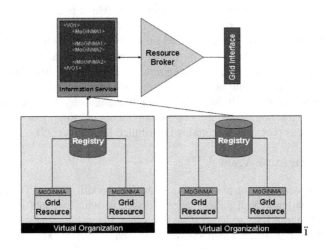

**Fig. 1.** Basic Architecture for Semantic Sharing of monitoring Data in Semantic

In Figure 1 we have explained how the Autonomous Grid Resource Management Agent, Service Registrar Agent, Information Services Agent and Resource Broker Agent are interconnected and how and what do they communicate? This architecture which we have designed for the monitoring of Semantic Grid systems is based the features of agent platform which is used for the basic environment for the execution of agents in the system. This architecture is totally based on the agents ability to transfer the code dynamically (mobility) and the concept of negotiation.

## 5  Monitoring System Architecture

The monitoring system architecture of our proposed system is discussed in this section. The main components of our system are ontology repository, subscriber handles, directory service, self-monitoring and self-organizing, negotiation module and decisions making module. In this section we will be explaining each and every module in detail. In our current architecture the ontology is centralized. The ontology repository is accessible by all the involved agents to enable understanding the negotiations terms. Subscriber handler is also a repository that is there in each monitored resource, this repository actually contains the information of the consumers to which the trap/event data is to send after certain time intervals. The time intervals are specified at the time when the consumer subscribes to certain service. The directory service is an important part of this architecture.

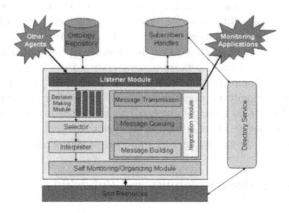

**Fig. 2.** Architecture of the Monitoring System

In the directory service all the services that monitored devices provide are published. The service discovery algorithm that the consumers have is destined to these directory services. The self-monitoring and organizing module is used to monitor the resource parameters like (CPU Utilization, Memory Utilization etc) and keep the monitoring information in some persistent storage. The next is the negotiation module that is used by the agent to negotiate with other agents. The purpose of negotiation could be to share ontology information and to resolve monitoring and management problems. The negotiation module has further three layers message building, message queuing and message transmission. The message-building layer is responsible to build a message in a specific format and send the message to other peer agents or the subscriber for negotiation the parameters of monitoring and monitoring policies. The message is then encapsulated into an ACL header and sends to the next message queuing layer. The message queuing layer is than responsible to queue the messages and send to the upper layer when appropriate to send. The upper layer is message transmission layer this layer is actually responsible to send the message to the desired recipient. The message transmission layer check for the destination ID and transmits the message accordingly. The decision-making module is responsible to take decisions in case of any unwanted event occurred in the resource. This decision-making module is highly scalable as we can always-new intelligent components to make this module more and more intelligent and specific. If some unwanted event has occurred and the decision making does not know what action is to be taken in that specific conditions, in such cases that particular monitoring agent will negotiate with its peers agents and if possible solution is found then this new decision making module will be integrated to the existing. In this way we take full advantage of the mobility feature of the agents. This feature is also explained in detail in the next section.

## 6  Scalability Issues

In our architecture we will enable negotiation between different grid components. All the monitoring parameters will be decided on run time while negotiation. This is all explained in the above mentioned architectures. Now in this section we will be discussing that how scalability will be ensured. With scalability we mean the possibility of dynamic addition of monitoring logic to allow the monitoring of additional parameters. Initially the parameters to be monitored will be finalized though negotiations. The logic for monitoring those parameters need not be available there on the resource initially. Monitoring logic for some of the parameters may already be there but the additional monitoring logic required will be needed to fulfill the monitoring request for all the agreed upon parameters. This is where the mobile agents contribute by exploiting the notion of mobile code. The mobile agents will bring the required logic to the resource thus allowing the monitoring of all the requested parameters.

## 7  Dynamic Service Availability and Publishing

If in the grid any resource can measure memory and CPU utilization. But the system cannot monitor the network, we have to provide a service at runtime that enhance the capability of the system. Now the system has the capability that it can monitor the network using the service that we have made available and published. How we will provide and publish the service? We will provide the service according to the way as described above in scalability issues portion. For publishing the service we will follow publish and subscribe model. Publish and subscribe model is a mechanism for sharing data between applications and for workgroup collaboration. Applications can "publish" their data to a file, which will automatically notify all documents that have "subscribed" to that file, and those documents then update to reflect the most recently published data. Networking technologies and products enable a high degree of connectivity across a large number of computers, applications, and users. In these environments, it is important to provide asynchronous communications for the class of distributed systems that operate in a loosely-coupled and autonomous fashion, and which require operational immunity from network failures. This requirement has been filled by various middleware products that are characterized as messaging, message oriented middleware, message queuing, or publish-subscribe. Applications that communicate through a publish and subscribe paradigm require the sending applications (publishers) to publish messages without explicitly specifying recipients or having knowledge of intended recipients. Similarly, receiving applications (subscribers) must receive only those messages that the subscriber has registered an interest in. In our case we will publish the service by using "Directory Facilitator". Directory Facilitator (DF) is an optional component of multi agent system. It is responsible to provide yellow-pages directory service to other agents. Agents may register their services to the DF or query the DF to find out what services are offered by other agents. Agent is responsible to provide information related to service e.g. servie_type, service_name etc. Furthermore, an agent can also deregister or modify service.

## 8  Conclusion

Semantic Grid is an ambitious and exciting global effort to develop an environment in which individual users can access computers, databases and experimental facilities simply and transparently, without having to consider where those facilities are located and the resources could dynamic configuration of components and coordination with other resources to solve issues. The resources are the most critical part of Grid systems. Grid systems are complex and highly scalable so there is a need to develop systems that is autonomic [13] in nature and aims at bringing a new level of automation like self-healing, self-optimizing, self-configuring and self-protection functions [14]. This paper focus on resource monitors and management middleware infrastructure for semantic resource grid using mobile agents negotiation and mobility property. We are carrying out the implementation of the proposed system. This concept can provide strong foundation that lead toward autonomic computing realization environment. Negotiation is a key to scalable and adaptive autonomous distributed systems and mobility property can provide with self and dynamic configuration. In future we plan to implement peer to peer system which wills middleware independent and monitoring and management will be totally local and distributed. The ontology information will also be distributed on each resource.

## Acknowledgement

We would like to thank participants of Grid Computing and Multi-agent systems workshop held at NUST Institute of Information Technology, Pakistan for their comments on the paper. We would like to thank Mr. Kashif Iqbal and Mr. Aamir Shafi for there guidance and support in writing research paper and implementation of our system.

## References

[1]   Adriana Iamnitchi, Ian Foster. On Fully Decentralized Resource Discovery in Grid Environments.

[2]   Carl Kesselman, Ian Foster, editor. The Grid: Blueprint for A New Computing Infrastructure. Morgan Kaufmann Publishers, San Francisco, 1999.

[3]   S. Tuecke I. Foster, C. Kesselman. The anatomy of the grid: Enabling sdalable virtual organizations. International J. Supercomputer Applications, 15(3), 2001.

[4]   David De Roure, Nicholas R. Jennings and Nigel R. Shadbolt: The Semantic Grid: A Future e-Science Infrastructure

[5]   David De Roure, Mark A. Baker, Nicholas R. Jennings and Nigel R. Shadbolt: The Evolution of the Grid

[6]   GridForum. http://www.gridforum.org.

[7]   R. Wolsky, M. Swany, and S. Fitzgerald. White Paper: Developing a Dynamic Performance Information Infrastructure for Grid Systems. February 2000. Available at http://dast.nlanr.net/GridForum/Perf-WG/.

[8]   B. Tierney, B. Crowley, et al. A Monitoring Sensor Management System for Grid Environments. In High Performance Distributed Computing (HPDC-9, Pittsburgh (Pennsylvania), August 2000.

[9]   Antonio Puliafito, Orazio Tomarchio, Lorenzo Vita: ACTIVE MONITORING IN GRID ENVIRONMENTS USING MOBILE AGENT TECHNOLOGY

[10]  L. DeRose and A. Reed. SvPablo: A Multi-Language Architecture-Independent Performance Analysis System. In Proceedings of the International Conference on Parallel Processing (ICPP'99), Fukushima (Japan), September 1999.

[11]  Karl Czajkowskiy Steven Fitzgeraldz Ian Fosterx{ Carl Kesselmany:Grid Information Services for Distributed Resource Sharing_

[12]  http://www-106.ibm.com/developerworks/grid/library/gr-ipmds.html

[13]  Roy Sterritt, Dave Bustard. Autonomic Computing-A Means of Achieving Dependability

[14]  Roy Sterritt, Dave Bustard. Towards Autonomic Computing Environment

# A Service-Oriented Framework for Traffic Information Grid*

Guozhen Tan, Chengxu Li, and Jiankun Wu

Department of Computer Science and Engineering,
Dalian University of Technology, 116024, China
gztan@dlut.edu.cn

**Abstract.** Intelligent Transportation System (ITS) refers to the use of information technologies to address and alleviate transportation problems. The challenges of ITS exist mainly in synthesizing information from geographically distributed, dynamic and heterogeneous databases, specialized sensors and other systems. This synthesis process is computation and communication intensive. Computational Grid is a promising platform for such large-scale data-intensive applications. Building on grid computing technologies, this paper presents a novel infrastructure referred to as Traffic Information Grid (TIG) for ITS development and deployment. The service-oriented and layered system architecture of TIG is introduced and described. Two implementation modes-request/response mode and subscribe/notify mode are presented and evaluated with real traffic data respectively. In addition, an example application is given to illustrate how the TIG works. Based on the practice of TIG, Grid computing is proved to be an effective solution for data-intensive applications.

## 1   Introduction

Modern society is becoming increasingly information-oriented at the global level, and the road traffic is no exception. The use of information technologies on roads, traffic and vehicles has been promoted in order to solve numerous urban transportation problems, such as traffic accident, congestion and environmental deterioration. This trend results in an increased focus on the research and development of Intelligent Transportation System (ITS)[1, 2]. ITS is a typical data-intensive, computing-intensive and mission-critical application. Its realization highly depends on large-scale sharing and collaboration of traffic information resources[1]. However, these requirements could not be satisfied by any existing computational and data management infrastructure due to its geographically distributed, heterogeneous, large dataset size and dynamic characteristics.

---

* This work was supported in part by Grand 60373094 of National Natural Science Foundation of China and Grand 2002CB312003 of High Tech. Research and Development (973) Programme, China.

P. Herrero, M.S. Pérez, and V. Robles (Eds.): SAG 2004, LNCS 3458, pp. 197–206, 2005.

Problems related to information sharing and cooperative use have been of central concern in distributed application development, and have led to a new form of information technology known as the Grid computing[3, 4]-an infrastructure supports the sharing and coordinated use of diverse resources in dynamic, distributed Virtual Organizations (VO)[5]. In the first phase, Grid was proposed for scientific and technical computing applications. Now the focus is going to shift to commercial distributed computing applications [5, 6]. In this paper, we apply Grid technologies to ITS development and deployment, in order to meet the information sharing and collaboration requirements of ITS. This novel infrastructure is referred to as Traffic Information Grid (TIG) [7].

TIG is a hardware infrastructure and distributed software, which integrates traffic data from various resources and turns it into information by interconnecting high-performance computers, huge storage systems, various traffic instruments, databases and other transportation systems in the heterogeneous, dynamic and geographically distributed environment. The rest of the paper is organized as follows: Section 2 presents and describes the service-oriented and layered architecture of TIG. Section 3 discusses the traffic information services in more detail and implements them with the Globus Toolkit 3.0. Section 4 gives an example application to illustrate how the TIG works. Section 5 concludes the paper.

## 2   System Overview

Information technology forms the basis for TIG, and the traffic data can be divided into 3 categories according to their different sources: Dynamic Traffic Data (DTD), Static Traffic Data (STD) and Public Traffic Data (PTD). DTD is collected by dispersive traffic sensors in real-time, including traffic flow data indicating the crowded degree of roads, traffic light state data indicating light colors, traffic camera data indicating the real-time traffic video, etc. STD is stored in various databases with different formats, including geography data, road network data, traffic management data, etc. PTD is about airplane flight, railway, public transportation, etc., which is provided by different departments around the city. Traffic data has following characteristics:

- Data-intensive. The volume of traffic datasets needs to be measured in terabytes and are still generated every seconds. Thus, there must be enough storage resources to save such large amounts of data, as well as enough computational resources to dispose them.
- Computing-intensive. Problems in traffic domain are usually complex problems or difficult problems, especially in order to meet people's more and more rigid requirements on real-time and accuracy. Solving such problems requires high-performance computing abilities.
- Distributed. Traffic data is scattered dispersedly because of the distribution of resources and the distribution of data consumers. It is impossible to find such an exclusive data owner who manages the whole traffic data in a city.

- Heterogeneous. Heterogeneity means diversity in data sources, data formats and data management systems. The heterogeneity makes the information platform development cannot assume a specific target environment, but an open system.
- Dynamic. The content of traffic data is changing frequently, and the frequency is range form year (such as digital map information), day (such as airplane flight information), to second (such as the traffic flow information).

TIG fuses distributed traffic data from different sensors or stored in different databases with different formats, and turns it into various kinds of information, which makes it possible to access them in a more flexible and convenient way.

### 2.1   Physical Elements

TIG is comprised by the following physical elements, as shown in Fig. 1:

- A large number of different traffic sensors, which are spatially dispersive in the city and linked to the modems by voice lines, then connected to the TIG through the sensors and actuators management systems (SAMS).
- A large number of Internet sites providing public traffic data as airplane, train, bus, etc., which are connected to the TIG through gateways.
- A large number of database servers, which installing with different database management systems (DBMS) and running on different kinds of software and hardware platforms.
- A large number of information servers, which are the main parts of TIG and responsible for data integrating and information publishing.
- A large number of transportation systems, which are the information consumers.
- Networks, which provide (hopefully high performance) connectivity among the various elements just listed.

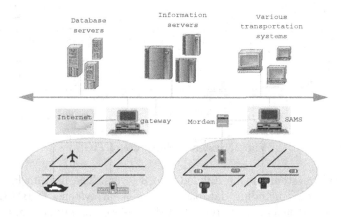

**Fig. 1.** Physical elements of TIG

## 2.2     System Architecture

The system architecture of TIG presented in this paper is based on the Open Grid Services Architecture (OGSA) [8]. OGSA defines a uniform exposed Grid services semantics and mechanisms for creating, naming and discovering transient Grid service instances, provides location transparency and multiple protocol bindings for service instances, and supports integration with underlying native platform facilities. In OGSA, everything is treated as services, including computational resources, storage resources, networks, programs, and so on [8].The system architecture of TIG presented in this paper is based on the Open Grid Services Architecture (OGSA) [8]. OGSA defines a uniform exposed Grid services semantics and mechanisms for creating, naming and discovering transient Grid service instances, provides location transparency and multiple protocol bindings for service instances, and supports integration with underlying native platform facilities. In OGSA, everything is treated as services, including computational resources, storage resources, networks, programs, and so on [8]. The service-oriented, layered system architecture of TIG is illustrated in Fig. 2 and described in the following:

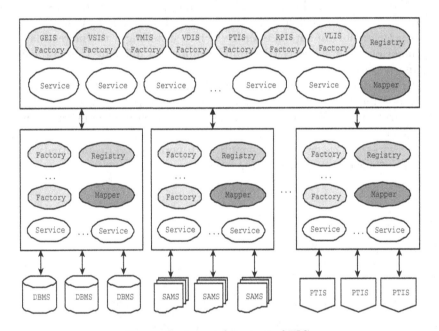

**Fig. 2.** System architecture of TIG

The overall system can be divided into 3 layers. The bottom layer is multiple data sources, including database management systems (DBMS), sensors and actuators management systems (SAMS), as well as public traffic information systems (PTIS), which provide all kinds of traffic data. The middle layer includes several heterogeneous and geographically distributed simple hosting

**Table 1.** The service contents of TIG

| Service name | Service contents |
| --- | --- |
| GEIS | Highroad, street, building, schools, place name, etc. |
| GSIS | Optimal path selection, driving assistant, etc. |
| TMIS | Vehicle amount, road status, road flow, etc. |
| VDIS | Vehicle driving condition, road congestion, etc. |
| PTIS | Car navigation, car scheduling, car parking, etc. |
| RPIS | Road status within or across the city, etc. |
| VLIS | Car location, accident location, congestion location, etc. |

environments. Each hosing environment is responsible for a specific kind of data fusion services. Its user interface can be structured as a registry, one or more factories, and a handleMap service. Each factory registers with the registry service. When a factory receives a request to create a Grid service instance from above, the factory invokes hosting-environment-specific capabilities to create the new instance-usually a process, assigns it a handle, registers the instance with the registry, and makes the handle available to the handleMap service. The top layer provides a new abstraction based on the middle level. Its user interface also can be structured as a registry, several factories and a handleMap. However, once a factory receives a createService request from the user or another service, it delegates the request to a corresponding factory in the middle level. In other word, the top layer is just as a facade, which hides the complex and trivial details of middle layer from its users and provides an impression of one homogeneous and centrally managed environment.

The TIG, until now, provides 7 different kinds of traffic information services, which are characterized by 7 different factory services in the top layer of the architecture. Each information service has several operations. The contents of the services are illstrated in Table 1.

## 3   Implementation

The traffic information services provided by TIG fall into 2 categories: static traffic information services (STIS) and real-time traffic information services (RTIS). The information provides by STIS is nearly time invariant-such as geography information, transportation infrastructures information, etc. And the information provided by RTIS is time variable-such as the road traffic flow information, traffic accidents information, etc. According to this difference, we design two different information grid service implementation modes respectively: request/response mode for STIS and subscribe/notify mode for RTIS. We also implement and evaluate both of them based on the Globus Toolkit version 3.0 [9].

### 3.1   Request/Response Mode

The information provided by STIS is nearly unchanged, so the information consumers needn't query if the information has been changed while running. Fig. 3

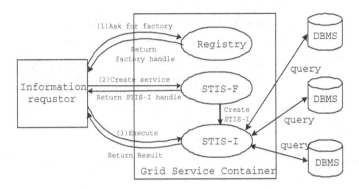

**Fig. 3.** Request/response mode for STIS

illustrates the structure and a possible workflow of STIS. The numbers on the arrow represent the sequence in which actions are executed:

(1) Communicating with the registry of the VO (Registry, a standard grid service instance supporting the Registry interface for registration) and requesting the grid service handle (GSH) for the static traffic information service factory (STIS-F).
(2) Calling the factory (STIS-F, a user defined grid service instance supporting the Factory interface for service creation), which creates the static traffic information service instance (STIS-I) and returns the GSH for it.
(3) Calling the STIS-I (a user defined grid service instance) and submitting the request. The STIS-I executes the query against the database and encapsulates the result into corresponding information, then return to the requestor.

The curve of time cost with different amount of data transfer is illustrated in Fig. 4.

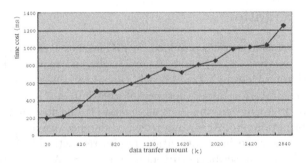

**Fig. 4.** Data transfer performance

## 3.2   Subscribe/Notify Mode

In contrast with static traffic information, the real-time information changes frequently. If we still adopt the request/response model mentioned in section 3.1,

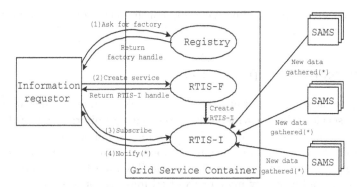

**Fig. 5.** Subscribe/notify mode for RTIS

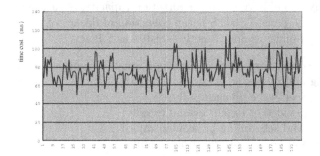

**Fig. 6.** Data notification performance

the information requestor must periodically ask the service instance if the information is changed while running. This is very inefficient, especially when the query interval is short or there are dozens of applications aware of the change. Subscribe/notify model, which is also named as notifications or observer/observable [8], provides a more efficient approach to solve this problem. The requestor makes an initial call asking the service to notify whenever there are any changes, and the service will contact the requestor as soon as a change occurs, then the requestor can act accordingly. This approach decreases the network traffic and CPU use.

Fig. 5 illustrates the structure and a possible workflow of the real-time traffic information service. The numbers on the arrow represent the sequence in which actions are executed:

(1) Communicating with the registry (Registry) and requesting the GSH for the real-time traffic information service factory (RTIS-F).
(2) Calling the RTIS-F, which creates the real-time traffic information service instance (RTIS-I) and returns the GSH for it.
(3) Subscribing to a specific service data element (SDE) of the RTIS-I.
(4) The SDE notifies the requestors as soon as the RTIS-I receives new data form SAMS.

The curve of response time with 200 continuous traffic flow information is illustrated in Fig. 6.

## 4   An Example Application

From the application's point of view, TIG is a collection of middleware traffic information services that provide applications with a uniform view of distributed resource components and the mechanisms for assembling them into systems. Building on TIG, traffic application developers needn't to be aware of the underlying distribution and heterogeneity of the TIG, but treat the TIG as a single homogeneous and centrally managed virtual information system.

Dalian rapid response transportation systems (DRRTS) are developed based on TIG to enhance Dalian's rapid-response abilities under urgent conditions. Consequently, to enhance the transportation capacity, release traffic congestions and avoid traffic jams. DRRTS is the collection of dozens of sub-systems, which have 12 main rapid-response functions listed as follow:

- tracking congestions by road transportation TV automatically;
- detecting and disposing congestions rapidly;
- creating green-wave plans rapidly;
- gaining the video of urgent events rapidly;
- arranging and scheduling policemen rapidly;
- checking policemen's distribution rapidly;
- scheduling guard tasks automatically;
- detecting and disposing suspectable vehicles rapidly;
- detecting overtime parkings rapidly;
- diagnosing equipments rapidly;
- passing messages rapidly;
- gathering real-time mobile images.

Fig. 7 illustrates the architecture of the DRRTS. Whenever sub-systems need information while computing, they simply tell the TIG what they want, but not necessarily where it is located.

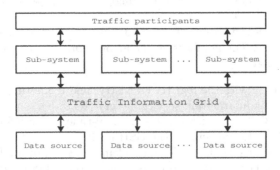

**Fig. 7.** DRRTS architecture

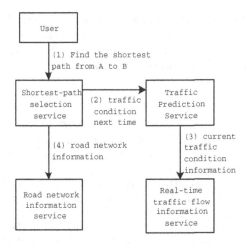

**Fig. 8.** An example of TIG at work

Fig. 8 gives a more detailed scenario to explain how the TIG supports the DRRTS. It depicts a situation in which user wants to find the shortest path form A to B with the help of DRRTS. The figure illustrates the following steps:

(1) The user-a driver or a tourist-issues a request to the shortest-path selection service specifying details such as the beginning point, the destination and the time.
(2) The shortest-path selection service issues a request to the traffic prediction service to query the possible traffic condition in that time.
(3) The traffic prediction service subscribes to the real-time traffic flow information service (a RTIS provided by TIG) and accesses the latest traffic flow information for traffic forecasting [10], then return the results to the shortest path selection service.
(4) The shortest-path selection service accesses the road information via the road network information service (a STIS provided by TIG) and computes the optimal path according to both the forecasting result and the road network [11]. Then return the optimal path to the user.

## 5   Conclusions

In this paper, we have described our research work related to traffic information grid, which applies Grid technologies to solving intelligent transportation systems problems-information sharing and coordinated use. We described the TIG's physical elements, a service-oriented and layered architecture and two different implementation modes as well as their experimental results. An example application was given to explain how the TIG works. TIG integrates data from distributed sources with different formats together and turns it into fine-defined information services, which hides the underlying distributed, heterogeneous and dynamic characteristics form the information consumers. On the other hand, TIG also provides the complex information processing with high-performance computation abilities. Based on the practice of TIG, Grid is proved to be an effective solution for data-intensive applications.

# References

1. National police Agency, Ministry of International Trade and Industry, Ministry of Transport, Ministry of Posts and Telecommunications, Ministry of Construction: System Architecture for ITS in Japan (1999)
2. System Architecture Committee of ITS America: National ITS Architecture (1997)
3. I. Foster and C. Kesselman: The Grid: Blueprint for a New Computing Infrastructure, Morgan Kaufman, Pub. (1998)
4. I. Foster, C. Kesselman and S. Tueche: The Anatomy of the Grid: Enabling Scalable Virtual Organizations. International Journal of High Performance Computing Applications, 15(3), 2001: 200-222
5. I. Foster, C. Kesselman, J. M. Nick, and S. Tuecke: Grid Service for distributed system integration. IEEE Computer, 35(6), 2002: 37-46
6. Z. W. Xu, and W. Li: Research on Vega Grid Architecture. Journal of Computer Research and Development, 39(8), 2002: 923-929
7. C. J. Jiang, G. S. Zeng, H. Z. Chen, et al: Research on Traffic Information Grids. Journal of Computer Research and Development, 40(12), 2003: 1677-1679
8. I. Foster, C. Kesselman, J. M. Nick and S. Tuecke: The Physiology of the Grid: An Open Grid Services Architecture for Distributed Systems Integration. http://www.globus.org/research/papers/ogsa.pdf, 2002
9. Globus Group, http://www.globus.org
10. G. Z. Tan and H. Ding: Research of generalized neural network and it's application to traffic flow prediction. Control and Decision, 17(s1) 2002: 777-780
11. G. Z. Tan and W. Gao: Shortest Path Algorithm in Time-Dependent Networks. Chinese Journal of Computers, 25, 2002: 165-172

# Author Index

Abawajy, Jemal H.  168
Ahmad, Hafiz Farooq  188
Ali, Arshad  188
Allan, Geoffrey  146
Alpdemir, M. Nedim  13
Altintas, Ilkay  120
Amoreira, Celine  120
Antonioletti, Mario  1
Atkinson, Malcolm  1

Baldridge, Kim K.  120
Birnbaum, Adam  120
Burki, Hamid Abbas  188

Cannataro, Mario  75
Carretero, Jesus  59
Chang, Elizabeth  86
Comin, Matteo  75

Egglestone, Stefan Rennick  99
Escolar, Soledad  59

Fernandes, Alvaro A.A.  13
Ferrari, Carlo  75
Fleming, Peter  146

Garcia, Felix  59
Garcia, Jose D.  59
Georgousopoulos, Christos  25
Gounaris, Anastasios  13
Greenhalgh, Chris  99
Grosu, Daniel  176
Guerra, Concettina  75
Guzzo, Antonella  75

Hadzic, Maja  86
Hamsphire, Alastair  99
Hanushevsky, Andrew  38

Herrera, J.  108
Herrero, Pilar  50, 158
Hong, Neil Chue  1
Huedo, E.  108
Humble, Jan  99
Hume, Alastair  1

Jackson, Mike  1

Kadirkamanathan, Visakan  146
Kant, Umesh  176
Karasavvas, Konstantinos  1
Krause, Amrey  1

Li, Chengxu  197
Li, Peter  13
Llorente, I.M.  108
Ludaescher, Bertram  120

Miladinovic, Igor  134
Miller, Mark  120
Montero, R.S.  108
Mukherjee, Arijit  13
Muller, Henk L.  99

Nazir, Fawad  188

Ong, Max  146

Palansuriya, Charaka  1
Paton, Norman W.  13
Perez, Jose M.  59
Pérez, María S.  50, 158
Peña, José M.  50
Potier, Yohann  120

Radenkovic, Milena  134
Rana, Omer F.  25

Ren, Xiaoxu    146
Robles, Víctor    50, 158

Sakellariou, Rizos    13
Sánchez, Alberto    50
Stockinger, Heinz    38
Sudholt, Wibke    120
Sugden, Tom    1
Suguri, Hiroki    188

Tan, Guozhen    197
Tarar, Tallat Hussain    188
Thompson, Haydn    146

Veltri, Pierangelo    75

Watson, Paul    13
Wu, Jiankun    197

# Lecture Notes in Computer Science

For information about Vols. 1–3397

please contact your bookseller or Springer

Vol. 3525: A.E. Abdallah, C.B. Jones, J.W. Sanders (Eds.), Communicating Sequential Processes. XIV, 321 pages. 2005.

Vol. 3517: H.S. Baird, D.P. Lopresti (Eds.), Human Interactive Proofs. IX, 143 pages. 2005.

Vol. 3516: V.S. Sunderam, G.D.v. Albada, P.M.A. Sloot, J.J. Dongarra (Eds.), Computational Science – ICCS 2005, Part III. LXIII, 1143 pages. 2005.

Vol. 3515: V.S. Sunderam, G.D.v. Albada, P.M.A. Sloot, J.J. Dongarra (Eds.), Computational Science – ICCS 2005, Part II. LXIII, 1101 pages. 2005.

Vol. 3514: V.S. Sunderam, G.D.v. Albada, P.M.A. Sloot, J.J. Dongarra (Eds.), Computational Science – ICCS 2005, Part I. LXIII, 1089 pages. 2005.

Vol. 3510: T. Braun, G. Carle, Y. Koucheryavy, V. Tsaousidis (Eds.), Wired/Wireless Internet Communications. XIV, 366 pages. 2005.

Vol. 3508: P. Bresciani, P. Giorgini, B. Henderson-Sellers, G. Low, M. Winikoff (Eds.), Agent-Oriented Information Systems II. X, 227 pages. 2005. (Subseries LNAI).

Vol. 3503: S.E. Nikoletseas (Ed.), Experimental and Efficient Algorithms. XV, 624 pages. 2005.

Vol. 3501: B. Kégl, G. Lapalme (Eds.), Advances in Artificial Intelligence. XV, 458 pages. 2005. (Subseries LNAI).

Vol. 3500: S. Miyano, J. Mesirov, S. Kasif, S. Istrail, P. Pevzner, M. Waterman (Eds.), Research in Computational Molecular Biology. XVII, 632 pages. 2005. (Subseries LNBI).

Vol. 3498: J. Wang, X. Liao, Z. Yi (Eds.), Advances in Neural Networks – ISNN 2005, Part III. L, 1077 pages. 2005.

Vol. 3497: J. Wang, X. Liao, Z. Yi (Eds.), Advances in Neural Networks – ISNN 2005, Part II. L, 947 pages. 2005.

Vol. 3496: J. Wang, X. Liao, Z. Yi (Eds.), Advances in Neural Networks – ISNN 2005, Part II. L, 1055 pages. 2005.

Vol. 3495: P. Kantor, G. Muresan, F. Roberts, D.D. Zeng, F.-Y. Wang, H. Chen, R.C. Merkle (Eds.), Intelligence and Security Informatics. XVIII, 674 pages. 2005.

Vol. 3494: R. Cramer (Ed.), Advances in Cryptology – EUROCRYPT 2005. XIV, 576 pages. 2005.

Vol. 3492: P. Blache, E. Stabler, J. Busquets, R. Moot (Eds.), Logical Aspects of Computational Linguistics. X, 363 pages. 2005. (Subseries LNAI).

Vol. 3489: G.T. Heineman, J.A. Stafford, H.W. Schmidt, K. Wallnau, C. Szyperski, I. Crnkovic (Eds.), Component-Based Software Engineering. XI, 358 pages. 2005.

Vol. 3488: M.-S. Hacid, N.V. Murray, Z.W. Raś, S. Tsumoto (Eds.), Foundations of Intelligent Systems. XIII, 700 pages. 2005. (Subseries LNAI).

Vol. 3483: O. Gervasi, M.L. Gavrilova, V. Kumar, A. Laganà, H.P. Lee, Y. Mun, D. Taniar, C.J.K. Tan (Eds.), Computational Science and Its Applications – ICCSA 2005, Part IV. XXVII, 1362 pages. 2005.

Vol. 3482: O. Gervasi, M.L. Gavrilova, V. Kumar, A. Laganà, H.P. Lee, Y. Mun, D. Taniar, C.J.K. Tan (Eds.), Computational Science and Its Applications – ICCSA 2005, Part III. LXVI, 1340 pages. 2005.

Vol. 3481: O. Gervasi, M.L. Gavrilova, V. Kumar, A. Laganà, H.P. Lee, Y. Mun, D. Taniar, C.J.K. Tan (Eds.), Computational Science and Its Applications – ICCSA 2005, Part II. LXIV, 1316 pages. 2005.

Vol. 3480: O. Gervasi, M.L. Gavrilova, V. Kumar, A. Laganà, H.P. Lee, Y. Mun, D. Taniar, C.J.K. Tan (Eds.), Computational Science and Its Applications – ICCSA 2005, Part I. LXV, 1234 pages. 2005.

Vol. 3479: T. Strang, C. Linnhoff-Popien (Eds.), Location- and Context-Awareness. XII, 378 pages. 2005.

Vol. 3477: P. Herrmann, V. Issarny (Eds.), Trust Management. XII, 426 pages. 2005.

Vol. 3475: N. Guelfi (Ed.), Rapid Integration of Software Engineering Techniques. X, 145 pages. 2005.

Vol. 3468: H.W. Gellersen, R. Want, A. Schmidt (Eds.), Pervasive Computing. XIII, 347 pages. 2005.

Vol. 3467: J. Giesl (Ed.), Term Rewriting and Applications. XIII, 517 pages. 2005.

Vol. 3465: M. Bernardo, A. Bogliolo (Eds.), Formal Methods for Mobile Computing. VII, 271 pages. 2005.

Vol. 3463: M. Dal Cin, M. Kaâniche, A. Pataricza (Eds.), Dependable Computing - EDCC 2005. XVI, 472 pages. 2005.

Vol. 3462: R. Boutaba, K. Almeroth, R. Puigjaner, S. Shen, J.P. Black (Eds.), NETWORKING 2005. XXX, 1483 pages. 2005.

Vol. 3461: P. Urzyczyn (Ed.), Typed Lambda Calculi and Applications. XI, 433 pages. 2005.

Vol. 3460: Ö. Babaoglu, M. Jelasity, A. Montresor, C. Fetzer, S. Leonardi, A. van Moorsel, M. van Steen (Eds.), Self-star Properties in Complex Information Systems. IX, 447 pages. 2005.

Vol. 3459: R. Kimmel, N.A. Sochen, J. Weickert (Eds.), Scale Space and PDE Methods in Computer Vision. XI, 634 pages. 2005.

Vol. 3458: P. Herrero, M.S. Pérez, V. Robles (Eds.), Scientific Applications of Grid Computing. X, 208 pages. 2005.

Vol. 3456: H. Rust, Operational Semantics for Timed Systems. XII, 223 pages. 2005.

Vol. 3455: H. Treharne, S. King, M. Henson, S. Schneider (Eds.), ZB 2005: Formal Specification and Development in Z and B. XV, 493 pages. 2005.

Vol. 3454: J.-M. Jacquet, G.P. Picco (Eds.), Coordination Models and Languages. X, 299 pages. 2005.

Vol. 3453: L. Zhou, B.C. Ooi, X. Meng (Eds.), Database Systems for Advanced Applications. XXVII, 929 pages. 2005.

Vol. 3452: F. Baader, A. Voronkov (Eds.), Logic for Programming, Artificial Intelligence, and Reasoning. XI, 562 pages. 2005. (Subseries LNAI).

Vol. 3450: D. Hutter, M. Ullmann (Eds.), Security in Pervasive Computing. XI, 239 pages. 2005.

Vol. 3449: F. Rothlauf, J. Branke, S. Cagnoni, D.W. Corne, R. Drechsler, Y. Jin, P. Machado, E. Marchiori, J. Romero, G.D. Smith, G. Squillero (Eds.), Applications of Evolutionary Computing. XX, 631 pages. 2005.

Vol. 3448: G.R. Raidl, J. Gottlieb (Eds.), Evolutionary Computation in Combinatorial Optimization. XI, 271 pages. 2005.

Vol. 3447: M. Keijzer, A. Tettamanzi, P. Collet, J.v. Hemert, M. Tomassini (Eds.), Genetic Programming. XIII, 382 pages. 2005.

Vol. 3444: M. Sagiv (Ed.), Programming Languages and Systems. XIII, 439 pages. 2005.

Vol. 3443: R. Bodik (Ed.), Compiler Construction. XI, 305 pages. 2005.

Vol. 3442: M. Cerioli (Ed.), Fundamental Approaches to Software Engineering. XIII, 373 pages. 2005.

Vol. 3441: V. Sassone (Ed.), Foundations of Software Science and Computational Structures. XVIII, 521 pages. 2005.

Vol. 3440: N. Halbwachs, L.D. Zuck (Eds.), Tools and Algorithms for the Construction and Analysis of Systems. XVII, 588 pages. 2005.

Vol. 3439: R.H. Deng, F. Bao, H. Pang, J. Zhou (Eds.), Information Security Practice and Experience. XII, 424 pages. 2005.

Vol. 3437: T. Gschwind, C. Mascolo (Eds.), Software Engineering and Middleware. X, 245 pages. 2005.

Vol. 3436: B. Bouyssounouse, J. Sifakis (Eds.), Embedded Systems Design. XV, 492 pages. 2005.

Vol. 3434: L. Brun, M. Vento (Eds.), Graph-Based Representations in Pattern Recognition. XII, 384 pages. 2005.

Vol. 3433: S. Bhalla (Ed.), Databases in Networked Information Systems. VII, 319 pages. 2005.

Vol. 3432: M. Beigl, P. Lukowicz (Eds.), Systems Aspects in Organic and Pervasive Computing - ARCS 2005. X, 265 pages. 2005.

Vol. 3431: C. Dovrolis (Ed.), Passive and Active Network Measurement. XII, 374 pages. 2005.

Vol. 3429: E. Andres, G. Damiand, P. Lienhardt (Eds.), Discrete Geometry for Computer Imagery. X, 428 pages. 2005.

Vol. 3427: G. Kotsis, O. Spaniol (Eds.), Wireless Systems and Mobility in Next Generation Internet. VIII, 249 pages. 2005.

Vol. 3423: J.L. Fiadeiro, P.D. Mosses, F. Orejas (Eds.), Recent Trends in Algebraic Development Techniques. VIII, 271 pages. 2005.

Vol. 3422: R.T. Mittermeir (Ed.), From Computer Literacy to Informatics Fundamentals. X, 203 pages. 2005.

Vol. 3421: P. Lorenz, P. Dini (Eds.), Networking - ICN 2005, Part II. XXXV, 1153 pages. 2005.

Vol. 3420: P. Lorenz, P. Dini (Eds.), Networking - ICN 2005, Part I. XXXV, 933 pages. 2005.

Vol. 3419: B. Faltings, A. Petcu, F. Fages, F. Rossi (Eds.), Constraint Satisfaction and Constraint Logic Programming. X, 217 pages. 2005. (Subseries LNAI).

Vol. 3418: U. Brandes, T. Erlebach (Eds.), Network Analysis. XII, 471 pages. 2005.

Vol. 3416: M. Böhlen, J. Gamper, W. Polasek, M.A. Wimmer (Eds.), E-Government: Towards Electronic Democracy. XIII, 311 pages. 2005. (Subseries LNAI).

Vol. 3415: P. Davidsson, B. Logan, K. Takadama (Eds.), Multi-Agent and Multi-Agent-Based Simulation. X, 265 pages. 2005. (Subseries LNAI).

Vol. 3414: M. Morari, L. Thiele (Eds.), Hybrid Systems: Computation and Control. XII, 684 pages. 2005.

Vol. 3412: X. Franch, D. Port (Eds.), COTS-Based Software Systems. XVI, 312 pages. 2005.

Vol. 3411: S.H. Myaeng, M. Zhou, K.-F. Wong, H.-J. Zhang (Eds.), Information Retrieval Technology. XIII, 337 pages. 2005.

Vol. 3410: C.A. Coello Coello, A. Hernández Aguirre, E. Zitzler (Eds.), Evolutionary Multi-Criterion Optimization. XVI, 912 pages. 2005.

Vol. 3409: N. Guelfi, G. Reggio, A. Romanovsky (Eds.), Scientific Engineering of Distributed Java Applications. X, 127 pages. 2005.

Vol. 3408: D.E. Losada, J.M. Fernández-Luna (Eds.), Advances in Information Retrieval. XVII, 572 pages. 2005.

Vol. 3407: Z. Liu, K. Araki (Eds.), Theoretical Aspects of Computing - ICTAC 2004. XIV, 562 pages. 2005.

Vol. 3406: A. Gelbukh (Ed.), Computational Linguistics and Intelligent Text Processing. XVII, 829 pages. 2005.

Vol. 3404: V. Diekert, B. Durand (Eds.), STACS 2005. XVI, 706 pages. 2005.

Vol. 3403: B. Ganter, R. Godin (Eds.), Formal Concept Analysis. XI, 419 pages. 2005. (Subseries LNAI).

Vol. 3402: M. Daydé, J.J. Dongarra, V. Hernández, J.M.L.M. Palma (Eds.), High Performance Computing for Computational Science - VECPAR 2004. XI, 732 pages. 2005.

Vol. 3401: Z. Li, L.G. Vulkov, J. Waśniewski (Eds.), Numerical Analysis and Its Applications. XIII, 630 pages. 2005.

Vol. 3400: J.F. Peters, A. Skowron (Eds.), Transactions on Rough Sets III. IX, 461 pages. 2005.

Vol. 3399: Y. Zhang, K. Tanaka, J.X. Yu, S. Wang, M. Li (Eds.), Web Technologies Research and Development - APWeb 2005. XXII, 1082 pages. 2005.

Vol. 3398: D.-K. Baik (Ed.), Systems Modeling and Simulation: Theory and Applications. XIV, 733 pages. 2005. (Subseries LNAI).